# THE CIVIL WAR LETTERS OF
# SARAH KENNEDY

# THE CIVIL WAR LETTERS OF

## *Sarah Kennedy*

## LIFE UNDER OCCUPATION
## IN THE UPPER SOUTH

*Edited by Minoa D. Uffelman, Phyllis Smith,*
*and Ellen Kanervo*

Voices of the Civil War • Michael P. Gray, Series Editor

The University of Tennessee Press / Knoxville

The Voices of the Civil War series makes available a variety of primary source materials that illuminate issues on the battlefield, the home front, and the western front, as well as other aspects of this historic era. The series contextualizes the personal accounts within the framework of the latest scholarship and expands established knowledge by offering new perspectives, new materials, and new voices.

Library of Congress Cataloging-in-Publication Data

Names: Kennedy, Sarah, 1823–1899, author. | Uffelman, Minoa D., editor. | Smith, Phyllis (Historian), editor. | Kanervo, Ellen, editor. | Gray, Michael P., 1968- writer of foreword.
Title: The Civil War letters of Sarah Kennedy : life under occupation in the Upper South / edited by Minoa D. Uffelman, Phyllis Smith, and Ellen Kanervo.
Other titles: Voices of the Civil War series.
Description: First edition. | Knoxville : University of Tennessee Press, [2023] | Series: Voices of the Civil War | Includes bibliographical references and index. | Summary: "Sarah Kennedy (1823–1899) was the wife of a wealthy slaveowner, D. N. Kennedy, at the outbreak of the Civil War. D. N. Kennedy was a major supporter of secession in Tennessee who was rewarded for his devotion to the new nation with a job (though vaguely defined) in the Confederate Treasury Department. He shipped off for Mississippi, leaving Sarah Kennedy to care for six young children (including a son, 'Newty,' with special needs) and watch over numerous slaves on a large plantation in Clarksville. She was burdened by ill health (both her own and her children's), slaves that, one by one, disappear under federal occupation, and by the lack of consistent contact with her beloved husband owing to the Confederate mail system—which comes under surprising scrutiny here. Her letters are mostly about personal matters, but they offer significant insight into slavery and social relations in Clarksville under occupation"—Provided by publisher.
Identifiers: LCCN 2022056906 (print) | LCCN 2022056907 (ebook) | ISBN 9781621907268 (paperback) | ISBN 9781621907275 (Kindle edition) | ISBN 9781621907282 (Adobe PDF)
Subjects: LCSH: Kennedy, Sarah, 1823–1899—Correspondence. | Married women—Tennessee—Clarksville—Correspondence. | Women slaveholders—Tennessee—Clarksville—Correspondence. | United States—History—Civil War, 1861–1865—Personal narratives, Confederate. | United States—History—Civil War, 1861–1865—Women. | Clarksville (Tenn.)—Social conditions—19th century—Sources. | LCGFT: Personal correspondence.
Classification: LCC F444.C6 K46 2023 (print) | LCC F444.C6 (ebook) | DDC 973.7/82—dc23/eng/20221209
LC record available at https://lccn.loc.gov/2022056906
LC ebook record available at https://lccn.loc.gov/2022056907

# CONTENTS

# ILLUSTRATIONS

# FOREWORD

The historiography of the Civil War has no longer left the voice of women unheard. Indeed, a primary mission of the Voices of the Civil War series has been to keep pace with current trends in the secondary source scholarship, so that "left out voices" might be amplified in published primary source material, making them more accessible for both scholars and popular audiences. Dynamics of class, culture, gender, and region, mingled with political and military matters, tell a much more complicated story about the Civil War. As scholars further delve into the long Civil War, findings have shown how women dealt with their occupied locales, strained relationships with family, friends, or neighbors, and the handling of intimidation by an enemy, whether soldiers or non-combatants. Moreover, recent scholarship examines a crucial question: what tactics might women employ to help their cause? Fending off guerillas, taking on the management of their home, family situations, disease, death, and loneliness—all of these challenges undeniably validate women as not passive, but rather active agents on their respective home fronts—providing stability, solace, relief, and more, which only begins to unravel the complicated story women have to tell. Previous publications in the Voices of the Civil War series help demonstrate such themes.

In 1996, *A Very Violent Rebel: The Civil War Diary of Ellen Renshaw House* was published under the skilled editorship of Daniel E. Sutherland. While in East Tennessee, the nineteen-year-old Ellen ardently supported the Confederacy in US held Knoxville. Moving from Savannah, Georgia, to Knoxville, Ellen's parents instilled in her a sense of Southern nationalism. The self-proclaimed "very violent rebel," with ferocious devotion to the cause, carried out her own fight against "the Yankee Occupiers." Ellen was middle class, held deep Confederate convictions, and her volatile nature melded with the unstable region, which had an uneasy balance of Federal occupiers and Confederate supporters in Appalachia. She witnessed fellow neighbors being arrested, inhospitable Federal soldiers stealing, and deprivations of both

Southern citizens and soldiers being incarcerated. When Ellen attempted to alleviate their suffering by donating provisions to those captured, Federal authorities suspected she was a spy, and she was promptly banished back to Georgia.

The 2004 *Sanctified Trial: The Diary of Eliza Rhea Anderson Fain, a Confederate Woman in East Tennessee* saw similar hardships in a familiar locale for the series. John N. Fain edited his distant relative's work, tracking Eliza, who lived in Rogersville, Tennessee, between Bristol and Morristown. When Eliza's husband and five of her six boys left their farm for the Confederate army, she was left to manage the household, as well as overseeing their nine slaves. Eliza, an ardent supporter of slavery, secession, and the Confederacy, was also a firm believer in the Bible. She fought especially with the instrument of scripture. Eliza's sanctified trial put her on defense against her Unionist neighbors as well as Christian Northerners, as she felt they misconstrued the Bible with regard to slavery and believed, in turn, that this misinterpretation helped bring on the war. No matter how she viewed the war's origins, in the end, this devout Presbyterian would have to defend her home against bushwhackers and looters in 1865, as she watched her plantation burn. Her interpretation of the South's losses was also theological—mournfully, she speculated that the sins of Southerners, particularly miscegenation, had brought on defeat.

In 2010, the series ventured beyond the western borderlands, with a female voice from the Eastern Theater. *In the Shadow of the Enemy: The Civil War Journal of Ida Powell Dulany*, Mary L. Mackall, Stevan F. Meserve, and Anne Mackall Sasscer chronicled the intriguing private life of their subject. When Ida Powell Dulany's male family members left to join the Confederate army, she was left alone and isolated as the lone proprietor of a plantation in piedmont Virginia, around Loudon and Fauquier Counties, near border state Maryland. In this hostile area, fears over harassment from either side placed Ida in a precarious setting near Federal forces on the edge of uncertain borders. Her husband, progressive in mind, allowed Ida to be the "decision maker," and she oversaw the plantation. As Ellen House and Eliza Fain had done in Tennessee, at one point Ida had to stand face-to-face with the enemy. Faith in God, "demonization" of Yankees, and the "exploits" of John S. Mosby, helped her battle for her plantation while living in the enemy's shadow.

In 2014, Minoa Uffelman, Ellen Kanervo, Phyllis Smith, and Eleanor Williams collaborated on a volume that has since won academic acclaim. *The Diary of Nannie Haskins Williams: A Southern Woman's Story of Rebellion and Reconstruction, 1863–1890*, focused on a young, elite woman living in Middle

Tennessee. Nannie Haskins Williams's writings are witty, if not precocious, as she reflects upon the long Civil War. Nannie's complete story was almost lost to posterity, if not for the skillful researching and editing of the Uffelman, Kanervo, Smith, and Williams team. Prior to their collaboration, only short portions of Nannie's diary were known and utilized by historians—most notably, Haskins's words appeared as voice-overs in Ken Burns's PBS series *The Civil War* (1990). The book's setting is in Clarksville, on the Cumberland River, where the privileged Nannie received a private-school education as she honed her writing skills. For all intents and purposes, she became a local historian, recording names and stories of people throughout the community who had sacrificed in war, detailing those killed, wounded, or taken captive. As she detailed a war-torn South, from Clarksville and beyond, she highlighted how Reconstruction brought financial challenges, while the Gilded Age embraced industrial growth and diversification in a labor force that included women, but in so doing, wrought new dangers.

Some seven miles from where Nannie Haskins grew up, a handwritten ledger had been discovered in a smokehouse in the latter years of the twentieth century. It was composed by a young woman named Serepta Jordan, who lived, during the Civil War, in a community known as New Providence, which over time, was eventually merged with Clarksville. After the moderately damaged ledger had been transported to various places for rehabilitation, it found its way into the capable hands of Uffelman, Kanervo, Smith, and Williams—and in the spring of 2020, *The Diary of Serepta Jordan: A Southern Woman's Struggle with War and Family, 1857–1864* was published to the same acclaim of their previous work on Nannie Haskins Williams. There are similarities between Nannie and Serepta in terms of proximity and lively prose, and of course they share the same editors, but they have little else in common. Jordan despised elite women like Williams, and her disdain shows in her diary. Orphaned at a young age, Serepta was challenged by being raised by an extended family. She began writing her diary at age eighteen, collecting her thoughts from 1857 to 1864. This tart volume fills in voids of local history that Williams had left out. Jordan's descriptions of antebellum life are enlightening, including details about the Montgomery County's first agricultural fair and a professor leading students from a nearby college into war, a group that evolved into the 14th Tennessee. In addition, Jordan relates how she helped a Confederate prisoner escape and writes about Fort Defiance for the training of African American soldiers. A lot of her diary has an underlying theme: her bitter class resentment toward the elite ladies of Clarksville. Indeed, "Rep" even mentions Nannie's mother, among others, as she scoffs at those who exuded pretentiousness. Both communities partook in class warfare, during and after civil war, as old-monied Clarksvillians were pitted against the merchant class of New Providence.

In the fall of 2020, *The Civil War Diaries of Cassie Fennell: A Young Confederate Woman in North Alabama, 1859–1865* was published. Whitney Snow's adept editing fleshed out the diarist's character. Better known as Cassie, Catherine was well educated, and her account begins with her attendance at a prestigious female academy in Washington, DC. After moving back home to Guntersville, the trajectory of her social standing continues to rise until it is disrupted by civil war. As the war devolves for the Confederacy, so did the family's prosperity. Moreover, Cassie's family members are killed, taken prisoner, or suffer other deprivations. The diary also details the Federal bombardment and burning of Guntersville, which had been mostly overlooked, in January of 1865, giving a rare glimpse into this incident. Consequently, Cassie's diary is not only an engaging social history through the eyes of an advantaged young woman prior to war, it also demonstrates how she was humbled by the struggle. The diary is also notable since there are only a handful of war accounts written by contemporaries from northern Alabama.

Previous volumes were in the form of diaries and journals. The present volume, this time ably edited by Minoa Uffelman, Ellen Kanervo, and Phyllis Smith, comprises letters. *The Civil War Letters of Sarah Kennedy: Life under Occupation in the Upper South* spans from August 1862 to February 1865 with some familiar settings and scenarios and some new ones. Like Nannie Haskins Williams and Serepta Jordan, Sarah Kennedy lived in Clarksville. But unlike the two previous journals, Sarah was writing to someone—in her case, to her husband, David Newton Kennedy, who went by his initials D. N. His financial acumen as a local banker earned him a station in far-off Mississippi, where he was ordered to help run the Confederate Treasury Department. Sarah writes to D. N. about local college students being enlisted, disruption in the postal system, and ruptures in family life, including everything from the loss of children to loss of men in war. The subtitle of their work is especially significant, as the letters copiously describe Federal occupation—from curfews to loyalty oaths to pillaging. Also, the seizure of the press caused a dearth in newspaper production, so Sarah's letters are especially valuable in piecing together a narrative of the times. In addition, Sarah sends descriptions to D. N. about the routines of home life, including gardening, knitting, sewing, taking care of their six children, and running a household that included slaves. She reflects on the turning tides of emancipation in the upper South, Clarksvillians that fled to Canada because of it, and the isolation of being away from her beloved husband. There is inspiration in her prose—and also embitterment—as the Confederacy fell apart.

Recent scholarship includes distinguished examples of volumes of correspondence between couples, revealing particularly how deeply women influenced men. These volumes often describe fluid relationships, letters from family members divulging an intimate story in various layers, sometimes leading up the chain of command. Indeed, the editors of the present volume point out that "historians realized that women could deeply influence their husbands in important ways. Correspondence between couples shed light not just on relationships but also on the numerous ways men and women could confirm, challenge, support, or dissent from each other." They continue, "Historians have begun to realize the influence of husband-wife relationships on military officers. Far from being passive spouses, women could exert influence on their husbands. . . . The women were partners, giving advice, providing information, offering support, encouraging, or even challenging them." Ultimately, "marital influence," in the past (just as in the present), mattered. Scholars are now uncovering this, with couples' private spheres influencing our understanding of the political and militarily realms. The publication of this volume marks the completion of a unique trilogy, each with a distinctive voice, that presents as detailed a history of Civil War–era Clarksville as we are ever going to have.

Michael P. Gray
East Stroudsburg University of Pennsylvania

# ACKNOWLEDGMENTS

We would like especially to thank Jill Hastings-Johnson, Montgomery County Archivist, for her invaluable assistance. Ronald W. Vinson, executive director of the Presbyterian Heritage Center at Montreat, North Carolina, provided information on D. N. Kennedy and his role in the Presbyterian Church of the Confederate States of America. We would like to thank Austin Peay State University faculty members, Professor Emeritus Phil Kemmerly and Professor Greg Zieren, for assisting, sharing leads and expertise. Civil War scholars Kenneth Noe, Barton Myers, Candice Shy Hooper, Tim Wesley, and Raymond Steward offered much-needed suggestions on sources. Former Austin Peay State University librarian Nicole Wood and Clarksville-Montgomery County librarian Raymond Rosado offered valuable assistance. We would like to thank local historians Brenda Harper and Jim Long for sharing their knowledge. Clarksville attorney Jane Sharpe Olson explained legal issues. Neisha Wolfe and Ann Waddle provided helpful information on real estate transfers. Sarah's descendant, Paul Plunket, gave us updated information on the family.

Professors Antoinette van Zelm at Middle Tennessee State University and Aaron Astor at Maryville College acted as readers for the manuscript; they provided valuable insights and suggestions and improved the manuscript tremendously. Glenna Schroeder-Lein not only made this book more convenient for researchers through her thorough index, but she also offered suggestions that made our footnotes more accurate and complete. We would like to thank the team at the University of Tennessee Press, especially Scot Danforth, director, and our excellent editor, Jonathan Boggs.

# EDITORIAL DECISIONS

Sarah Kennedy had clear, legible handwriting that was easily transcribed. Letters by their very nature are intended for someone else to read. She was well educated and her letters are literate, grammatically correct, polished, and well organized. Only minimal editing was required for these letters. The editors corrected names in the few instances of misspellings. For example, we standardized the three spellings of Macrae (McCrae, MacCrae). We did not indicate our changes. If Sarah Kennedy misspelled a name in a letter, we left it as she wrote it, but we used the correct spelling in the endnote. Additionally, we added punctuation that eased reading but did not change the meaning. We inserted in brackets words Sarah appeared to have inadvertently left out.

We favored the term *enslaved people* to capture their humanity, though we did use the term *slave* occasionally. We did not refer to Yankees in our citations, employed *Union* very restrictively, and used the terms *Federal* and *US* interchangeably. Using the most widely accepted practice, we capitalized *Black* and *White* and used the term *Black* interchangeably with *African American*. We consistently used the modern name *Fort Defiance*, though the fort had two earlier names, "Fort Sevier" when it was built and "Fort Bruce" under Federal occupation. Despite our best efforts we were unable to transcribe a few words, and in those instances we used {*indecipherable*}.

Sarah wrote two letters dated September 2, 1864. The content of the two letters suggests that the second letter was perhaps written on October 2, 1864. However, we chose not to second-guess her dating and made the decision to use "September" just as she did. When researching the people mentioned in the letters, we consulted as many sources as we could find. We were not able to identify every person mentioned. If a person does not have a citation, it is because we could not find information on him or her. We used censuses; marriage, birth, or death records; newspaper accounts; city directories; cemetery lists; and published local histories. Ancestry.com has expanded tremendously with family trees constructed by descendants. Sometimes the trees link to traditional sources already mentioned and sometimes they do not. We acknowledge these nontraditional sources may include errors, but they contain useful information that helped us make connections. In fact, traditional sources can contain errors. We also used Find A Grave when possible. Headstones could confirm birth and death dates. We made every attempt to ensure accuracy in our research, and if mistakes occurred, we apologize.

# Introduction

Sarah Kennedy's Civil War letters to her husband, David Newton Kennedy,[1] who went by D. N., provide valuable insights into the home front in Clarksville, Tennessee, during Federal occupation. Because newspapers were not published during occupation, everything we know about the Clarksville home front comes from surviving diaries and letters.[2] Sarah Kennedy's letters chronicle the experience of an elite, slave-owning woman who deeply loved her husband and was devoted to her children. The letters passed to her granddaughter Mary Burney of Denton, Texas,[3] and are now housed at the Tennessee State Library and Archives.

We do not know what Sarah and D. N.'s relationship was like when they were together. Did he talk to her about his business dealings? Did she offer advice? Did she have a sense of humor? What was she like in public settings—quiet and retiring, or vivacious and outgoing? We do not have D. N.'s letters to Sarah to give us any answers to these questions. We have this one set of letters at a very specific, stressful time in her life. We can glean some of the dimensions of her life through public sources. We know about many events she took part in because they were recorded in newspaper articles about her prominent husband's community activities. The decennial censuses also allow us to know who was living in the household when and in what households children and grandchildren resided. As scattered as these bits of information seem, they provide a much more complete portrait of her life story than what we might expect from the old adage that a lady's name should only appear in the newspaper three times, her birth, marriage, and death.

D. N. was a prominent and influential banker and community leader and was part of the upper echelon of society in Clarksville and Montgomery County. Therefore, he left an extensive public historical record. By contrast, Sarah's public record is limited. Her Civil War letters were intended as private missives to her beloved husband, but because they were donated to the

Tennessee State Library and Archives, historians and those interested in the war have access to words she never intended for eyes other than her husband's. Her private words are now public.

Sarah's letters to her husband allowed her to stay connected by relaying the news they both would be interested in. Writing is a creative as well as an informative act. Amy L. Wink in *She Left Nothing in Particular: The Autobiographical Legacy of Nineteenth-Century Women's Diaries*[4] explores why nineteenth-century women wrote diaries. Sarah's letters seem to have served functions similar to those described by Wink for diarists. Sarah Kennedy was "a woman in the act of writing, physically placing pen to paper in order to write and give her thoughts a physical and concrete existence." She was "spinning thought into the potent and empowering web of written language— language styled differently than language used in speech or even immediate thought."[5]

In writing, Sarah drew upon her education, vocabulary, and talent as a wordsmith. She had agency in creating the narrative she wanted to give. Letters allowed her to share experiences, give opinions, and seek advice. Perhaps she was even able to clarify and work through the issues as she articulated them in writing. She determined how much anxiety and stress she would share with her husband. She was recreating in words her experiences, fears, hopes, and information about family, friends, and the enslaved. Unlike diaries, letters are meant to be read and therefore tend to be more polished. The letters in this volume required much less editing than the diaries these editors previously published. They are more formal and grammatically correct. Wink concludes that reading the writings of a nineteenth-century woman means a woman is speaking to the reader across the generations.[6] Today, generations after she wrote the letters, we read her words and probably relate to universal feelings of love for her children and concern for her husband. But other aspects of her life, her attitude toward her enslaved, we find abhorrent.

Traditionally, male historians wrote about men in history with little regard for the women in their lives. More recently, historians realized that women could deeply influence their husbands in important ways. Correspondence between couples shed light not just on relationships but also on the numerous ways men and women could confirm, challenge, support, or dissent from each other. Historians have begun to realize the influence of husband-wife relationships on military officers. Far from being passive spouses, women could exert influence on their husbands. Candice Shy Hooper's study of the wives of Lincoln's top four generals shows that overlooking the important influence of wives on their husbands renders incomplete our understanding of the men.[7] The women were partners, giving advice, providing information, offering support, encouraging, or even challenging them. Hooper's study points out that ignoring the dynamics of marital influence diminishes what was perhaps one of the most important influences on public decision-making.

Drew Gilpin Faust, in *Mothers of Invention: Women of the Slaveholding South in the American Civil War*,[8] devotes a chapter to letters between husbands and wives. Indeed, Faust refers to Sarah Kennedy's letters several times. Poor women, desperate with hungry children as the war worsened, sometimes wrote and encouraged their husbands to return home and stop fighting a lost cause while their families starved. Sarah did not offer D. N. advice, nor did she even reference any decisions he might have been grappling with while at war. Her letters reveal an unwavering partnership and unwavering love and support. Her letters contain home front news and she always wrote words of love and support. No matter what was happening in D. N.'s life, he knew his wife was committed to him and she was caring for the home.

The fifty-two letters span from August 16, 1862, to February 20, 1865, from sixteen months after the firing on Fort Sumter and six after Clarksville surrendered to the US military. Sarah moved her family out of the city either before or early in the occupation, retreating to a friend's home on the Kentucky/Tennessee border. A week after Clarksville surrendered, Nashville surrendered too, becoming the first Confederate capital to fall. The US Navy controlled the Cumberland River, a major blow to the CSA. The letters reveal how this well-connected slave-owning mother of six young children survived, keeping the large household running in US-occupied Clarksville. Sarah saw to the health, education, and welfare of her large brood. Rarely were they all healthy at the same time, and she constantly assessed what form of education was best for each child. While she struggled to keep everyone fed and warm, her situation was not dire because of their pre-war wealth and connections. Yet, as she wrote of loving and caring for her children, she also held a worldview that believed White people could own Black people. She believed the enslaved should be submissive, obedient, performing the work they were told to. As slavery broke down in Clarksville and the African Americans she owned began to assert their independence, she became a cold, calculating, embittered slave owner. In the waning months of slavery, she tried to extract as much labor as possible and made decisions based only on the financial benefit to her family. Sarah used the term "servant" in the earlier letters but as she lost control, she resorted to using "nigger." As her enslaved grew more independent, she became evermore resentful and harsh. Yet, in the same letters she wrote lovingly of her children and her husband.

Nineteenth-century women's lives were determined by race, class, and stage of life. Young elite white women had few household responsibilities and their lives were consumed with school, friendship, and courtship. Working class young women assumed more household responsibilities but also participated in courtship rituals. Marriage and motherhood meant that the wife ran the household, reared the children, and oversaw their household's enslaved people. The three published diaries and letters of Clarksville women vividly demonstrate this point. Nannie Haskins was sixteen when she began her diary. She recorded few household tasks and described many social gatherings, writing of the various young men she met and became interested in.[9] Serepta Jordan was a young unmarried woman whose parents had died. She lived with her maternal aunt and uncle. She had to earn her keep and her diary chronicled exhaustingly long lists of labor she performed to keep the household going.[10] Though well off, Sarah Kennedy was at the most labor-intensive time of her life with heavy responsibilities. She had young children, one with special needs, oversaw the enslaved, and was in charge of every aspect of maintaining the household. She managed the family finances, including trying to maintain the value of her human property. She alone was the economic manager of the family.

Her letters described dealing with ordinary issues of feeding, caring for, and educating her children in spite of the extraordinary circumstances of war. Sarah wrote about the policies and practices of the occupation, including curfews, passes, loyalty oaths, violence, the appropriation of goods and produce, and the scarcity of some goods as prices rose. She told of some Clarksvillians going to Canada to escape Federal occupation. She related the dangers of robberies, violence, and arson. She gave updates on the weather, her garden, sewing and knitting, and other news she thought would interest D. N. She wrote him of births, illnesses, and deaths in the community.

Clarksville, Tennessee, is located at the confluence of the Cumberland and Red Rivers. In 1860 the population was about 5,000. The area was strategically important for transportation and for products such as iron and livestock. Clarksville and New Providence, across the Red River from each other, were thriving market towns, shipping goods in steamboats across the South. Today the town of New Providence is incorporated into Clarksville. Tobacco was the main crop, and the city processed and stored tobacco in massive warehouses along the river until ready to ship to market. Pig iron was an important industry with hundreds of workers, including slaves, refining vast quantities of ore in the area's seven iron furnaces. Foundries in Montgomery and the adjacent counties were among the nation's leading iron producers. The area also boasted numerous slaughtering houses. When war began, both American and Confederate militaries would want the resources the area provided; however, it was the US Government that would benefit.[11]

The Kennedys lived in a handsome red brick structure that stood on an incline at 221 South Second Street. The residence was built in an L-shape with an entry doorway off-center to the right. The front door opened to a hallway from which a flight of stairs led to the bedrooms on the second floor. The servants' room and kitchen were on the first level and there was a full basement. Sarah's letters indicate that there were slave cabins on the property. The large home had plaster walls, an asphalt shingled roof, and a front porch and large windows. It was an impressive private residence.[12]

As the nation careened toward war, Montgomery Countians supported staying in the Union, but that stance changed with the firing on Fort Sumter. Opinion changed quickly and dramatically toward secession. This turnabout was typical for many Tennesseans who opposed secession until Fort Sumter, when their support moved overwhelmingly toward the Confederacy and creating a new nation. D. N. Kennedy was originally a "Union man" but his opinion changed, and he led the secessionist movement in the county. His obituary said he "went with his people and supported with all his energy the cause of the Confederacy."[13] In preparation for war, citizens established four recruiting and training camps.[14] By the time Fort Donelson fell in February 1862, the Confederate soldiers that trained at these camps had moved to other sites. The loss of Fort Donelson, which had a water battery overlooking the Cumberland near Dover, Tennessee, was the beginning of the end for the Confederacy because it opened the entire Cumberland Valley to US forces. The US controlled both the Tennessee and Cumberland Rivers. On February 19, a Federal gunboat and steamer approached Fort Sevier, now known as Fort Defiance,[15] at New Providence. Clarksvillians understood that the gunboats could destroy downtown Clarksville and despite the name of the fort, local dignitaries raised the white flag and promptly surrendered without a shot being fired. Flag Officer A. H. Foote issued a proclamation that residents could expect safety but also outlawed Confederate flags and demanded the surrender of military supplies. Federal occupation would last until the end of the war.

Perhaps seeing the handwriting on the wall or simply acting on good fiscal sense, D. N. Kennedy had moved audaciously to protect the bank he had founded with partner James L. Glenn, the Northern Bank of Tennessee.[16] He removed the bank's gold and assets, secreted them out of Clarksville to New Orleans and sent them to England.[17] He would not risk the bank he co-founded falling under the control of US occupiers. The gambit paid off.

After the war the assets were returned and the Northern Bank reopened. The building was damaged during occupation but it was rebuilt and the bank thrived.[18]

The Kennedys were active members of First Presbyterian Church, Clarksville. The Presbyterian denomination split along sectional lines during the war.[19] Kennedy continued his leadership in the Presbyterian Church of the Confederate States despite being in exile. He was listed as a trustee of the first General Assembly of the Presbyterian Church of the CSA in Augusta, Georgia, in 1861 and again at the 1862 General Assembly that met in Montgomery, Alabama, in May.[20] The next year David N. Kennedy was replaced as a trustee for the General Assembly of the Presbyterian Church of the Confederate States because he was "within the lines of the enemy."[21] These notes in Presbyterian records add to the mystery of Kennedy's whereabouts during the war. He was not listed as a trustee again until 1868[22] when First Presbyterian Clarksville was part of the renamed Presbyterian Church in the United States. The southern and northern branches of the Presbyterian Church did not reunite until 1983.[23]

In December of 1862 Sarah wrote that she had talked to a Clarksville resident, Joe Broaddus: "He had expected to meet you in Montgomery but you had passed through before he arrived there."[24] It is unclear if this related to the May 1862 conference but does indicate that D. N. was moving within the Confederate territory. In the same letter she wrote, "I do hope you will see all our Woodville friends and write me particularly of Bro. Willie's family."[25] The next letter Sarah wrote said she was giving a letter to someone in the 49th Tennessee Infantry Regiment to be delivered. By November of 1862, the 49th was at Port Hudson, Louisiana,[26] which was less than 40 miles from Woodville, Mississippi. The letters from December 1862 through April 1863 indicate that D. N. was in Woodville, near Sarah's family.

It appears that D. N. Kennedy's movements may have been loosely connected with those of the 49th Tennessee, the second Confederate infantry regiment organized in Clarksville, with Sarah's cousin, James Edmund Bailey, as its colonel. As we try to trace D. N.'s steps through Sarah's letters we might connect them to the battles the 49th fought.[27]

Members of the 49th were captured with the fall of Fort Donelson in February 1862, taken to Vicksburg, Mississippi, in September 1862, and exchanged on November 10, 1862. The 49th remained in Mississippi until General Joseph E. Johnston pulled out of the state in late July 1863. In the February 12, 1863, letter, Sarah asked her husband to try to find Clarksville soldiers at a camp near Granada, Mississippi, a distance of 240 miles from Woodville—not close, but the family hoped that Kennedy could manage to get a letter to the recipients. In fact, she frequently mentioned contact between D. N. and members of the 49th during the first half of 1863.

D. N. may have left Mississippi before the 49th's July departure because of the increased level of combat in the state. US and Confederate forces met in skirmishes almost daily. The city of Jackson fell to the Federal Government on May 14, 1863. Two days later the US won the Battle of Champion's Hill, halfway between Jackson and Vicksburg. By June of 1863 Sarah asked D. N. to keep a lookout for a Clarksvillian who was believed to be in Chattanooga.[28]

Kennedy's leaving Mississippi for Chattanooga may have been like jumping from the frying pan into the fire. Beginning with a Confederate victory at the Battle of Chickamauga, just south of Chattanooga, on September 1863, Southerners held the high ground and seemed in a good position to take command of this river/rail/highway center. However, the three-day Battles of Chattanooga resulted in one of the most dramatic turnabouts in American military history. When the fighting at Missionary Ridge stopped on November 25, 1863, Federal forces had driven Confederate troops away from Chattanooga, into Georgia, clearing the way for Union General William T. Sherman's march on to Atlanta.

Letters through October 1863 indicate D. N. was in Chattanooga. He would have been ahead of the 49th, which arrived at Missionary Ridge in late November, just after the battle. In November Sarah sent letters by flag of truce, suggesting that this was the best way to ensure that D. N., still in Confederate territory, received mail from US-occupied Clarksville.

Letters from the first eight months of 1864 give no information on D. N.'s whereabouts. We know the 49th was headquartered in Mobile, Alabama, while Johnston and Sherman battled through northern Georgia. In May of 1864 the 49th joined Johnston's army for the Georgia Campaign. D. N. must have been in Georgia for some of this time. In September 1864 Sarah wrote, "Three weeks since I received your first letter advising me of your change of address."[29] Then she wrote that she supposed the letters addressed to Atlanta had been lost. They had been cross-referencing letters sent and received by this point in the war.

Sometime in 1864, D. N. and the 49th went their separate ways. The 49th was with General John Bell Hood—who succeeded Johnston—when Atlanta fell in July 1864. It was with him as he marched back up into Tennessee and his army was annihilated in the Battle of Nashville in December 1864, ending the existence of the 49th. On September 21, 1864, Sarah wrote that she was glad to have received the good news of her Mississippi family being in good health, suggesting D. N. may have personally seen them in Mississippi. In one of the last letters, February 6, 1865, Sarah wrote that she had received letters from D. N. from October and January sent from "the Carolinas and the rest from Augusta." Together the references indicate that Kennedy moved several times from Woodville to Chattanooga to Atlanta to somewhere in one of the Carolinas and finally to Augusta.

By the end of his life, Kennedy was one of the most important and influential men in Clarksville. He was involved in every aspect of civic activity acting as an elder, trustee, officer (usually recording secretary or treasurer) in practically every committee of importance. He drew up resolutions at critical points in history, he was unanimously elected to the constitutional convention. All these activities are listed in his biographies. Yet, his wartime service is vague. Kennedy served in the Confederate legislature in 1861, on the Committee of Finance of Military Affairs. He offered his services to the Confederate Treasury Department where his knowledge of banking and finance would be needed. Late in the war, May 30, 1864, Jefferson Davis appointed D. N. Kennedy as "Collector of Taxes for the State of Tennessee."[30] It is unclear how Kennedy collected taxes in a US-occupied state, especially as he appeared to be outside of the state for most of the war. Nevertheless, a 1901 article about the history of the Confederate Treasury lists D. N. Kennedy as "reappointed" in 1864 to be state tax collector for Tennessee;[31] therefore he seems to have had the same position in the Treasury before 1864. A list of letters sent to the Confederate Treasury mentions one letter written by D. N. Kennedy.[32]

Sarah Ann Bailey was born to James and Lucinda Brown Bailey on November 2, 1823, in Woodville, Mississippi, located in Wilkinson County, in the far southwest corner of the state. Her mother died when Sarah was only one year old and her father died when she was ten. Sarah, along with her older sister Mary, moved to Clarksville to live with their paternal uncle, Charles Bailey.[33] Both Sarah and Mary married men they met in Clarksville: Mary to Wiley Blount Bryan in 1837 and Sarah to D. N. Kennedy in 1843.[34] Sarah always signed her letters S. Kennedy, S. K., or S. A. and was called Sallie by friends and family.

David Newton Kennedy was born in Elkton, Kentucky, February 28, 1820. His father also died when he was young and at age fourteen young D. N. began working as a clerk in a dry goods store. He became the junior partner with John S. Hart in a retail business, Hart and Kennedy, and built it into a successful dry goods firm. The next year, after eight years in the retail business, he left the business because of bad health, and began his banking career as a cashier. In 1854, with James L. Glenn, he organized the Northern Bank, serving as president for forty-five years. Kennedy also was active in the insurance industry, not just selling policies but also serving as an officer in insurance governing boards. He held numerous leadership positions in utilities, philanthropies, professional organizations, First Presbyterian Church, Southwestern Presbyterian University, and Greenwood Cemetery.

Prior to Fort Sumter, Kennedy was a southern Unionist and in the 1860 election, he supported the Constitutional Union Party that was opposed to secession. They nominated East Tennessean, John Bell, with vice-presidential nominee, Edward Everett of Massachusetts. In July 1860, D. N. attended a "meeting of friends of the Union" called the Bell and Everett Club, where he served as chair and wrote the article for the paper, signing it, "D. N. Kennedy, Chairman." Upon taking the chair Mr. Kennedy made a short speech explanatory of the object of the meeting and further said he had thought he would never again interest himself in politics, but his mind had undergone a change. He thought this was not the time for the friends of the Union to falter, every man should be at his post, and do his duty in an effort to save the Union. As for himself, he was ready to come forward and try it once more.[35]

After the firing on Fort Sumter, Kennedy, like most Tennesseans, became a secessionist and served as the president of the Southern Rights Association. He hastily called a meeting to be held at the Montgomery County Courthouse in April 1861. He said that citizens were united to defend "sister Southern States, against Lincoln's Abolitionist hordes." The large crowd enthusiastically cheered in approval to "override the despot," and the "freedmen" of Clarksville would "resist oppression." The secession resolutions passed unanimously and D. N. Kennedy, along with the other committee members, agreed to present the resolutions to the Tennessee Legislature in Nashville the next day. In the passionate, heated secession discussion, someone announced that the *Louisiana Journal* urged neutrality and the news "was received with curses upon a traitor who could be so recreant to every feeling of honor—*neutrality was assistance to our enemies*." (Italics in the original.) Kennedy adjourned the meeting around midnight but the crowd left reluctantly.[36] The die was cast. Clarksville and Montgomery County, led by D. N. Kennedy, enthusiastically supported joining the Confederate States of America.

In September of 1861, Kennedy was a fervent proponent of the rebellion and actively recruited young men at Stewart College to enlist. As a trustee of the college,[37] he worked with the president and faculty to recruit the young college students to the Southern army. At a barbecue to drum up support for the Confederacy, Stewart College president, Dr. R. B. McMullen, opened with a prayer. Judge James Quarles followed with an "earnest, patriotic and eloquent speech." The newspaper article continues: "Mr. D. N. Kennedy next came forward and urged upon the patriotic sons of Stewart to enlist in this, the second war for independence. He depicted, in strong colors, all the horrors of the civil war about to be precipitated upon us by an invasion of Lincoln Hessians into Kentucky. He sketched the causes of the war—read numerous statistics showing the difference between the sections, and the relative positions of both the north and south. His was a matter-of-fact kind of speech, and was well delivered and well received."[38]

The enlistment efforts were successful and devastating for the young Stewart College men, for the war brought death to many. Of the twenty-nine students who joined, sixteen were killed and seven died of disease or wounds. The unit the college students joined, the 14th Tennessee Infantry, elected Stewart College math professor William Forbes as captain. The 14th fought in virtually every major battle in the Eastern Theater.[39]

Hundreds of young men joined the CSA and filled the hastily con-structed camps in Montgomery County. President Jefferson Davis declared June 13, 1861, a day of fasting and prayer. First Presbyterian held morning services as did the various training camps. Kennedy served as treasurer of the Military Fund and raised money to supply the camps. With funds raised, they purchased meat, bread, meal, and flour. Employers were encouraged to continue to pay the salaries of the enlisted men. Women joined aid groups to contribute to the Southern cause.[40]

In 1861, Sarah and D. N. had been married eighteen years and had suf-fered the heartache of burying three children. In November 1849 their four-year-old daughter, Lizzie, suffered a horrible death after her cotton dress caught fire while she was playing with a lit candle. At first the injuries did not appear fatal but the next morning she died. According to the article in the paper, the young girl said, "good-bye mamma, I am dying.' And in a few moments sunk quietly to rest."[41] In September of 1850, the paper carried the death notice of their infant son, Edward Bailey.[42] He may have been named Edward David and called by his middle name because his tombstone reads "David, three months old." William "Willie," born in 1848, was counted in the 1850 census but died shortly thereafter. In the span of two years Sarah and D. N. lost all three of their children.

Sarah resumed childbearing immediately and was perhaps pregnant when Willie died. By 1861 she had six children and was left alone to care for them and run the household. Mary was born in 1851, James "Jimmy" in 1853, Sally in 1855, David N. "Newty" in 1857, Clara in 1859, and Ellen in 1861. All her letters contain news of the children. Sending the letters between two warring nations, Sarah's from US-occupied Clarksville to her husband in Confederate-controlled Mississippi, was complicated.

Americans were used to a dependable postal system. By declaring itself a new nation, the Confederate States of America faced the challenges of creating a postal system out of nothing.[43] The pre-war assumption that a letter or package mailed from any post office in the US would reach the intended recipient was shattered at the very moment that people were desperate for reliable mail delivery.

The CSA formed a post office on February 21, 1861, naming John H. Reagan, a Texas congressman, as postmaster general. Confederates controlled about 30 percent of the postal service with 8,535 post offices out of 28,586. Reagan encouraged postmasters and employees to bring with them their equipment, maps, forms, reports, and plans. Reagan hoped to negotiate an agreement that mail would be delivered through enemy lines throughout the war, but US Postmaster Montgomery Blair instead cut off mail service to the South on March 31, 1861.[44]

Letters addressed to the South were sent to the Dead Letter Office and returned to senders. Because using postage stamps as currency was common practice, Blair cancelled all stamps, therefore denying Confederates use of US stamps and also preventing their use as money. He authorized new US stamps. Border States that stayed in the Union but whose citizens often had friends and relatives both fighting for and living in Confederate states had to rely on smugglers to deliver their correspondence. As control of territory changed sides, the borders were constantly moving. Post offices sometimes passed from USA to CSA to USA control.[45]

Some postmasters improvised and sold their own provisional stamps or marked "paid" by hand. A Richmond firm, Hoyer & Ludwig Lithography, printed the first CSA five-cent stamp featuring the image of Jefferson Davis. This green stamp was of inferior quality as Hoyer & Ludwig had no experience and subsequently lost the contract. Southerners next turned to a London printing firm, Thomas De La Rue & Co. In 1863, Archer & Daly, a Southern firm, began producing stamps.[46]

As Confederate territory fell to Federal control, the USPS was restored. Because Clarksville surrendered to US troops after the defeat of Fort Donelson, Sarah had to find ways to get her letters from US-occupied Clarksville to her husband in Confederate Mississippi. Her letters are silent on how she knew who the carriers were, but obviously there was a network of people sharing information about who was leaving and when, right under the noses of occupying forces. There were some Southern independent firms that transported mail. After August 1861, mail could also be sent between the two countries under a flag of truce. Under this system, mail could only cross the lines at designated exchange points. Mail from the North to the

South primarily passed through City Point, Virginia, and from the South to the North primarily through Fortress Monroe, Virginia.[47]

A flag-of-truce letter had to be enclosed in an unsealed inner envelope and sent in an outer envelope with postage paid to the exchange point. Authorities examined the letter and discarded the outer envelope. Delivery required payment of the postage by stamps of the other side or by an attached or inserted coin. Therefore, USA and CSA postage could be paid on a single envelope if the sender possessed stamps of both sides.[48] Sarah seemed particularly adept at navigating the various ways to send letters to D. N., sending them covertly by someone she knew was traveling south, perhaps using a private company or under flag-of-truce. She needed both CSA and USA stamps depending on the method she used. Only the letters survived, not the envelopes she mailed them in. Those may have shed light on how she managed to get the letters delivered to her husband.

Toward the end of the war, Sarah realized some letters were not arriving. Therefore, she began to write in the letters the dates of all the letters she wrote and the dates of the letters she received so that they could cross-reference any missing letters. During this time her letters became repetitious because she did not know which ones would arrive and which would disappear into the confusion of war. Cross-referencing her dates indicated that a few letters did not arrive and she was able to figure out which of D. N.'s letters went awry. Letters could take weeks to be delivered with long periods of no correspondence and suddenly several letters coming at once. By 1865 almost five hundred routes had returned to the USPS.[49]

This was the complicated and fractured mail system that Sarah and D. N. used to exchange letters. They dealt with both USA and CSA postage stamps and had to know which particular one was needed. Sarah depended on a network of local people to get the mail out of occupied Clarksville to Confederate-held post offices. It seems that at times the appropriate stamps were somewhat difficult to obtain, as she listed in postscripts how many stamps she was sending D. N. or asked for him to send her stamps.

Sarah deeply loved and respected her husband. She expressed great sorrow at being separated from him with the added anxiety of worrying about his health and well-being. She called him their "presiding genius,"[50] which perhaps to a modern reader may seem like teasing or loving sarcasm. It is not. To Sarah, D. N. was indeed the family's "presiding genius." She instilled in her children a devotion for their father. Sarah's letters followed a pattern. Each one contained family news, particularly of the children with an emphasis on how much the children loved and missed their father. She always related their health, including her own, and she was often sick. She discussed business dealings and local news. She told D. N. who had taken the oath of allegiance, who refused, and who went to Canada to escape occupation. She related news of weddings, illnesses, and deaths of friends and neighbors. She included requests from friends for D. N. to find information about local soldiers, especially men in the 49th Tennessee Infantry. The 49th served mainly in the Western Theater while the 14th fought in the East.

Southern women were active participants and essential to economies and education in urban centers. In *Constructing Townscapes: Space and Society in Antebellum Tennessee*, Lisa C. Tolbert shows how merchants were dependent on women's trade. Therefore, store owners would cater to their preferences.[51] Female education was an aspect of Southern towns both for the girls attending schools and the mothers choosing the best schools for their daughters.[52] Nannie Haskins, Serepta Jordan, and Sarah Kennedy reflected this significance; all of these women received excellent educations. Nannie attended Clarksville Female Academy,[53] an important educational institution, and she wrote a history of her alma mater in 1896 for Tennessee's state centennial.[54] It is unknown where Serepta obtained her fine education, but she had a tutor at some point and mentioned meeting a favorite former teacher. Sarah attended Nashville Female Academy.[55] As an upper-class woman, Sarah was determined to provide the best education for all of her children, not just for her sons but for her daughters as well, with training in spelling, reading, history, geography, French, and piano. Eventually, the couple would have to determine how to educate their special needs child.

In the early letters, Sarah and the children were living at a farm named Cloverlands, near the Kentucky state line. They must have hastily moved out of their downtown Clarksville home to be safe from Federal soldiers and for fear of what occupation would bring. They had rented their home to a Unionist Kentucky family named Parker and left the Kennedy slaves in Clarksville. By August, Sarah was eager for the Parkers to move out so that she could return to her home. She wrote of them with annoyance tinged with anger as she thought the renters were trying to take advantage of her because the Parkers did not remove their furniture after they departed for Kentucky. She was unhappy with the financial arrangements Parker offered regarding rent reduction and the storage of their furniture. Sarah's letters reveal the complex business of managing all the finances of a household of fifteen people, white children and enslaved men, women, and children. She made decisions about every purchase for the household, her family and the enslaved.

Sarah returned to the large downtown house with children, Jimmy, Newty, Mary, Sally, Clara, and Ellen, along with the enslaved Aunt Lucy,

Phil, Tom, Fanny, Cheney, and Patsy, whom Sarah had hired from another owner. Sarah was in charge of running the household, including managing the household expenses and organizing the labor of the enslaved, hiring out different slaves and contracting with other owners for slaves to meet her needs. She also managed a number of rental properties. She wrote to D. N. of the provisions she had secured including food and fuel, often telling him quantities and the amount she spent. As the war progressed and scarcities developed, she related to him the inflated costs she was forced to pay. Because the occupying forces appropriated goods, she thought it prudent to buy supplies in smaller quantities as needed so that she would not lose all her stored food to the military in one fell swoop. She wrote of their family's business interests, both personal and interests of the Northern Bank. She was increasingly concerned about the financial losses that freedom for enslaved people would bring and realized selling the slaves had become impossible. Sarah not only sent information but also asked for advice from D. N. and shared with him what other people had advised her. She considered all advice given to her and then took action that she thought was best, even if it was contrary to what her husband recommended.

The normally mundane but essential procurement of food and coal for heat became more difficult during the war. She maximized energy efficiency by moving bedrooms and serving two meals a day instead of three. She wrote of violence and arson and knew both could happen to her. She prepared for the potential of arson, keeping a bag of essential paperwork handy to grab in case someone set her house on fire. She worried that when D. N. left, she forgot to pack his slippers. Later biographies of D. N. stated that ill health prevented him from joining the Confederate military. As the war progressed, Sarah was concerned about him not having shoes and shirts, and she tried to send him needed supplies.

In her early letters, Sarah described occupation. Kentuckian Colonel Sanders Bruce, who headed Clarksville's occupation, commanded about three thousand soldiers. His policies had two sometimes contradictory goals. He wanted to stop and stamp out resistance from local Confederate families who had friends and loved ones fighting against the US, but also not to alienate the local Whites. Pickets were stationed "at every inlet and outlet of the town and no one, white or black is allowed to ingress or egress without a pass from the Col."[56] Bruce prohibited molesting private residences. However, the soldiers foraged and appropriated goods and produce throughout the county, causing resentment. Sarah saw soldiers daily "bringing in wagon loads of corn, pork and hay."[57] The situation made her anxious and nervous and she related hearing noises in the night and checking the house. She, however, wrote that the "servants seem entirely right, and if they have any notions of freedom, they keep it concealed."[58] Each slave kept plans for freedom secret from Sarah, yet by the last letter seven of her eight enslaved people had left slavery for freedom.

As with most Clarksvillians, Sarah held deep antipathy for Federal soldiers. Locals had daily interaction with soldiers who were on the streets, were billeted around town, frequented local businesses, and even attended the same worship services. Churches were monitored since Colonel Bruce understood Confederate congregations could make plans to provide aid and comfort to the enemy, plan insurrections, and even foment rebellion. Sarah related that her Presbyterian church service was well attended because the "Chaplain of the Yanks" preached at the Methodist church that Sunday.[59] She saw Federal officers who "looked mean enough" and the armed guard on the steps made her "mad enough to run the bayonet through him."[60] Clarksvillians may have avoided hearing a Union man of God, but they could not avoid seeing a US soldier guarding the church. This type of hostile peace lasted throughout the war.

Each letter listed the family members' sicknesses. Sarah herself mentioned suffering numerous illnesses, including ones modern Americans know: colds, smallpox, whooping cough, and chills. Additionally, she wrote of several illnesses using archaic terms: typhoid pneumonia, bilious remitting fever, torpid liver, cholera morbus, and a bone felon. She mentioned weight loss once saying she was forty pounds lighter. She sometimes stayed sick for days if not weeks. Additionally, she admitted to emotional problems of depression, anxiety, and worry. By far, Newty was the child that required the most care. She referred to "Newty's affliction,"[61] and while his condition remained unnamed, and presumably undiagnosed, it was extremely serious. She described him suffering numerous "spasms," one of which lasted four hours. In May 1863, she said he had gone two weeks without spasms but became "indisposed for three days and is in a never ending nervous state tonight" and could not sleep.[62] Caring for him drained her physically and emotionally and she became ill herself. In one letter, she despaired that this was a lifetime condition and he would never get better. She knew he needed a nurse but it was impossible to find one, despite being willing to pay the expense. Caring for him wore Sarah down: "My own nervous system is almost prostrate."[63] She did get help from Aunt Lucy. "I think Newty has improved under Aunt Lucy's care," she wrote in one letter.[64]

Still life carried on and she did normal activities like taking her children to have photographs made to send to their father. Unfortunately, none of those could be found in public archives nor with descendants. Sarah decided which type of education suited each child, schooling at home under her tutelage or at one of the local schools. She ensured that Mary, who was talented musically, received piano lessons and wrote of how well she played. A war was raging but Sarah made sure her children received the best education possible for each one's particular needs. Sarah also taught practical skills such as knitting, even to her son, Jimmy.

The 1860 Slave Schedule lists eight enslaved in the Kennedy household. Only the sex and the age of slaves were listed, not names. D. N. and Sarah owned three females, ages 60, 40, and 37, and five males, ages, 37, 30, 25, 20, and 4. Through the context of the letters we can deduce the age of the people Sarah wrote of. Slavery remained legal in occupied Tennessee until January of 1865; however, in practice slavery gradually ended in Clarksville with the absence of Confederate troops and the presence of US troops, which facilitated African Americans leaving their White owners.

Enslaved town people had much different lives from those enslaved on large plantations. While enslaved people did not leave diaries recounting their daily activities, their White enslavers sometimes recorded their activities. Some enslaved people labored in their owners' homes. Other times, the enslavers hired out the slaves so that while still enslaved they were working for someone who did not own them. Lisa C. Tolbert documented the activities of town slaves in Franklin, Tennessee, where a Black man was accused of murdering two White men. Through court testimony the enslaved man recounted his day's activities showing a certain amount of autonomy as he completed his tasks. He traveled through town, interacting with other enslaved people, talking with several people, and playing cards. The Black and White communities in Southern towns were intertwined and complex. People would have known each other by name or at least been familiar with who everyone was.[65]

Enslaved people might hire themselves out for jobs and earn their own money. Serepta Jordan made references to enslaved people visiting and interacting. In the first letters in this volume, Sarah had rented out their Clarksville home and left the enslaved people there. It is not explicitly stated what they did with their time when not taking care of the house, but it could be presumed that they might have hired themselves out to other Clarksville families for particular jobs. That was certainly true as the war progressed and White mastery diminished. Sarah wrote of Tom working for himself and she even tried to get his wages sent to her. The enslaved had communication networks Whites were not privy to. Therefore, enslavers would sometimes wake to find their human property had left under the cover of darkness.

The letters describe the incremental end of slavery. Sarah struggled to maintain her mastery over the enslaved people of her household as they began asserting independence. The letters were written from an owner's perspective and we must read between the lines to suss out the African Americans' perspectives. She wrote of the annoyance and financial calamity of losing their human property. We, however, must imagine the totally opposite attitudes of the enslaved as they planned their precarious and uncertain steps toward freedom. While Sarah was weighing all her options to try to minimize losing money on her human property—considering selling, renting, and trying to collect the wages of a former slave from his job with the US Army—the enslaved must have felt elation, excitement, and hope at the probability of freedom. Until they acted, they kept their plans secret. They bided their time, weighed their options, and left when they decided it was best for them. Each enslaved person and family decided when and where they would leave based on their individual circumstances, perhaps influenced by age, health, family, friends, skills, and their courage to leave, and strike out on their own. The letters illustrate the varied and individual responses to choosing freedom. By the end of the war only one elderly enslaved woman, Lucy, remained in the Kennedy household.

Sarah knew that Lincoln's Emancipation Proclamation would go into effect January 1, 1863. Though Clarksville was not included in the proclamation, Kennedy seemed to understand the grave import to her slaves and slavery in general. She wrote of her anxiety and how neither Black nor White in the household revealed to each other their true feelings. "I feel very lonely though, quite anxious sometimes, at the events that are likely to take place the first of January. I give no evidence to the servants that I am looking for any excitement, and they have shown none. They all perform their duty...."[66] Troops patrolled the streets and enforced a curfew. Tensions were high.

Federals used a neighbor's home to house what the military called contraband, people who left slavery and sought protection under the auspices of the US Army. Early in the war runaways were returned, but the military soon realized they were aiding the Confederacy by returning slaves. Instead, the military hired those laborers as they deemed necessary, and eventually contraband camps were established throughout the South under Federal control. Local citizens would hire people from the contraband camps to work in their households or in the fields. Sarah's enslaved people could see free people nearby.

By November 1863 the US Army began recruiting African Americans as United States Colored Troops (USCT). Sarah was particularly incensed at the thought of former slaves as soldiers. She wrote, "All negrodom is in a fluster here on account of the opening of a recruiting office for male niggers."[67]

Fort Defiance served as a recruiting station for African Americans. The opportunity of becoming a USCT, wearing a uniform, bearing arms, and earning money to fight the Confederates was an exhilarating prospect for many African Americans.[68]

Federal troops impressed large numbers of African Americans and needed labor to complete the fortifications at the camps. Clarksvillians hired semi-free men and Tom took advantage, hiring himself out to other people for wages while he still lived in the Kennedy household. He seemed hesitant to leave the home, and to counter his anxiety he took to drink. Sarah wrote, "He frequently lies at home on Sunday too drunk to stir, loses much time in the week from this cause." She tried to sell him, but by this time buyers were unwilling to purchase a recalcitrant person, "men not being willing to buy unless the subject is willing to go."[69] Tom was not. He eventually took a job with the quartermaster for $15 a month. Sarah toyed with the idea of applying for his wages but that came to naught.

Fanny and her husband John, two among the Kennedys' enslaved, had a "troop" of children. According to Sarah, Fanny had "tantrums" and was a "perfect terror."[70] Sarah asked John what to do about his wife; he said to whip her. We can only imagine the stress and anxiety Fanny felt to behave in the way Sarah bemoaned. Did John really want her whipped or was he placating Sarah? We will never know. We only have Sarah's account of the events. In July, Fanny left with the children and Sarah declared she had been "so quarrelsome and disagreeable that the whole family hated the sight of her." John joined her three weeks later. Aunt Lucy, the elderly enslaved woman, said she was glad Fanny was gone. Perhaps it was true, but it is possible that she employed Brer Rabbit–trickster type dialogue.[71]

Phil remained but also worked for wages around town. His other employment took so much time he neglected the labor at the Kennedy home. Historian Drew Gilpin Faust describes the disgust and anger female enslavers felt as they realized the people they owned were far from the obedient faithful slaves that they believed they should be. It was a shock to learn that the White perception of mutual benefit in the institution of slavery was not held by the enslaved. In the absence of the male heads of the household, women often found it difficult to control their human chattel.[72] Sarah tried to reason with Phil and talked to him about not working, apparently hoping to remind him that he was a slave owned by her and therefore needed to perform as such. But this nominally enslaved man could reject mastery and he tried to explain reasonably to her why he divided his labor in a way to benefit himself. "'Miss Sally, you don't consider how many men are working for themselves and doing nothing at home.'" The justification that this is the new normal did not make Sarah any less annoyed. "He thinks I should consider it a great favor done me that he has not left entirely."[73] Clearly, when a master can no longer demand obedience, slavery is over, in practice if not law.

Sarah regularly related to her husband names of local Blacks as they left for freedom. The slave-owning community was well apprised of the whereabouts of some of the newly freed people. News seemed to travel between African American networks to White communication networks. Sarah heard that Cheney had moved to Cincinnati and was working as a chamber maid. Fanny and her family moved to Nashville, which was a place of particular opportunity. "Nashville seems to them Paradise, and to get there the height of their aspiration."[74] Only Aunt Lucy remained, apparently saying, "'I will die with you, unless they take me by force.'"[75] Aunt Lucy seemed to have gained status and prestige over the series of hired laborers, both White and Black. Sarah wrote that Aunt Lucy "reigns (as ever) supreme."[76]

After the war, D. N. returned to Clarksville. As a public figure, businessman, and a leader in the community, news of his activities, honors, and achievements were chronicled in the newspaper. Sarah had no public role in the community; she ran her household and reared the children. She had no newspaper articles marking the private milestones of her life. The articles about D. N. give us hints, clues to describe her life through him. An article from May 1877 announced the "ladies of the Presbyterian church will give their moonlight picnic, strawberry and ice-cream entertainment," at the home of the Hon. D. N. Kennedy. Certainly this was Sarah's church group, and surely she oversaw the planning of the event, yet she was not mentioned.[77] When their children married, news of the weddings and receptions appeared. James went into the tobacco and insurance business, and the paper carried newspaper ads of his businesses.

In 1893, Sarah and D. N. celebrated their golden wedding anniversary with a large party attended by relatives. The newspaper carried an astonishingly long article about the event, listing attendees and printing in full the poem, speeches, and tributes to the elderly couple. The "Address of Mr. Kennedy" to his wife sounded more like a formal speech to a banking board than a love letter, as he acknowledged that Sarah deserved credit for the success of their long and fulfilling partnership. "You are entitled to a full share of praise for whatever of success we have had. You have done well your part. I do not feel it improper to say for fifty years of life together, which God in mercy has permitted us, we have been faithful to each other; we have ever recognized the identity of our interests—the oneness of our lives."[78]

Six years later, at age 76, Sarah died, survived by D. N. and five of their nine children. Her obituary stated, "She passed quietly away; after, a long and useful life, leaving the record of a noble life." That record must have been in the rearing of children because her public record consists of being mentioned as D. N.'s wife. It said she was "an earnest practical Christian woman who did good quietly and shunned all parade." She was "considered one of the pillars of the Presbyterian church of Clarksville and her death will be felt the length and breadth of the social and religious life of the city."[79]

D. N. and Sarah had a long and successful marriage. The letters in this volume cover only a brief but tumultuous time in their fifty-six-year marriage and in our nation's history. As a couple, they shared joys, as well as devastating losses. Because of the nature of public and private spheres of nineteenth-century men and women, we know a great deal of D. N.'s life. Even with events they shared together, Sarah was absent from newspaper accounts. It is only because of Sarah's Civil War letters that we know this short chapter in her life. The letters reveal one woman's unique experiences but also shed light on life in Civil War Clarksville. As a loving wife and mother, Sarah was devoted to rearing healthy, happy, and educated children. She was loved and cherished by her family. Importantly, she also recorded the stories of the Kennedys' enslaved as they decided which path to freedom to take, providing us information on the end of slavery and the various ways people entered freedom. It may be jarring for modern readers to see the bifurcated nature of a mid-nineteenth-century woman, who loved and cared for her children, almost beyond measure, and at the same time was cold-hearted and calculating about the people she owned. Yet, thousands of women across the slaveholding South exhibited the same, seemingly contradictory, impulses.[80]

# THE CIVIL WAR LETTERS OF
## SARAH KENNEDY

# 1

## August 16, 1862–
## January 20, 1863

*Sarah Kennedy was concerned with conveying local news to her husband; therefore, her letters contain very little about overall war events. To provide context, general war news is summarized at the beginning of each chapter.*

*Six months before Sarah wrote the first letter to her husband, on February 16, 1862, Fort Donelson had fallen. Clarksville surrendered a few days later. Nashville surrendered on February 25, 1862. Although an occupied city, Clarksville did not have a permanent garrison until after the Battle of Shiloh, which occurred April 6–7, 1862. The 71st Ohio, commanded by Colonel Rodney Mason, became the permanent garrison unit. On August 27, 1862, Confederate Partisan Ranger units under Colonel Adam Rankin Johnson and Colonel Thomas Woodward bluffed the Federal garrison into surrendering. After a failed attempt to retake Fort Donelson, the Confederates were chased into Kentucky, and Clarksville returned to Federal control on September 7, 1862. On December 24, 1862, Union Colonel Sanders D. Bruce took command of Clarksville.*

Cloverlands[1] August 16th, 1862

My Dear Husband:

Mr. G.[2] came out this evening to inform me that there would be an opportunity of sending a letter to you and I with delight avail myself of it. I have for several days suffered great anxiety of mind, at the thought of your not hearing from us, although I strongly hope that ere this you have received at least one letter. It seems unaccountable that my letters do not reach you. I fear that in your despair, you will put your thought of not writing again into execution. I am anxiously looking for another letter from you, and if I do not hear that in a short time that you have read one from me, I shall be very miserable. For several days, I have had a severe cold, which has almost laid me up. I am now some better and think I will be relieved in a few days. All the children have improved in health and spirits, being extremely jaded in both respects when we arrived. Clara[3] is as fit as a fig. Newty[4] is better than he has ever been and improving every day though he occasionally has his spells. Ellen[5] has improved very much in a few days, though it is likely she will not be well until cool weather sets in. You would scarcely know her; she is so thin. We are getting along very pleasantly indeed and heartily enjoy the hospitality of our host and his good lady. I think the latter, the best woman[6] I ever saw. We are now having cool weather, and tonight a fire would be agreeable.

Lizzy and John Hickman[7] called on me day before yesterday, the first visit. John kindly offered to assist me in any way, and offered to drive me to town in his Rockaway,[8] whenever I wish to go. Lizzy is looking better than I have seen her since her marriage. She informed me that Patty Hollingsworth[9] has become a great business woman. She gives her personal attention to her mother's farm having taken it into her own hands, goes to Clarksville frequently, and always on horseback. She informed me that Mary Clark[10] and Tishy K.[11] were in Clarksville last week and are expecting me to visit them. I have not heard from our friends in town since my visit there last week. I am looking every day for a letter from someone, I expect they are waiting for me to write first. Mary[12] has written several letters to you, but on account of the difficulty of transmission,[13] I have persuaded her not to send them. She thinks it very hard as she has the utmost confidence in her ability to write as interesting a letter as anyone else. She is improving rapidly in music and is greatly interested. Her teacher gives her praise for her industry in practicing. She has commenced knitting a pair of socks for Newty and has finished one and thinks that she can knit a pair for your next birthday present. Sally[14] says tell Father that I have nearly finished the leg of a negro sock and will soon knit as well as sister. In the absence of more manly employment, I have had Jimmy[15] learning to knit, and Clara has been begging me to teach her. I think we will all become so attached to country life that we will prefer it to the city. I have been alone all day. Mrs. B.[16] having gone to spend the day at Mr. Ferguson,[17] and I have been engaged in thinking of you and grieving at the necessity of our separation. I hope that the day is not far distant, when we will meet around our own fireside and be able to sing the beautiful words. . . .

Home again, from a foreign shore
And oh! It fills my soul with joy
To meet my friends once more.[18]

I have nothing of interest in the way of news, not having heard from Miss Carrie[19] or Cousin Mill, and Cousin Lucy Bryan[20] has not yet come home. Mr. G. tells me that Dr. McMullen[21] has opened a school in the basement of the church[22] and has seventeen scholars. I have not seen Mr. G. since he returned until now. He tells me that you wish the servants[23] taken from Parker.[24] I weighed this subject well and concluded it best for them to remain. The house I could rent had not a comfort for the servants, nothing but a cellar room that is wet half way all the time, and I thought it would endanger their lives to put them there. They are comfortable at home and do not have more than half the work to perform that they do for us. The family is small and live in a close yankee fashion.[25] It is hard I know to think of their being with so mean a man, but I thought it our interest to let them remain. I think it likely that he will not remain long. He is getting in worse odor every day he stays. I have learned that all his clerks have left him. Be sure to write me your opinion of my action on the part of the servants, and advise me what to do. I know it would be very hard to get them a home if at all. I told you in a former letter that I have hired Phil[26] to Dr. Acree.[27] If I am not fortunate enough to get the house before Christmas, if there should be any difficulty about it, I am determined to go in as soon as his time expires and make it too hot for him to remain. I feel quite certain that if Dr. Cobb[28] was a southern rights man, I would have had possession without difficulty. I have drawn a long letter out of nothing and I know it cannot interest you. I will have to close when G. is ready to start and this goes today, 16th. All the children send love and a kiss to Father. I hope to hear from you soon and often. Your letters are my one consolation.

Your devoted wife
SK

Cloverlands Sept 16th, 1862

My dear Husband:

I have just received a note from cousin L. Bailey[29] informing me of an opportunity of sending a letter to you and I hastily embrace it.[30] I sent one to Ben[31] last week but have not been advised of its being sent. If it has not it will go now. In it I told you of the sickness of the family. Jimmy and Patsy[32] had both been very sick with bilious remitting fever.[33] They have both recovered but had a return of chills last Saturday which I have succeeded in stopping by quinine.[34] Jimmy went to school today. Clara was very sick for a week with the same fever and since her recovery has had a very sore mouth, which has caused her great suffering and me a great deal of care. She is now getting well of that, but is much reduced. I am almost broken down with nursing the sick and having to attend altogether to Newty and Ellen beside. Newty is greatly improved and talks intelligibly.[35] Ellen is fattening every day and looks rosy and saucy. The good news of the success of our army everywhere[36] makes me think so much of your speedy return to us that I am so restless I can scarcely eat, sleep, or perform any work of any kind. When will the long-desired event arrive? Since my last, Clarksville has gone through the rubbins.[37] A large force of Yankees went in on the seventh,[38] and committed all kinds of villainous deeds exceeding any thing that I have heard of during the War. They staid only one day being too cowardly to stay longer. They swept everything before them as they went. I have been here two months and a half and have not been to Clarksville but one day in that time. I feel very anxious to see our friends there but cannot leave my family. All night and the days are so hot, and the dust so disagreeable that I cannot get around. Indeed, I have become as accustomed to the quiet of the country that I have not much disposition to change, and do not care to be in Clarksville unless I could be at our own house; and I thank Providence for giving me this quiet retreat this Summer, and for being shielded from the abuse I could have received from the advent of the Northern Demons[39] that visited at C. last week. Mary says she is glad that our house had a Yankee in it. I do so long for a letter from you and have almost given up all hope of getting one. We have had a long dry season. The crops are suffering for rain, and the dust is intolerable. All nature is putting on the livery of autumn, and the cold nights make us think of Winter clothes. I have a fire every morning and evening, but the noon day is hot enough for August—yesterday ranging to 68 in the hall. Mrs. Barker has been very ill with bilious fever. She is now up and recovering. I shall be perfectly satisfied if I only escape it. Mary and Jimmy go to school to Mrs. Brockman[40] at Mr. Fergusons. Mary takes music lessons and improves rapidly. Sally learns at home. I hope my dear Husband that your health is still good and that we shall be able to visit before very long. I must be brief as this must go to C. this evening. I hope that you have received my letters, and that I shall have the pleasure of reading one from you soon. God protect you and bring you back safely to us soon is the constant prayer of your Devoted wife.

S. Kennedy


Clarksville Nov. 27th, 1862

My Dear Husband,

Last Saturday I went with the children to pay a visit to Dr. Bailey.[41] On Monday at noon I received a letter from Mr. Glenn stating that Parker was called suddenly to Louisville to see some sick friend and as he did not expect to get back before Jan. He would condescend to let me have the house if I would clear it rent, and give him a room for his furniture for the balance of the year.[42] I thought it best to get the house before any thing else happened to prevent. So, I wrote to Mr. G. the same evening to send for me next morning, and on Tuesday we all came in. I could not get Phil yesterday or I would have gone home last night. We are at Uncles.[43] I will prepare a room at home to-day, and sleep there tonight. I feel very thankful that we are able to get settled before the bad weather sets in, and while I have Patsy to help me as Fanny[44] is down. She has a boy one week old. The health of the children has been better. Jimmy and Clara still look badly and they are in fact far from well, but they have wiped chills. I have had a bone felon[45] which for two weeks caused me intense suffering. Dr. J.[46] opened it to the bone which relieved me, and it will be well as soon as the wound heals, but it will be some time before I can use it, it will be so tender. I have been very miserable lately. I have thought that I was in the way ever since Mollie[47] came into the family. She has always been very cold and distant to me. Then Father takes no notice of her child and is very attentive to Ellen which exceedingly galls both the old lady and Mollie. Nothing has been said but the saying is "actions speak louder than words." I have suspected such a state of feeling on their part and my suspicion has been confirmed by Miss Cal Merriweather[48] who told Virginia Bailey[49] that Mollie and Mrs. K.[50] did not get along well together. I have always shown the utmost friendship and attention to Mollie but have been met with cold-ness. Miss Cal's communication shows that they have talked about it. The old man[51] filled the wagon with eatables[:] a barrel of flour, a bag of meal, hams, sausages, spare ribs, dried peaches, etc., apples and turkey so you see I am in no danger of starving for a while at least. I have heard not a word from Ben. He seems to be avoiding us. I have sent him word by every one I have seen that I wish to see him but have had no answer. I would like very much to write you of what is transpiring in the military line but cannot. I can tell you that the old man's son C B[52] was arrested and held one day. When asked if he would take the oath to support the constitution, he replied I have not broken the constitution.[53] Will you swear to support the government? If I support the government, I break the constitution. If I support the consti-tution, I am not supporting the government. With this they let him off. My dear Husband, how much I miss you and how much I regret our separation I can never express. I am miserable at the idea and look forward with gloom at the lonely time I shall have this winter. Dr. Acree has let me have Phil for the balance of the year. If I could not have gotten him, I would have been very much put out. I shall give Patsy up at Christmas and get rid of her expense in the event of trouble with the colored ones.[54] I will have to do the best I can perhaps hire a biddy.[55] The children send love and a kiss to Father.

Your devoted wife

S. Kennedy

Clarksville, Dec 6th, 1862

My Dear Husband

I am sitting by our own fireside tonight, the children are in their own little beds asleep and although we are at home, I have not yet felt entirely at home. The presiding genius that it requires to make my home happy is away. A wanderer. And when I suffer myself to meditate on the hardship and inconveniences to which he has to submit, the tears will gather and I send many a sigh for him and many prayers for his safety during exile and for his safe return to us before many days or weeks or months shall have passed. I wrote you last week that we were enabled to get our house. Parker's family having gone to Louisville. They retain a room for their furniture until first January and deduct rent for the time I am in it. We have been living at home a week last night. I found Fanny in bed with an infant a week old, and I miss her services in putting the house in order. Dr. Acree kindly consented to give Phil up and I have him to assist me. I find things very much out of order, a great many lost, and the house somewhat injured; yet I rejoice that we are comfortably settled before the bad weather sets in. The weather has been very cold, and we have been burning wood in the grates with very little comfort. Today we have had a good coal fire. Mr. Glenn purchased for me a hundred bushels from Dortch,[56] who is selling off his stock at the mill at forty cents a bushel. It is good Breckenridge coal.[57] I have had the cooking stove set up in the servant's room so that the fire that does the cooking, washing, and ironing keeps the room warm without an extra fire in the kitchen. I burn a fire in my room night and morning and sit in the dining room through the day so we have virtually but one fire. We eat two meals a day. Breakfast at the usual hour and dinner and tea together at four. Uncle has procured a cow for me, but it has not yet come as the calf is too young. Mr. Ferguson was in town last Friday. Uncle was inquiring of him for a cow. He informed Mr. Barker that I had none, and today Mr. Jordan came in with a note from Mr. B. saying he had sent me a cow which I could keep until I could get one, or in the event I had one, I could send it back. I chose to do the latter as I am looking for mine every day. This has prepared me to call on him for aid in any matter during your absence. His kindness is unlimited. He desires to be remembered when I write to you. I received your letter of twelfth Nov. last night. Mr. Joe

Broaddus[58] told me that he expected to meet you at Montgomery, but that you had passed through before he arrived there. A company of five hundred Yankees visited us last Saturday.[59] They behaved remarkably well taking nothing but corn and hay from the private stables and some who did not relish cold food went to the private residences for supper and breakfast. I luckily escaped a visit from them which was singular as they called on all my neighbors. They were hunting Woodard[60] and his men. They left Sunday morning crossing the upper ferry in pursuit and in crossing had some men drowned. It is reported that a company of Jayhawkers[61] are hourly looked for. I do not know or hope they will not come. I have not heard a word from Ben. I have sent him word by every conceivable opportunity to come to see me and have not been able to get a clue to his whereabouts. It is rumored that he is engaged in smuggling goods. Jimmy's health is improved from the change from country to town. Clara has had a chill followed by fever of three days duration, but I think she seems better than before we came home. The children enjoy themselves finely. Mary, Jimmy, and Sally recite their lessons every day to me. Mary is continuing her music with Miss Margaret Ring.[62] Ellen is as fat and rosy as when you left. Newty is about the same. Mr. B's growing fondness for and constant attention to Ellen was arousing the jealousy of Molly and the old lady to such an extent that I was glad on that account to get away as soon as possible. In his letter today, he says remember me affectionately to all your children and especially to my little Green as he calls her. I do hope that you will see all our Woodville[63] friends and write me particularly of Bro Willie's family.[64] I have written a scrawling letter, but you will excuse it. I have had neuralgia[65] for several days from exposure in cold rooms and yesterday we had a heavy fall of snow. I have taken cold and am so nervous I can scarcely steady my nerves to write. The children join me in love to Father. Ellen when asked where Father is says away down in Dixie far away from the Yankees. Pray for me, my husband, that I may trust in God and not be afraid.

Your devoted wife,
S. Kennedy


Home Dec 11th, 1862 Thursday

My Dear Husband:

I wrote to you on Saturday by Mr. Jordan[66] belonging to the 49th regiment.[67] Mr. Glenn starts today for Murfreesboro[68] and I will drop you a few lines by him. I have nothing new since my last except that we have had another visit from the Yanks who burnt the upper Red River bridge[69] night before last at nine o'clock. We saw the light distinctly from here. Their object is supposed to be to prevent the escape of those whom they come to take prisoners, and to cut off supplies. They also destroyed the pump and chain of the large cistern on the square. They seem to have a particular spite at Clarksville, that secesh hole,[70] as they call it. We are now having lovely night weather, not very cold. The ground is still sloppy from the snow but is drying very fast. All are well. I spent yesterday with Lizzie Lewis.[71] All her children have whooping cough.[72] Laura[73] is assisting me with my sewing. My finger has not recovered from the felon sufficiently for use, and I am very awkward with my needle in consequence. A society has been formed here for supplying the poor with necessaries. The visiting committee have some very amusing things to tell at the meetings. One poor woman cannot eat corn bread, another cannot eat wheat bread, another must have coffee and tea with brown sugar for the coffee and loaf sugar for the tea. Time passes dully enough. Every body is low spirited.

I have the news of the contemplated Armistice[74] with feelings of joy but am slow to believe that such a thing will really take place. Will the time ever come when all will be restored to their homes and loved ones? I hope to receive another letter from you very soon. I had a dream a few nights since which has rendered me very uneasy. I fear that it is ominous of evil to you. All the children join me in love to Father. Mary, Jimmy, and Sally are learning very well at home. Hoping that you are well and will continue so and soon be restored to us. I remain your ever devoted wife

S. Kennedy

Clarksville Dec 22nd, 1862

My Dear Husband:

I have just received your letter of 29th Nov. from Woodville. You can judge of my delight at hearing from you and of learning that you are well and so pleasantly situated. I am delighted to hear so fully from Bro Willie's family.

We have been settled at home three weeks last Friday, are all well, and enjoying a feeling of independence which has been so many months a stranger to mine and the children's hearts. I feel very lonely though and I give no evidence to the servants that I am looking for any excitement, and they have shown none.[75] They all perform their duty. Phil is very attentive. I have heard of several instances of their expectation and what they say will happen if any opposition is offered to their freedom. I have informed Mr. Keer[76] that I will not hire Patsy for the next year. She has been very troublesome to me, and I long for the time to come for her to go. I am confident that she will go off at the first opportunity. What a pity for so excellent a girl to be spoiled by circumstances. We have had three visits from the Yanks lately. They come for the purpose of arresting southern soldiers. They were here yesterday and got Bill McCall,[77] Bob Johnson,[78] and several others and took them to Hopkinsville.[79] Our town looks almost like a wilderness and every face looks sad. Our friends are all well. Dr. McMullen is having the College[80] cleaned up for a residence as he will have to give Mrs. Forbes'[81] house up 1st Jan. One of Mrs. Robb's[82] men who was assisting in the cleaning has small-pox[83] supposed to have been contracted there, some of the Yankee leavings. I am afraid that other servants will have it and that it will be dangerous for the family to occupy it.

George Lewis has left the McKeage[84] house and moved to Bill Resees country house on the Charlotte Road.[85] I am very sorry they have left town as Lizzie and Laura were a great deal of company for me. Ben is now here. He came to see me yesterday. He was not aware of my being at home until he got here. Sam Kennedy[86] and Mr. Clark[87] have been rearrested and taken to Russellville.[88] John Lewis has taken the oath. The Parkers have not removed their furniture yet, and I shall not feel at ease until every vestige of them is gone. They pretend to be trying to rent a house for the next year, but I imagine they are only waiting for the river to rise that they may convey their chattels to Louisville by boat. I feel restless and was anxious for the inter-view to be over. O how I do yearn for your presence at home. I lie awake at night and think of you being compelled to wander and be deprived of your comfortable home and then the idea that you may never return comes often into my mind and I am so distressed that I have to get up, and I spend hours at night in this way. But I strive to calm my apprehensions and think of the tens of thousands who are in a state of destitution and their husbands who have died in battle and of disease in camp and feel ashamed to complain. I heard from Mr. Barker[89] yesterday. Mr. Ferguson[90] was in and came to see me. They are well. I have not received your letter of 24th. I wrote to you on the 27th or 28th Nov, I do not remember which. Again, on the 6th and 12th of this month. I hope my dear husband that you will receive my letters and not be subjected to so much uneasiness as you experienced last summer. There was great joy in the family yesterday. The cow came and today we had the first sweet milk we have had to drink since we came home. I have not vis-ited any one being so busy getting straightened up. I find a great many things are missing. Every day some article that I have not seen comes into my mind and on inquiring for it the answer is, the Yankees took it with them. I have barely a change of sheets for the beds in my room and if I should have any one to sleep upstairs could barely cover them. I miss the articles in my cedar chest and hope I may get it when the river rises. The children all have good health. Mary exhibited her musical proficiency on Friday night at a review of Miss Ring, her teacher. She did quite well. I have not entered the children at school, it being so near the end of the session.[91] I think I shall send Mary and Jimmy as I will have more care of the little ones after Patsy leaves. I heard late this evening of an opportunity of sending a letter. I am writing this by candle light and have lost my specs, so you will have to excuse the bad writing. I should like to write to sister by this opportunity, but have not time. The children send love and many kisses to Father. May God protect my dear Husband is the prayer of your wife,

S. Kennedy

Clarksville Dec 29th, 1862

My Dear Husband:

Just one week ago today, I sent you a letter by Patrick Henry.[92] I write to you today not knowing when or how I am to send the letter as our town is now garrisoned by about three thousand Federals and command of Bruce.[93] They came in on Christmas Day. Their pickets are at every inlet and outlet of the town, and no one, white or black, is allowed ingress or egress without a pass from the Col. They seem determined to cut us off from everything and everywhere. I learned this morning that they are preparing for the reception of the confederates under Morgan[94] and Forrest[95] thinking that they are within five miles of the Seven Mile Ferry.[96] They are not allowed to molest private residences, and if they call on us for something to eat, we have only to inform on them. I fear that this stringency will not last, and that before long we will have to feed if not board them. They are foraging in the country everyday bringing in wagon loads of corn, pork, and hay.[97] I feel sometimes very badly and at night can scarcely sleep. When I hear a noise at night, I get up and go all over the house. I have done this three times but have never found anything wrong. The servants seem entirely right, and if they have any notions about freedom, they keep it concealed.

Patsy is gone and myself and the children are alone. We have all been sick with influenza colds but are now better. The weather has been very warm and damp, and colds are prevalent. I met Jim Davie on the street last Monday on his way south. I told him to tell you that we were all well and at home. The next day, Mr. Barker sent in a letter to be directed to you for Tex.[98] I am sorry it did not come sooner as Mr. Davie was the last chance that I know of. It will accompany this. Ben was in town last week. He called, gave me a bill of expenses, made a settlement with me, and this was all I saw of him. I do not know whether he has left. He seems entirely unconcerned about the

Parker affairs, and when I told him that he and Parker differed to the amount of a hundred dollars in the rent, he did not say a word. They have not yet removed their furniture and have said nothing about it. I notified them that I would not keep it longer than 1st Jan and that I would not let it go until the bill is paid. One of them had the impudence to tell me that he was to sleep in the room with the furniture. I told him that he should not that they had imposed upon me all along. I was now in possession of my house and would do as I pleased. He has not been back since. The idea was to save paying for a sleeping room. Old Bruce has been in town for a week. He keeps very close. I suppose he is ashamed to show his face. He come to take his family north. I think his wife has refused to go because her father is much opposed to it.[99] We have had the most quiet Christmas I ever knew.

The darkies seem afraid of the strict rules over them. They are not allowed to go out after dark or talk in squads on the street in the day. Every street is guarded and you cannot walk a square without coming up with the guard. Mr. McCullash[100] yesterday invited the Chaplain of the Yanks to preach at the Methodist Church[101] and in consequence we had a large congregation.[102] Some of the brethren not fancying the arrangement as much as the aforementioned brother. Some of the officers were at our church and looked mean enough. The guard was on the steps with his gun, and I felt mad enough to run the bayonet through him. The children have good health. Mary and Jimmy are very impatient to start to school. I am waiting for the beginning of the session as it is so uncertain whether the schools will continue. The Feds say that they intend to finish the forts[103] and prepare to shell the town if the Confederates attempt to take the place.

Mary continues her music with Miss M. Ring and is learning very fast. I send a letter from cousin J. E. B.[104] to his family in which he tells them not to despair that the Feds will hold Tennessee this winter but that next summer, they will every one be driven from the soil. I do hope it may prove so. No goods will be allowed to come here, and we will have to get clothes the best way we can. I will need none and the children very little. I will try to have a set of shirts for you as I think you will be quite threadbare by the time you get home. I have the domestics and will get the linen best way I can manage. I found your slippers after you left which I had overlooked. I hope you will not be seriously inconvenienced by the want of them. Dr. McMullen's family are still at Mrs. Forbes' house.[105] They will have to leave it in a month as Mrs. F. contemplates moving into it. Nannie Garland[106] seems almost gone with consumption. Mrs. Frank Beaumont[107] is failing daily. I have been so much at home that I hear very little local news. I shall have to stir around and get up something interesting to tell you in my next. Mr. Barker sent us a turkey for Christmas, eggs, apples too. If he could send to town, I would want for nothing. He is so very kind. I had a long visit from Mr. J. S. Hunt[108] last week. He made many inquiries of me and sends his regards to you. I judge from the way he talks, he has taken the oath. Sam Kennedy, Mr. Clark, and John Lewis have all taken the oath to save them from being sent to Johnsons Island.[109] The children send much love and kisses to Father. May heaven preserve my husband is the prayer of his devoted wife

S. Kennedy

Clarksville January 4th, 1863

I have just this moment learned of an opportunity of sending you a letter. I have had one written for two weeks, but our town, being occupied by the Federals, and no one being allowed to pass out, I could not send it. On Christmas day, Col Bruce took possession of us with a force of fifteen hundred men. He is lenient and kind, but some of his officers are very severe. He does not allow his men to molest private residences.[110] Still we all feel very badly and would much rather they were not here. Last Sunday, Mr. Wardlaw,[111] Bryce Stewart,[112] and Aleck Barker[113] were arrested and requested to take the oath. They all refused and after appearing before the Provost Marshal for several days in succession and remaining firm, Mr. W. was unconditionally released and the others are on parole. No other arrests have been made in town, but the men are all on thorns. John L. Johnson[114] and Robert Humphrey[115] were waited on at their homes, brought to town, and both took the oath.[116] All the negro men have been pressed to work on the fortifications.[117] Phil has escaped them thus far. They have dug a trench reaching from Dr. Drane's[118] house (by the pond[119]) all round the college. Morgan is in Kentucky, has torn up the rail road, burnt bridges, and blown up the tunnel at Muldrow's Hill.[120] It is said that he is now surrounded without any possible means of escape.[121] I am very anxious to get a letter from you and feel very anxious to know whether you have received my letters. We have been at home four weeks last Friday. Every thing is in so excited a state that I cannot settle my mind to feel at home. Jimmy and Clara are both complaining to day. Clara has a very sore mouth and Jimmy has neuralgia over his eye. The rest are well. Mary and Sally have gone to church. I remain at home with the sick. Mrs. Wardlaw[122] acted very heroically when her husband was on trial. She told him that if he made the least concession, she would give him no peace as long as he lived. Neither would allow of any intercession by friends, and Mr. W. was so sure of being sent to prison that he packed his trunk and was ready to start. I must close as the lady who is to take this is waiting. I will enclose this in my other letter. I hope to hear from you soon and shall feel very restless until I do. Adieu, my dear Husband. I pray heaven to protect you.

Your devoted wife

S. Kennedy

Clarksville January 7th, 1863

My Dear Husband:

On the fourth I started a letter to you which had been written more than a week. I will have a good opportunity of sending another tomorrow and hastily embrace it. As I have mentioned in several letters, we have been comfortably settled at home since the twenty ninth November. We are all delighted to be at home once more and I feel that nothing (short of being forced out of the house by the Federals) can tempt me to leave home again. Jimmy and Clara have been complaining from the effects of their summer fever and though not well, seem to be improving. The changeable weather keeps us with colds, with this exception, the rest of us have good health. I am very lonely, but try to keep my spirits up. I have not heard of you since your letter of 29th Nov. from Woodville. We cannot get letters since the occupation of our town by the Federals. I wrote you in my last that Col. Bruce had been here with his command since Christmas day. They are fortifying with the intention of holding it. The citizens have fared very well considering their power to do us great harm, but they are doing the farmers very badly, taking all their bacon, flour, corn, hay, etc. They last week arrested our kind friend Mr. J. W. Barker and ordered him to report to Shackelford[123] at Hopkinsville. Mr. Wardlaw has been with him to console and counsel him. I saw Mr. W. this morning. He told me that he had Col. Bruce's consent for Mr. B. to stand his trial here, and as he (Col. Bruce) seems very lenient, I have no doubt that he will get off well. The old man is very much afflicted with rheumatism, and I fear that this misfortune will tell sadly on his failing constitution. The family are in great distress. I wrote you in my last that Mr. Wardlaw, B. Stewart, and Aleck Barker had been arrested but stoutly refused to take the oath and have been released. No other arrests have been made in town. The Feds declared their intention of arresting all the prominent men, and some of the gentlemen have been saying that they are very much disappointed at not being considered prominent citizens. The river has risen sufficiently for light draught steamers.[124] Several have been here from Nashville and are taking all the flour with promise of pay when the war is over. The Feds have taken possession of all the mills in the country. Mary and Jimmy have started to school. Mary to Dr. Ring[125] and Jimmy to Miss

Sally. Sally is learning to spell and read very well at home. Clara is anxious to begin to learn and has been to Sunday School once. I think Newty has improved under Aunt Lucy's[126] care. He came near losing his life a few days ago. He stole off to the lot, got into the stable (at the back door where the cow was confined). Two negro men hearing his cries and the noise made by the cow, came to his assistance and whilst they were breaking the door, the cow tapped him three times. He was so much frightened, he did not get over it all day and has not budged from the house since. He is a little, but not seriously, bruised. Ellen is the picture of health and life. I shall write to sister, to your address, and you will forward it to her. Hoping and praying that you are well and happy. I will close. All the children send a great deal of love and many kisses to their Father. I hope to receive a letter, yours, very soon. Your devoted wife

S. Kennedy


Clarksville January 19, 1863

I have spent many anxious days and sleepless nights since I received your last letter from Woodville dated 29th Nov. I do not even know that you have received one from me since you left. Our situation here renders it almost impossible to get letters. I send one to you by every opportunity that I can get, but have no knowledge that one of them has reached you. Mr. G called today to inform us that he had received one from you dated 29th Dec. I was gratified indeed to hear from you and deeply grieved to hear that your health is only tolerably good. I have greatly feared that your health would fail you, and picture to myself sometimes that you are really sick and needing my care. I sometimes think that it would be best for you to come home and do all that would be required of you to stay here than run the risk of your life where you are; for I do fear that you will lose your health entirely. Then again, I imagine that you had better remain at the neighborhood of Woodville, where you will be more comfortable and more pleasantly situated than where you are. It is delightful to be at home once more on account of the children. They have never enjoyed home so much. Their long separation from it seems to endear it to them, and I have not half the trouble and care with them that I had in the country. Their health has been injured by travel, and the summer's sojourn in the country, but nothing serious, and they are all improving. Newty, I have reason to believe is improving almost daily. My hope for him is very strong. My own health has been good with the exception of colds. Since I dismissed Patsy, I have all the care of the little ones at night and sometimes, I am easily tired, getting up with first one and then another. We have had some bitter cold nights; and you know that our room

14

is not very warm after the fire dies out. The water in the pitcher has frozen several times sitting on the hearth. I am looking daily for Clara and Ellen to take whooping cough. It is all over the neighborhood, and I think one of Fanny's children has it. All Lizzy's have it. All of Uncle's family are coughing.

As usual, Uncle is in very bad health and is frequently laid up. I have not heard from Mr. Barker's family in some time. The old man has not yet been in. Mr. and Mrs. Wardlaw, Mrs. McMullen, and Miss Carrie were here to-day. They all told me to give their love to you when I wrote. Miss Carrie is as interesting as ever, and says she would be delighted to see you. Our town is very dull and uninteresting except to certain people. We are as yet unharmed from surrounding circumstances, but there is no telling what a day may bring forth. We are comfortable at home and wish that you could be here to enjoy its comforts. I visit my neighbors more than I ever did before. I go to drive away the blues and while away some of my lonely hours.

Mary is improving rapidly under Dr. Ring's tuition and it is the first time that I have ever been satisfied that she was learning at all. Sally is learning to read at home and Clara has commenced her ABCs, Jimmy I think he is learning fast. Ellen is as fat and saucy as ever but is very bad. The children spoil her sadly. Mrs. Munford[127] wishes you to let me know if you know anything of Julia Anderson.[128] She has not heard from her in a great while. I was out to see Mrs. Bemiss[129] last week. She told me that she had not heard from her husband since October. Lizzy Lewis dined with me yesterday. She is very much displeased with her country residence. She is looking very badly and says she believes the care of her two babies will kill her. I long for pleasant weather that I may begin to trim my rose bushes and fix up the garden generally. Everything looks sadly neglected and putting things to rights will give me some occupation now, if no pleasure afterwards. I hope my dear husband that an opportunity will soon offer for you to send me a letter and be assured that if you do not receive any from me that the fault is not mine. I have written regularly and my letters have been sent by those considered as responsible. The children send love and a kiss to father. May God protect and bless you is the constant prayer of your

Devoted Wife
S. Kennedy

Clarksville January 20th, 1863

My Dear Husband:

You can imagine my feeling of gloom and suspense when day after day passes by, and I receive no tidings of you. Many letters are received every week from the army, but I do not get any from you and do not see any one who can tell me where you are or that you are well. Your letter from Wood-ville of 29th Nov. is the last news I have of you. I have been very gloomy for a week. Clara has been quite sick and Mary very complaining. Clara had another chill last Friday and was very ill for three days, and Mary had a severe cold and cough. Both are now much better, and I think will be quite well in a few days. I feel very uneasy about Mary. You remember she had a fall from a swing at the Academy two years ago. It is now developing in an enlarged shoulder and a slight curvature of the spine. It is so perceptible to me that I got Dr. Haskins[130] to examine it. He does not seem to think it very serious, but I very much fear that at her age it will prove more so than he would lead me to think. The rest of them are well. Newty is about the same as when I wrote you last. We have had a miserable spell of weather for eight days. On Tuesday of last week, it rained heavily all day. Before bed time it was sleeting, and the next morning the ground was six inches deep with snow. It continued to snow until the whole face of the ground was two feet deep with it. Night before last it commenced raining and has not yet ceased. The snow is nearly all gone. Every one has been housed for the time, and I have never felt so lonely and blue in my life. A letter from you would cheer me, and I still hope to get one soon. Laura came to see me on Sunday and left today. I tried to prevail on her to stay a week with me, but Lizzy could not spare her so long. Last night we had a severe wind storm. We were sitting around the fire, when a dreadful crash caused us to start. I thought it was a slide of snow from the roof. Another crash and an examining found it to be the top of the dining room chimney blown down by the wind. The balm of Gilead[131] on the left of the front door was almost uprooted. I think with careful propping, it can be safely reset. Our town is still guarded by the Fed-erals, and it is evident that they fear an attack, and they send out a troop of Cavalry whenever a fleet of transports go up the river, since Wheeler burnt so many boats at the shoals.[132] A part of Shackelford's regiment[133] were here last week, among them a Maj. Kennedy,[134] one of your kin[135] from Garrard County, Ky.[136] I do not know which family he belongs to. I have been so con-fined at home during the bad weather and seen as few persons that I know very little of what is transpiring. One of the Yankee pickets was shot on the square last night, and to day an order was passed that any one white or black seen outside their gates after dark would meet with the same fate. Ben left town on Christmas day, and I have not heard of him since. Parker called on Mr. Glenn and offered to pay his rent and remove his furniture. He stated that he agreed with Ben to pay the rate of $300 a year with the servants thrown in with the use of all the furniture and deduct fifty dollars from it that he paid Kimble to be released from his house but that he would not require me to pay the fifty dollars. Uncle Charley and Mr. Glenn advised me not to receive it until Ben came down again and the matter investigated. He told Dr. Cobb that he was willing to act according to Ben's understanding of the matter, but was confident that Ben would agree with him. According to his account, there is $175 due me from him. He is an arrant scoundrel. He and Isabina[137] are now in Louisville after a stock of goods with a permit from Bruce. I learn that this authority is not sufficient and that their goods will be stopped at Smithland.[138] A letter has been received from Co. Bailey[139] as late as 28th Dec. and Mrs. Munford received one from Will[140] yesterday. O how I wish that I could get one from my husband. I was at the gate last week when Mr. Leonard[141] passed. He rode up and whispered to me that he would see you soon. I had only time to ask him to say to you that we were all well. I often imagine you sick and uncomfortable and am miserable but try to keep my spirits up, and show no fear of surrounding danger on account of the children. If I only knew tonight that you are well and comfortably situated, I could sleep soundly. I commit you and all of us daily and hourly to the care of a kind father in heaven and try to feel that he will do all things well. The children all send love and a kiss to father. Adieu and may heavens best blessings follow you and bring you back safe to us again is the prayer of your devoted wife

S. Kennedy

# 2

## FEBRUARY 2, 1863–
## JUNE 17, 1863

By 1863, changes were occurring which would alter the structure of American society forever. The Emancipation Proclamation took effect on January 1, 1863. Although Tennessee, under Federal control, was exempted from the proclamation, Federal attitudes toward runaway slaves had changed. No longer would the Federal soldiers return slaves to their enslavers. They were put to work as laborers for the Army. On May 22, 1863, General Order 143 was published; it established the Bureau of Colored Troops. Now the ex-slaves enlisted as soldiers, wore uniforms, and demanded to see passes. Federal treatment of civilians in occupied areas also changed. No longer did the US Government think rebel civilians would come back to the Union of their own volition. Civilians were required to take oaths of allegiance or move to Confederate-controlled areas. They were restricted in their ability to travel and were required to have a Federal-issue warrant to travel into or out of occupied towns. On February 3, 1863, Confederate Generals Joseph Wheeler and Nathan Bedford Forrest made an unsuccessful attack on Dover and Fort Donelson. Colonel Abel Streight left nearby Palmyra on April 11 with 1,500 Federal troops on an unsuccessful Deep South raid, which ended with the capture of his troops and Streight himself. Both the 49th and 50th Tennessee Confederate Infantry Regiments captured in the Battle of Fort Donelson had been exchanged in September 1862 and were stationed at Port Hudson, Louisiana, in the first part of the year. The 50th fought at the Battle of Raymond, Mississippi, on May 12. Both units fought at Jackson, Mississippi, on May 14. Other notable battles during this period of Sarah's writing were the Battle of Champion's Hill, Mississippi, on May 16 where Confederate General Lloyd Tilghman was killed. The Federal army unsuccessfully attacked Vicksburg, Mississippi, on both

*May 19 and 23 before settling into a siege. The Battle of Milliken's Bend, Louisiana, was fought on June 7. Two unsuccessful attacks were made on Port Hudson, Louisiana, on May 27 and June 14, 1863, before the Federals settled into a siege.*

Clarksville Feb 2nd, 1863

My Dear Husband:

I wrote you four days ago, but as another opportunity offers, I shall write again. As there is nothing transpiring except in the military world, I fear that I cannot interest you with news. Our town looks like desolation itself. All its glory has departed. I have staid at home without exercise until I have lost my appetite and am sad and gloomy. I have felt more sad than usual today. I have hoped to receive a letter from you until I feel that such a pleasure is not in store for me. I brood over the privations and anxieties to which you are subjected until my life is a perfect misery. The children are sick a good deal. I have written you again and again that Clara and Jimmy still had a spell once in a while. Clara's health is never good. Newty's affliction preys more and more upon my mind and heart every day. Yesterday Mary had a chill and has been quite sick all day. I hope by precaution to prevent another tomorrow. Sally and Ellen are the healthiest ones of the lot. They are a great care and none old enough to be much comfort. Aunt Lucy has been in bed for three days with her old complaints. To drive away dull care, I went out this morning to trim my evergreens. The sun was shining pleasantly and I worked away for about two hours when the clouds began to gather and a keen north wind with a feeling of snow in it drove me in. I shall have to resume the operation in more pleasant weather. The place is sadly out of repair. We have had very unhealthy weather, a great deal of rain and sudden changes, and a great deal of snow. B. W. Macrae & Lady[1] paid me a social visit one day last week. I enjoyed it exceedingly. They were both very agreeable. As I have but a short time to write, I will bring this to a close. The children send a great deal of love and a great many kisses to Father. And still hoping that I shall receive some letters from you, that you are well and in receipt of mine and many prayers for your safe and speedy return to us. I am your devoted wife

S. Kennedy

Clarksville Feb 9th, 1863

My Dear Husband:

I came down to Uncle Charly's this morning to drive away the blues, and fortunate enough it is that I am here. Mr. Bivens called to get letters and

I hastily write one to you. I have been in fine spirits since the reception of those letters from you. One of 24 Dec. and 13th & 25th Jan. The two last by Mr. L. They afforded me a good deal of pleasure and enlivened my hopelessness. We are all tolerably well. I have had a very hard spell of Neuralgia and am not entirely recovered. Mary's health is very bad and I feel very miserable without her. She is not confined but has fever every day, and I fear that it comes from debility occasioned by her weak shoulder and spine. I am giving her sarsaparilla.[2] Clara seems to be better. I am expecting her & Ellen to take whooping cough every day as one of Fanny's children has it. I believe there is nothing new of interest. George Marr[3] has been taken prisoner and started to Louisville but tonight it is believed that he will be sent to Johnson's Island. Henry Allen[4] was taken at the same time but has been paroled within the city limits, also two with the 14th who were sent with G. Marr. Our town is full of Yankees and they display themselves on every occasion. They say they have never before been treated so coldly as they are here. I have never spoken to them but twice. Two of them came for their breakfast. I told them that I would not do anything for a Lincoln soldier to save their lives unless compelled to do so. They came to take Phil to work on the fort. I told them they could not get him that they could work on the fort and leave Phil to cut wood for me as surely, they would not expect me to do it. Old Wines and Breed[5] have a stock of goods just opened. The Yanks have formed a board of trade here, who are to dictate who shall sell goods. I learned that Parker is a member of this board. We have a great many mushroom merchants[6] here. Mathill, Landon, Kane[7] are in the dry goods line but are expecting every day to have the rabble strike at them. There are a good many Yankee women here, wives of the officers. They are all quartered at old Peart's[8] elegant residence which has been taken as a Yankee boarding house. They are thus huddled together for safety in case of an attack. Dr. McMullen opened a female school today in the basement of the Presbyterian Church. The weather has been very bad indeed. A heavy fall of snow and the sloppiest time I ever did see. There has been a good deal of ice formed 4 to 5 inches thick. Mrs. Munford is very much interested about the fate of Port Hudson.[9] She says please try to find out where and how Julia Anderson is and write to me. I have not seen any one from Mr. Barker's since the Feds came in and do not hear from them. Mr. B. has not yet been in to his trial but I suppose he will put it off altogether. Uncle Charley's health is very feeble indeed; and he is confined mostly to the house. I learned this morning that the Yankees were to go round and divide our bacon amongst themselves. If they do this, what are we to live on? Marketing is very high and scarce.[10] I am becoming so impatient for the time to arrive when we can be again united. Oh, when will that time come? I sometimes think that this war will never be ended. Remember me kindly to E. J. McClure[11] & family. All our friends desire to be remembered to you. The children are not here but I will send their love and kisses to Father. Write often. I must close. Your devoted

S. Kennedy

Clarksville Feb 12th, 1863

My Dear Husband:

I again embrace an opportunity of writing to you. Nothing worthy of note has transpired here since my last. We are all well, in better health than for some time past. My own health is better now than since I came home. The reception of three letters from you has I think had a fine influence on me, and I think if I could receive all your letters regularly, I would not again be so complaining. We have miserably dull weather, either snow or rain continually. I hear very little that is going on. The children and the bad weather confining me at home. I have a lonely time, nothing to keep me company, but the noise of the children and that sometimes is very distracting. The weather keeps every one at home so there are few visitors. The only thing I have heard is Brandon's escape from the Yanks. They were after him for some of his devilment. He got into a box in the middle of a wagon and had a load of hay piled on top and so made his way out of town. You mentioned that Mr. L told you I was looking so very well. You need not attach any credit to his yarn for I was looking badly. He told me on his return that he never saw you looking so well or in better spirits. Now I know you cannot be looking so very well when you write that your health is not good. He is a real Yank at flattery not meaning any harm, but only taking pleasure in making others feel happy. I do not mean to detract from his virtues. I am very grateful for his favor in bringing your letters and in carrying one from me to you. I have not heard from Mr. Barker in a long time and have no idea when I will again. The country people do not come to town with the exception of a few warhaters. They are afraid of having the oath stuck at them. Mrs. Munford desires that you should look after her Will and write to me if you hear from him. She is very miserable about him since the rumor of the fall of Port Hudson.[12] She says please find out if you can if he is in need of money and let him have it if you can and she will refund the amount to me and be sure to try and learn where Ed Munford and Julia Anderson are. Tell E. J. McC.[13] that I saw her sister, Bene Van Culin[14] day before yesterday, I believe in shopping and dined at Uncle Charley's. They are all well. She and Cousin Sue Marr[15] came near being crashed in crossing the river on a ferry boat. I wrote you on Monday last by Mr. Bivens. I was very much hurried as I was and did not have time to be elegant in style of composition or penmanship. I wrote because I had the opportunity of letting you hear from home and because I know it gives you pleasure to hear. I have just received a note from Mrs. Munford in which she requests me to ask you to try to find out Bud & George Warfield[16] at camp near Grenada, Miss.[17] Tilghman's[18] division. Bud belongs to the Tenth and George to the 50th Tennessee. Also, in case of a battle to let her hear from them and if you can hear of Matt McClung's family,[19] let them know that their friends here are alive and well, and to please excuse her for troubling you so much. She is extremely anxious to learn where Ed Munford is. Uncle Charley is in a very feeble state of health. He seems to fail very fast. All his family sends its love to you and enjoy your letters extremely. Cousin Will[20] says to tell Mr. Kennedy what a treat his letters are to us, and tell him please to look after Charley. The children join me in love to Father. Hoping that you are well and comfortable and that you will be enabled to return to us again soon. I remain your

Devoted wife
S. Kennedy

Clarksville February 24, 1863

My Dear Husband:

I wrote you last week to send by Mr. L[21] and as he has not yet gone, I will write a few more lines. All are well with the exception of Mary, Jimmy, and Clara who are complaining as when I last wrote. Mary and Jimmy are not sick enough to stay from school but quite complaining. Clara has been quite sick for several days but I think is improving from the treatment she is now under. She is not confined to bed but not well enough to enjoy play. My health is very good. Our friends are all well except Uncle Charley. He has been confined to bed for several days and I fear is dangerously sick. Mr. Barker came in yesterday to stand his trial. He informed me that he was treated very kindly, and they gave him papers as security to his person and property. The old man seemed in fine spirits. His daughter, Ellen, has been dangerously sick with pneumonia.[22] He requested me to say to you that he had already in reply to your letter by Mr. L. said to you that he would rather have cotton than gold on such terms as please you.[23] But whilst cotton is advancing in New York, it is declining in England. English advices quoting———middling at 23 pence and New York at 92 cents per pound. The blank mark you can judge the meaning of as I do not remember the word. He thinks the skies look bright but dreads the horrible collisions that are likely to take place before the war ceases.

O I do pray that the war may soon come to an end and the joyful news of peace resound throughout the land. The children send a great deal of love and many kisses to Father. I was rocking Newty to sleep a few nights since, when he sat up and pointing to the door said "Mama, Father away in Dixieland and the Yankees won't let him alone." Uncle's family, Dr. McM., & Mr. Wardlaw send their love to you. Mr. L. was as kind as to call and let me know that he would go tomorrow and I write this in addition to the one I wrote last week. I pray God to protect you, preserve your health and return you safely to us again. Your devoted wife

S. Kennedy

Clarksville February 28, 1863

My Dear Husband:

I hastily embrace another opportunity of writing to you. My last was written to send by Mr. Leonard, but he failing to get off they were sent by a different route. I received yesterday a letter from you of date Jan 22nd with one enclosed to Maj. Elder[24] and was glad to send it. Although I have some from you of later date, I have not had one from you since Mr. L. left you. I heard today that Cousin Lucy White[25] has received a late letter from E J McC. in which she mentions that you were well. I am looking anxiously for letters from you & indeed I am getting quite blue again because I do not hear from you. The health of the family is tolerable. Clara is improving rapidly. Mary is much stronger and in better health than when I last wrote. Newty is as usual. Jimmy has been at home for several days complaining and this morning had a chill. It seems impossible for him to recover from his last summer fever. A few days ago, Ellen whilst running around the fire stumbled, and sat flat down on the hot fender burning a place under her right thigh about the size of the palm of my hand. Although it is not deep or seriously bad, she suffers a good deal in consequence of her running on it. I find it impossible to keep her still. Clara and Ellen both have whooping cough, and thus far it goes lightly with them. Sally is the only one who is not sick and she looks more puny[26] than I ever knew her in consequence of a very bad cold. We have the most miserable of weather so much rain and sultriness of atmosphere. Colds and sore throats are very prevalent, and I am reminded of the time that we had last spring with typhoid fever. The children have been so much affected and I have felt so great a weight of responsibility and so much care that this morning when Jimmy was taken with a chill, I took a hearty cry and have been nearly crying all day. I know it looks badly in me to give up so, but I cannot be always cheerful and I know I bear up under my trials with a great deal more fortitude than many do. Not being at all satisfied with Dr. Haskins's opinion of Mary's shoulder and spine, I got Dr. Lurton[27] to examine it. He is of my opinion that it is quite serious and demands instant and constant attention. Her shoulder is seriously injured and spine slightly curved. He prescribed a Douche bath[28] every morning, rubbing with liniment after the bath, and, putting her into strap, which treatment has already produced a fine effect. Uncle Charley's health is very bad indeed. He is suffering with gravel[29] and has been confined to bed nearly three weeks. The family are all alarmed about him. The rest of our friends are well. Dr. McM was to see me day before yesterday and the ladies the day before that. Mr. & Mrs. Wardlaw visit me frequently & Mrs. W. is not in good health and is in an interesting situation.[30] I have not heard a word from Lizzie Lewis for two or three weeks. Mr. L. comes to town but does not call on us. The Yanks here had a big scare last night. It was reported that Morgan was just beyond the fair grounds[31] with 10,000 men. The drum beat, and the soldiers were in the rifle pits all last night. Heavy cannonading was heard yesterday and today. It was reported that Fort Donelson had been again taken.[32] I wrote to you of Henry Allen's imprisonment here. He was taken with George Marr and paroled within the city limits. He was called on to report and when asked if he would take the oath, he with an oath, said no which so exasperated Col. Bruce that he ordered him into close confinement. On last Saturday night, he with two others made his escape by jumping from the second story window of Robb & Bailey law office[33] where they were confined. He went immediately to Uncle Charley's but Aunt told him he must not stay, and in fifteen minutes after he left the porch, the guard came to search the house for him. This was nine o'clock at night and at four next morning they searched again going into all the rooms where the women and children were all in bed. On the same morning, Cousin Lucy's maid, Zillah, took leave of them with bag & baggage for Nashville.[34] Caroline Pritchett[35] bid farewell to Clarksville on the same day. Molly Allen[36] is kept in town. They [are] refusing to give her a pass to go home until they get her brother. They pretend to think she and Uncle's family have a hand in his escape when they have not the least idea that he intended such a thing. There are two of our soldiers confined, none with handcuffs. They have taken the Academy[37] for a hospital and have between two and three hundred sick.

All the children send much love and many kisses to Father, and all your friends desire to be remembered. Your Devoted Wife,

S. Kennedy

Clarksville March 13, 1863

My Dear Husband:

After waiting a month for a line or some word from you, I had almost given up in despair. Mr. Macrae[38] called yesterday evening and handed me yours of 10th & 18th February. Words cannot express my joy and happiness. I am delighted with the cheerful tone of your letters and wish I could feel as buoyant and hopeful as you seem to be. We who are entirely in the power of and so entirely surrounded by the enemy without freedom of speech or action, and scarcely of thought cannot feel but gloomy. Every day the reins are tightened. Our whole country is becoming completely stripped of the necessities of life for man and beast. I find it next to impossible to get anything to eat for the family and my poor cow looks half famished. I have been looking forward to my garden for a supply, but they threaten to have the benefit of the gardens themselves and my only hope is that they will be compelled to leave before the vegetables mature. The health of the family is much improved since I last wrote. Indeed, there is no complaint except Clara & Ellen's whooping cough. We have all had severe colds but are now recovered from them. We still have changeable weather, one day bright sunshine and the next pouring rain. I wrote you of Uncle Charley's bad health. Since then he has rapidly declined and cannot live many days. His disease is a protracted case of gravel accompanied with typhoid fever. He has been confined to bed for four weeks suffering intense pain. For the past three days, his suffering has ceased and he has been gradually sinking. I was called at daylight yesterday morning to see him die but he survived and is yet alive. Dr. Bailey is with him.[39] Uncle has a great desire to have his absent male friends with him and calls incessantly for his sons & grandson. The family seem to regret that you are not here and feel quite desolate in the absence of so many of their friends. He said to me "Sally, tell Mr. Kennedy that I shall not see him again in this world but that he must meet me on the other side." He is calm and passive in view of death, and his mind is as clear as noonday. He seems anxious to go and he's rid of his suffering. I spend every day with him but am obliged to be with my children at night. I wrote to you that T. Munford[40] paid me eighty dollars. Mathill[41] paid his house rent, amounting to fifteen dollars. Roberts[42] paid me twenty dollars for John's hire. Ley[43] will not pay a cent for Tom's hire. Woodrum[44] will not pay house rent and the Abbotts[45] moved [a] month before I had a chance of making the rent off of them. Houses of this class cannot now be rented at all. Owners are putting tenants into them to prevent their being utterly ruined by the Yanks and bad boys who take pleasure in making a perfect smash. I have hired Tom to E. Broaddus[46] at two-and-a-half a month payable monthly and have had no difficulty in collecting it thus far. Parker paid me one hundred & seventy-five dollars and cannot be made to pay more. Ben has not been since Christmas. I have heard that he is married, but in a letter to me explaining the Parker matter he does not mention it. G. Lewis[47] (your nephew) has taken the oath and has the freedom of the town and even tiny Cousin Mollie Allen is still a prisoner. They refuse to give her a pass home until they recapture her brother. George Marr has been carried to the Nashville Penitentiary.[48] His brother Duncan[49] has just returned from a visit to him. Tell E. J. McClure that her mother is in town.[50] I see her every day. She and the family are all well. I am grateful that you have so many kind friends among the ladies. I think in case of my demise, you would have no difficulty in more than filling my place. Tell all the nice young ladies for me that they must not be too bewitching or they may make you regret your first choice and make you wish me out of the way. I will sit for my picture[51] as soon as possible but will not send it unless it gives better satisfaction than those taken in the past. When I last heard from Mr. Barker, they were in great distress at the news of Walton's being a prisoner.[52] He has been sent to Camp Moreton.[53]

SUNDAY, MARCH 14TH I left this open to give you the latest news of Uncle Charley. He declines every day. Every morning we think he cannot last till night and so on from night till morning. I do not see {An entire line of the letter is unreadable because a fold runs through it} is suffering intensely and seems not at all conscious of what is passing around him. His moans are harrowing to those who hear them. Mr. Van Culin[54] has permission from headquarters to be with him. Every body sends their regards to you. All the children send love and kisses to Father. Hoping to hear from you again very soon, I remain your Devoted wife

S. Kennedy

Clarksville March 29th, 1863

My Dear Husband:

I wrote you on the 15th relative to Uncle Charley's condition. He expired at six o'clock on the evening of that day. He was buried on Monday. His funeral was preached at the church by Mr. Wardlaw. It was the biggest funeral gathering that has ever been in Clarksville. The whole town seemed to be in mourning at the death of so honored and beloved a man. The stores were all closed and all business suspended.[55] The family are in the deepest affliction and feels it the more heavily on account of the absence of so many of its members. It will be a blow to his absent sons and grandson. Dr. Bailey and Virginia remained with them a week and are now looked for. The house looks lonely indeed and the inmates oh how sad. I wish you to write to them. It would afford them great pleasure, and they would feel doubly assured of your affection and sympathy. Cousin Margaret[56] and Lucy Donoho[57] arrived after the burial and are still here being unable now on account of events transpiring about Nashville,[58] to return home. Since my last to you, I have received your long and interesting letter of 9th March. I need not tell you of all the pleasure and comfort it afforded me and the children for you can imagine it. I sent it to Aunt and they were all grateful and very much interested though the girls laughed at the affectionate part of it. We are all very well and as spring advances, I see a steady improvement in the health of the children. Clara & Ellen are getting through with whooping cough very easily and will soon be well of it. There is little of interest transpiring in our town, except in the military line. We interest ourselves, talking over the various rumors from the seat of war, and our hearts beat high with hope as to the final result. There was a marriage in town last week. Miss Roxy Tarwater[59] & a Mr. Moody of Kentucky. Cousin Will says he is so tall & thin that he will not cast a shadow.

Mr. Parrish is very low with pneumonia, & it is thought he cannot recover. Ben was in town week before last and wrote to you. I enclose his letter with mine. We had a consultation about Tom, and with the advice of Mr. G. and Mr. Mc.[60] concluded that if he is not disposed of that he will be an entire loss. He has spoken of leaving, and aside from this, he is becoming a sot. He frequently lies at home on Sunday too drunk to stir, and loses much time in the week from this cause. Even if he should remain, he will be of little use and cause much trouble. Ben and others think that if he can be sold, it will prove a clear gain to you. If it meets with your views, you will write and give the necessary power to dispose of him.[61] The above persons think that if anything should happen before hearing from you, that it could be done by my representing you, but I hesitate to act thus. We have had some beautiful weather, and I have done a little gardening. Yesterday we had a heavy rain, and today we have real winter, with a keen north wind which cuts one through. I love to be in the garden, and a bad day gives me the blues. The Feds have pressed all the negro men to work for them,[62] but my man Phil is so unhandy that they will not have him, and I find that it is an advantage now to have a crippled nigger. I have not yet had my picture taken because I was looking badly. I have been dyspeptic[63] and my mouth and lips full of fever blisters, but I shall try to have it done this week. I dreamed last week that you came home and that I told you to go right off again and in a few minutes after you left the house was surrounded by soldiers come to arrest you. Ben was arrested in my parlor just at supper time. He went to headquarters, but they found nothing against him, and he was released. He thinks that some-one informed them that he was a soldier in the Southern Army. When he came up to supper it was almost dark. He was in company with some young men, acquaintances of the Capt. of the Provost Guard. They introduced Ben by name and in fifteen minutes the house was surrounded and he taken to headquarters. I think his name had something to do with his arrest.

The servants all said howdy to you and John.[64] Fanny says tell master that he has never mentioned one of his house servants in his letters, and she feels slighted. They were glad to hear from John. They all get along pleasantly and agreeably, and I find that Aunt Lucy is the most suitable person I ever had with the little ones and being relieved of Patsy is the greatest relief I ever had. I think that Aunt Lucy's kind management is proving a great benefit to Newty. She takes great interest in them and seems to try and do her duty.

Aunt Lucy and Will send their love to you. Mrs. Wardlaw was here the other day and read your letter. She is obliged for your kind remembrances and sends hers & Mr. W's in return, and Dr. McM's do the same. Mary says tell Lucy McClure to kiss you for her & give her love to Cousin Eliza[65] & Lucy and kiss Lucy for her. All the children talk a great deal about Father and send much love and many kisses. Clara says tell Father I kiss and hug Mother every morning and night for him and when I say my prayers, I say oh Lord take care of Father and bring him back safe to us again. Little Ellen is a bright little thing, but she has a temper. She was walking on the street yesterday and meeting a gentleman she stopped and said, "look here, me dot a new bonnet, a pretty bonnet, and mama sewed a string on it today, she did sure enough." She adds sure enough to everything she says. It's late and I must close. Good night. I pray God to preserve you and that you may be speedily restored to us and home. Your Devoted wife

S. Kennedy

Clarksville April 24th, 1863

My Dear Husband:

I have very much feared that you would become impatient at my long delay in writing to you. But one opportunity has passed since my last, and then I was very ill in bed. I took a severe cold in the garden last week, and for five days and nights I suffered intense agony from pain, soreness & swelling in my left jaw, gums and teeth. I am now up but very feeble and not able to eat more solid food than mush. I still have my jaws bound up in flannel but am im-proving steadily. The sadness and gloom thrown around everything at home by your absence, assumes a darker hue when I am sick. I deeply miss your coming to my bedside with the loving sympathy which so alleviates pain. Every family seems so occupied with its own trials that there is not much time to devote to others. There is much sickness in our town consequent at this season. The health of the children is now very good, though Clara & Ellen have both been very sick since I last wrote. They took severe colds with whooping cough which threw them into chills. Fanny's baby, I thought, would die, but all are recovering from the cough and will be entirely well when warmer weather gets in. I received yours by Tex B.[66] She arrived the next Friday after she left you. Went home that night. Since which I have not heard from the family. Mollie, Mrs. M. B., and Mrs. Trice[67] went to Camp Princeton to see Walton[68] whom they heard was sick. He had been exchanged before they got there and they did not see him. I learned that H. C., the man that accompanied Tex is likely to be put to much trouble on account of his trip.

I received yours of 1st April last week. I need not try to express how much comfort and pleasure I have had in perusing it for words cannot express my happiness. Aunt's family, Mrs. Munford, Miss Carrie, and Mr. W. have read it with great pleasure. Miss Carrie says tell Mr. K. that he is getting so poetical that she expects soon to hear that he has become an author. She says you must not make any arrangement in case of my death as she has a prior engagement. I have solicited her and others to write to you, but I believe no one has complied with my request. We are so tied down by despotism that we are afraid to write and it has to be done with the utmost secrecy as the writers, carriers, and receivers of letters from the South are subject to a heavy Federal penalty.[69] Spring has fairly opened upon us and though the mornings and evenings are cool, we have bright beautiful weather. Our home never looked more beautiful. The evergreens have grown almost out of knowledge. The shade trees are in full leaf & the roses are beginning to bloom. The garden is flourishing and the birds make melody in the trees. I so often wish you could take one peep at home and every day I more and more miss your coming at noon and at night to enjoy its comforts with us. The children are delighted at the reception of your letter and the servants seem much pleased at the notice you gave them. They are glad to hear from John. I made enquiries about John's children. Four weeks since they were at G. Brunson's[70] farm, all well.

Jimmie has not been at school for two months. His health continued so bad that I stopped him. He was learning nothing. I do not know whether to attribute it to bad health or bad teaching. I found it was money and health thrown away. He attends to all his studies at home, and if he does not learn more, he learns as much without the expense and his health seems to be permanently established. He is a great help to me, does all my errands, cuts wood, makes fires, and helps amuse the children. Mary is at hard study and one of Dr. Ring's best scholars. I wish she could have been with him sooner as she never knew before what it is to study. She is progressing rapidly in music. She is growing rapidly and I have to hold a tight rein to keep her under or she would be a little too fast for me. Sally shows a disposition to learn fast if kept closely at it but she does not progress at home like she would at school. I find that it takes all my time and strength to manage and take care of so many children and the older ones are a greater charge than the younger. Aunt's health is very poor, and they have had a lonely time there since Cousin Margaret and Lucy left them. They have a late letter from Col B. in which he gives a gloomy account of his health and says a summer south will kill him. Say to E. J. that Bene[71] was in town last week. All were well. Since my last to you, I think Tom has some what changed for the better. Phil tells me that he talked to him and he promised him he would do better and Broaddus has brought no charge against him since. I have a letter from Ben mentioning that he found it impossible to find a purchaser. Men not willing to buy unless the subject is perfectly willing to go which would not likely be the case.[72] Fanny has been in her tantrums for a week. She has been a perfect terror to the whole place. I consulted her husband with what I should do with her and he told me to have her whipped as she had been in need of it for some time. She is considerably cooled and if she boils up again, I shall act according to his advice. Lizzie Lewis[73] has just come. She sends her love to you. They are all well. {The rest of the line is indecipherable} what complaining as she expects to present another scion[74] to the family before long. I have not had an opportunity to have my likeness taken as McCormick[75] has been absent in the north and there is no other operator here. I will now have to wait until I get well. I succeeded in getting you a pair of shoes which Mr. B. W. M. thinks will suit and if they do not, he thinks you will have no difficulty in getting rid of them. I fear though that the chance for sending them is slim as few are willing to take a bundle. They cost four dollars and are the only pair here. They do not fill my idea of the thing you want but it is the only chance. All your friends send love to you. All the children join me in love to Father and Mary says she is going to write you a letter before long. She is ashamed of her writing or she would have written before. Remember me to E. J. and family. We all, and especially myself, miss you sadly and my only consolation during your absence is the letters I receive from you. I hope that this blessed privilege may not be taken from us. I pray that your health and life may be spared and that you may be able to join us at home before very long. Pray for me. Your devoted wife

S. Kennedy

Clarksville May 5th, 1863

My Dear Husband:

I very much fear that you are impatient at the intervals between my letters. Opportunities for sending letters are much less frequent now than formerly and the vigilance with which movements are watched makes it difficult to find conveyances. My last to you was dated 24 or 25th March, as well as I can recollect. Since that time, Mary has had a spell of a prevailing bloody diarrhea but has entirely recovered after five or six days of confinement to bed. Last Friday, the 1st, Clara had a chill, another Saturday, and another on Sunday. She was very ill and had convulsions with the fever. She missed the chill on the fourth day and is now up but owing to the wet chilly weather has not been out of the room. The rest of the family are well. I wrote in my last of my own indisposition. I was very reduced and very feeble and the care of the sick children has very much retarded my recovery. Poor little Newty after going two weeks without spasms has been very much indisposed for three days and is in a never endingly nervous state tonight, so much so that he cannot go to sleep. The Federals are pursuing the evil tenor of their way, but I have been thus far singularly free from their depredations. Whilst my neighbors are constantly annoyed by them in different ways, not one comes on our place or has anything to do with the servants. I think it owing to the secluded position of the kitchen and the privacy of the part of the house where the family stay. They look longingly into the garden as they pass and I expect every day to see them come over to gather flowers, but they have not done so yet. Some gardens they keep stripped of all the flowers that bloom. Cheney[76] goes out every morning with a basket of bouquets and brings me sixty and seventy cents each day. She says that she cannot get down in town before they are all taken by the Yanks who make a great fuss over them. Phil has my garden in fine order. I never had a finer prospect for vegetables. I think I shall beat every body in irish potatoes from a bed that was planted last spring and not disturbed during the summer. This spring it was ploughed and the potatoes will soon be large enough to use. Yesterday we were visited with a cold north wind which foreboded frost and today we have been sitting by a blazing winter fire. We were preparing to cover the garden tonight, but towards evening the weather moderated and it is now raining and unless the clouds clear away and it turns colder, the crops and gardens will be safe from frost. Ben was here last week. He came twice to see me but was so stupid from too much drink that his visit afforded no little pleasure. Last Thursday, Old Abe's great day, all the stores and schools were closed by order of the Military.[77] On Friday, the 1st, the young ladies had a coronation[78] at Poston's Spring.[79] There were a great many in atten-

dance, very select, no one but invited guests. Col. Bruce & Boone[80] with
their adjutants were among the number. They were invited for the purpose
of saving annoyance from the attendance of the soldiery. Miss Sally Lewis[81]
was crowned queen. Everything passed pleasantly and agreeably. I did not
attend. Mary, Jimmie, and Sally went under the care of Mrs. Munford and
Mrs. McMullen. Mr. Wardlaw has been quite sick but is now convalescent.
Dr. McM. filled in his pulpit last Sunday. Aunt's health is very bad. She has
chills and is looking very badly. I have so much sickness at home that I seldom go out, and I am grieved that I cannot visit them often. I started a pair
of shoes to you last Thursday which I hope may reach you. I sent them to
your address, and if the bearer should possibly not reach Atlanta, I gave him
J. A. Fisher's address at Chattanooga. McCormick's absence in the North
has prevented me from having my likeness taken, but I shall have it done
and send as soon as possible. I very seldom hear from Mr. Barker. None of
the family ever come to town and although I very much desire to pay them a
visit as soon as the health of the family will permit, I confess that I shall not
be able to do so. The last order is that no lady will be permitted to leave town
without signing the parole of honor which is a mild term for taking the oath
and having it paraded in the northern papers. I learned that this port will in
a short time be opened for the reception of dry goods and groceries. If it is
not, we will have to go barefoot as there is not a shoe in this town that will
fit one of the family. Jimmy is already barefooted and the little ones will be
turned out of shoes as soon as the weather will permit, but Mary and myself
cannot go unshod. I am troubled at the idea of your scant and threadbare
wardrobe. I have a set of shirts for you and would like to send them, would
do so if it were possible for anyone to take so much and a perfectly reliable
opportunity would offer. Mr. T. called to see me after his return to fulfill
the promise he made to you that he would do so. I was very glad to see him,
and his visit, as well as the information he gave, was very gratifying. There
is so little of interest transpiring that I fear my letters appear dull to you. I
am ashamed of my poor epistles when compared with the talent displayed
in yours. My dear husband, your letters afford me all the consolation I have
in the world with the exception of the thought of being so highly favored
in being permitted to be at home with my children for when I look back at
the mess we made last year and being so long deprived of home, it appears
doubly dear to me, and I am sincerely grateful to God for restoring it to me
again. It is the only place of happiness and comfort to a woman with a family
of children. And although the presiding genius is compelled to be separated
from us, the hope of his return keeps me strong to strive to do my duty alone.
And I do pray for strength from on high to do my duty in every relation

which I sustain in life. I have a bad pen & thick ink; this is my excuse for this miserable blotch. The children join me in love to you. May God protect you is the prayer of your devoted wife.

S. Kennedy

It would confer a great favor, not only to myself but to others who have friends to write to if you can send some Confederate stamps.[82] I am already out and there are none to be had here.

Clarksville May 25th, 1863

My Dear Husband:

I wrote you on the 5th this month and have since received your welcome favors of 18th April and 24th Feb. You mention that you have no letter from me later than the 18th March. I have written you three since the fifteenth which I hope you have received before this but fear that they are lost. Several of your letters have failed to come to hand and it is probable that some of mine fail to reach you. I have written by every opportunity offering except once and then I was sick in bed and in too much pain to write. I am afraid that my sad letters produce the melancholy pervading your last. You must not think that we are uncomfortable or without friends. Everyone shows sympathy and kindness to us and very many are the kind enquiries after your health and spirits. Mr. Q. & B {indecipherable} are very attentive to my wants and all your friends seem to feel a deep interest in my welfare. I shall endeavor hereafter to write more cheerfully. I am more unhappy about your condition than I am about anyone. My hands and time are fully occupied with my children and housekeeping, whilst you are unoccupied. My responsibility as a mother increases every day, and as I have no one to share this with me, I must strive the harder to do my duty. As the children increase in years and mingle more with the world, I have to be more watchful and look and beseech more for help from on high. My general health is pretty good, but I have frequent attacks of neuralgia. I have never felt so strong or so energetic since having Typhoid fever and my strength and spirits have been worn by the frequent sickness of the children. I look forward to settled summer weather for their entire recovery. Clara's health is better, and Newty seems to be slowly improving, his spasms are not near so frequent. Three weeks since I sent you a pair of shoes to your address at Atlanta, or if the bearer should not go to Atlanta, I directed him to leave them with J. A. Fisher at Chattanooga. I do hope you will get them. My picture and Mary's I have ready and will send as soon as possible. I am perfectly satisfied with mine and do not think you can make an objection to it. Mary's is a good likeness,

34

but has not a pleasing expression owing to the pain produced on her eyes by the light in the glass. Cousin Will says that mine is the finest picture she ever saw and that it looks like an authoress. I send one of each in this letter and will send one of each in a case so that you will be sure to get them. If those in the cases reach you, you must send the cards to sister. A week ago, I moved up stairs and am occupying the middle room as my own and the front room for the little girls. I like the change exceedingly, feel safer, and have a great deal more room. From the window, I can see all over town, and I am not so lonely. The Feds have quartered some of their negro hands in the Donoho[83] house, the idea of such neighbors is very disagreeable but thus far they have behaved with propriety and have given no trouble or offense to us or any of the neighbors. We live as quietly as if the war had never been heard of, that is, we are not at all troubled by the soldiers. I have been as little annoyed as any one whilst my neighbors have in some cases suffered insult. Whilst numbers of houses are left without a servant, and the family doing all the housework including cooking, washing, and ironing, I see no disposition on the part of our house servants to neglect a duty or to leave us. They appear faithful and cheerful. A week since Tom left E. Broaddus and set up for himself in the Quartermaster's department, wages 15 dollars a month. Yesterday (Sunday) he came strutting in as if the place and every one in it belonged to him. He spoke to Aunt Lucy and said how do you do? She answered, I do very well without you. I called to him and asked him how he dared show his face or put his foot on my place, and if he did not leave instantly, I should have him taken off. His answer was yes I can leave. Our friends here are usually well. Mrs. Wardlaw has a daughter three weeks old. Aunt's health is better than when I last wrote. It is a sad household. Aunt says tell Mr. K. that I am very grateful for his kind sympathy for me in my deep affliction and that he has shown more the affection of a son than of a distant relative. They all send love to you. Mrs. Munford says that it is impossible for her to express her appreciation of your kindness in regard to Will and if you meet or can in any way communicate with Ed M., let him know that she has his letters instructing her to send for Don and that she has written for him to come with Mrs. Elder[84] (who is in Memphis) and that nothing will be left undone to get him here. She would not trouble you with this but fears that her letters may not reach him. Rosecrans' order that all the men are to take the oath or go south with their families and all the women whose husbands are absent, sign the parole of honor or go south has cast a gloom over our town, not to be conceived by anyone not in our midst.[85] The men are not allowed to leave without their families, and I suppose this will induce many to take it, whilst others will utterly refuse. I have longed for your advice and regretted that I had not asked you long ago what I should do in the event I should be required to do so. Dr. McMullen & Mr. W. advised me to sign the parole and stay home with my children and protect my property. If I should be required to do anything more kindly let me know what I must do. The time will be out next Saturday. I expect Dr. Mc will go with his family. What Mr. W. will do, I cannot say.[86] Kathy Hollingsworth spent Saturday with me. She is looking very well and sends her love to you. Miss Carry was here this morning, is well, and sends her love. If they go south, you will probably see them. I hope you will as it would be a great pleasure to you to see such kind friends who could give you so much information about home. Mary, Sally, and Jimmie are well. Little Ellen is a sweet little miss. She sleeps with me and frequently during the night, she throws her arms around my neck and says don't me love you mama, out me feet, me feets in papa's place till he tums home. We all pet her a great deal, and I am afraid she will be spoiled. Remember me to E. J. and family. All the children send love to Father, and we all talk about you a great deal. Praying that you may have heavenly comfort and that you may be spared to return to us in health and before very long. I am your devoted wife

S. Kennedy


Clarksville June 2nd, 1863

My Dear Husband:

Cousin Sue Marr will leave tomorrow to join her husband away down in Dixie.[87] Fate has decreed that our separation be postponed for a longer period but hope points to a day not far distant when you will again be united to your family, home, and friends to enjoy peace and quiet made doubly dear by separation and the destructing scenes which we have been called to witness for two years past. Cousin Sue will give you all the information concerning us that you could desire to know. We are all well and comfortable and as happy as we could be under the circumstances. The days and hours drag wearily without your presence to cheer them, and our prayers rise daily for your health, happiness, and comfort in your lonely exile. I feel that a letter from me that has been inspected by other eyes cannot be of much comfort to you, but I must avail this opportunity to let you hear from your loved ones at home. We are all well and hope that your health continues to improve. I am very anxious to hear from you having no information from you later than 30th April. Aunt's health is improving. She and Cousin Lucy[88] send their love to you and say that you must write to Cousin Jamie[89] that they are well. All the children send love and kisses to Father and howdy to

Uncle John. The servants desire to be remembered to you. All our friends are well and make many kind inquires after your health. My love to E. J. Mc. and family.

Your devoted wife

S. Kennedy

Clarksville June 17th, 1863

My Dear Husband:

The children and myself wrote you on the 29th May accompanying the letters with pictures of myself and Mary, one of each of us in cases, and one of each in the letters. All of which I hope you have received. My last was by Cousin Sue Marr who started on the 3rd of this month. I did not know that she was going south until after the pictures had gone or I should have sent them by her. I received yours of a 9th May the day she left and have since received yours of 18th and 20th all of which have given me great comfort. And I am looking daily and with great anxiety to hear from you again. I am rejoiced to learn that your health is better and hope that you will soon be entirely restored. You do not mention having received the shoes I sent you in April and I find they have not reached you, I was very much disappointed at not being able to send you some clothing and do not despair of an opportunity to do so yet. The health of the children has improved since I wrote last and is better than at any time since we came home. My own health is pretty good, but I am growing thinner every day. We are cheered by the news from the south west and from Virginia, but many hearts are sad from the fear that loved ones have fallen either wounded or dead in the great battles.[90] Mrs. Munford is so anxious about Will that she is sick in bed nearly all the time, and she suffers great anxiety because she has no letters from him. She seems very much gratified that he has been offered the hospitality of Aunt Eliza's house, and her gratitude to you for your attention to him is unbounded. Charlie and Tex Barker came in yesterday. Tex came to our house and had been with me until this evening which she is spending at J. O. Shackleford's[91] with Col. Bruce and others. The Col. is very much taken with the family (Mr. B.) and invited himself there to spend a day. I went with Tex this morning to his office. She went for a permit to carry out some goods. He was very affable and kind and told her that she could carry anything she wished. I told him that I wished to visit in the country for a few days, but I was afraid to leave my place with no one but the servants to protect it. He told me to let him know when I wished to go, and he would have my place guarded until my return. I wrote you that Tom had procured employment in the quartermaster's department. Mr. Wardlaw advised me to apply for his wages and offered to ask for me (as some of the others were receiving the pay for their negroes). He told me today that the Captain said to him that according to the rules laid down that the slaves of such rebel sympathizers as you are must be used for the benefit of the government.[92] Cheney left on the night of the 2nd [with] bag and baggage. The other servants deny any knowledge of her intentions, and I had no intimations of it except in her neglect of her duties at home. She moved her clothing whilst Fanny & Aunt Lucy were in the house at suppertime, and when Fanny went down stairs, she met her with a cup in her hand saying that she was going to get some yeast to make bread for breakfast. She has not returned with the yeast yet. I learned from a negro man (who had seen her) that she was employed as a chamber maid on a Cincinnati Steam Boat, and a negro woman told Jimmie that she saw her in Cincinnati. I am now my own chamber maid. I clean out my own rooms every morning and do not feel any worse from it. I told the servants that I would not hire anyone to fill her place. I thought, at first, that I would not inform you of this for fear that you would be unhappy about it. You must not be distressed for I am not as her health was so bad and she was likely to have another three months siege and by her move, I will be saved the trouble of nursing her and the expense of a physician. I miss her less than I would any of the others. Negroes are leaving daily, and there will be few left behind when these Federals take their departure. If my health is good, I can do a great deal and feel it will be a benefit to myself and children to wait on ourselves. Their value, if we could get it, is the only loss. Cousin Lucy White and Bene V. C. I saw today. Cousin Lucy says please look out for her Nolan who she thinks is in Chattanooga and let her hear from him. Mr. Simpson and family were pleased to hear from their son. Old squire Johnson died last week, and Mr. Parrish died today.

Enclosed is a letter from Dr. Lurton which he desires you to forward to his brother-in-law, Rev. Dr. Harman at Enterprise, Miss. They have not heard from him for a long time and think he does not receive their letters sent in the normal way. Dr. L. wishes you to send him, Dr. Harman, your address so that he may direct his letters to you to be forwarded to Clarksville. I have employed Dr. L. as family physician and am exceedingly pleased with him. He and his wife are very estimable people and pious, devoted Christians. Mrs. Harman is a niece of my step-mother, Mrs. Adams. I also enclose a letter from old Mrs. Davidson to her son Ben which she desires you to forward to him, and she wishes you to write to me if you can learn any thing concerning him. The late news from our army leads me to anticipate your return home before long, and I do hope I shall not be disappointed. Aunt's health is very much improved. Mrs. Lusk[93] has been down. She took Maud and Jimmy Bailey to Nashville with her leaving Robb with Aunt.[94] If you wish me to send you any clothing, write, so that I may know what to do. I may have an opportunity and would dislike to send it unless you wish me to do so. Miss Carrie sends her love to you and says that she considers the old contract between yourself and her binding. Mrs. McM. is in very feeble health, so is Mrs. Wardlaw, the latter has an infant six weeks old and is in an alarming state of health. Phil's great desire for making money for himself makes him less attentive to home duties every day, and when I speak to him about it, he says Miss Sally, you don't consider how many men are working for themselves and doing nothing at home. He thinks I should consider it a great favor done me that he has not left entirely. Mr. Barker sent me yester-day, a barrel of flour as a present, also a nice quarter of lamb. He was in town last week and told me to call on him for any assistance that I needed, but I feel a delicacy in asking him for any thing after his kindness to me last sum-mer. Hattie Donoho[95] is with us tonight, and she and Mary are making so much fuss with this Rebel song in the parlor that I can scarcely write. I hope you will excuse this rambling letter. Remember me to W. McC. Family[96] and tell them that their friends are all well. Mr. L., the bearer of this, was so kind as to inform me that he was going and offered to take it. I pray hourly for your preservation and safe return to us. Your devoted wife

S. Kennedy

Mary expects to astonish every body with her musical attainments next Sunday night at a concert at the Presbyterian church given by Miss Margaret Ring. All the children send heaps of love and kisses to Father. Don't fail to send some Confederate stamps.

Undated portrait of Sarah Ann Bailey Kennedy (1822–1900)

Undated portrait of David Newton
Kennedy (1820–1904)

Sarah's paternal uncle, Major Charles Bailey Sr.
(1791–1863), reared Sarah and her sister when
they were orphaned as children.

Sarah's first cousin, James Edmund Bailey (1822–1885), served as a US Senator from Tennessee from 1877 to 1881.

Sarah attended the Nashville Female Academy and frequently mentioned her care for her children's education.

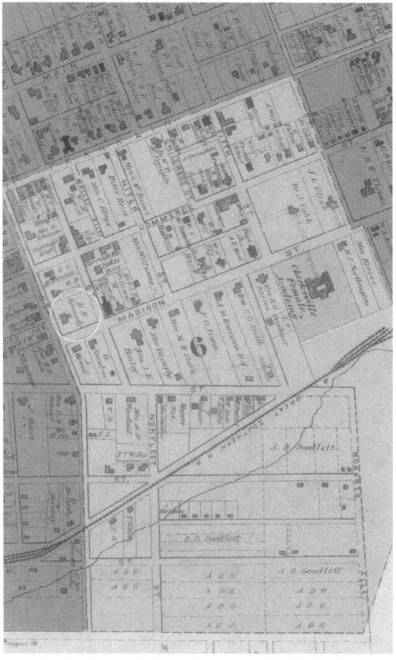

This 1877 Montgomery County map shows downtown Clarksville, including the Kennedy residence on the corner of Second and Madison Streets.

The Castle Building, constructed in 1850, on the campus of Stewart College,
was used by Confederate forces as a hospital until occupying Federal forces
made it their headquarters.

Stewart College was re-chartered as Southwest Presbyterian College
in 1875. In his eighties, D. N. Kennedy was instrumental in staving off a bid
to move it to Atlanta in 1901.

The Kennedys lived in a handsome red brick structure that stood on an incline at 221 South Second Street.

The Kennedys were active members of First Presbyterian Church of Clarksville. This early church building was replaced by a larger structure in 1878.

D. N. Kennedy and James L. Glenn founded the Northern Bank of Tennessee, located on the corner of Second and Franklin Streets.

After the fall of Fort Donelson, Sarah and her six children stayed for a while at Cloverlands, a farm about a mile from the Kentucky border owned by family friend John Walton Barker. This photograph shows the home as it is today.

# MRS. D. N. KENNEDY

## Passed Quietly Away At Her Home on Second St.

### After a Long And Useful Life, Leaving The Record of a Noble Life.

At ten minutes before two o'clock yesterday morning Mrs. Sallie Kennedy, wife of D. N, Kennedy, died at her home on Second street, in this city at the advanced age of seventy-six years. She leaves her aged husband, Hon. D. N. Kennedy, and five children, Mrs. Mary K. Owen, Mrs. Sallie G. Plunkett, James T. Kennedy, Mrs. Clara D, Burney and Mrs. Ellen B. Clapp. She was born in Wilkerson county, Miss., in 1823, the daughter of James Bailey, and was married in Clarksville November 22, 1843. She became the mother of nine children; and was noted as an earnest, practical Christian woman who did good quiet-

Sarah's obituary in the Clarksville *Leaf Chronicle* remembered her as "an earnest practical Christian woman who did good quietly and shunned all parade."

D. N. and Sarah Kennedy are buried near many of their descendants in Greenwood Cemetery in Clarksville. As D. N. spearheaded the cemetery's development in 1873, it is ironic that a tree was allowed to grow between their headstones.

A large family monument marks the Kennedy plot in Greenwood Cemetery, Clarksville.

# 3

## AUGUST 19, 1863–
## MARCH 19, 1864

On July 4, 1863, the Confederacy received a double blow. The Battle of Gettysburg, Pennsylvania, was lost, Confederate General Robert E. Lee withdrew, and combat returned to the South. Confederate armies would not fight on Northern soil again. Vicksburg, Mississippi, surrendered on that day as well, giving the US complete control of the Mississippi River. On July 9, 1863, Port Hudson, Louisiana, surrendered to the Federal army. However, things began to look up for the Confederacy in September. On September 19 and 20, 1863, Confederate General Braxton Bragg routed the US army at the Battle of Chickamauga, Georgia. When the Federals retreated to Chattanooga, the Confederates took the high ground, surrounding the city and cutting off the Federal supply chain. On October 16, 1863, President Lincoln appointed Union General Ulysses S. Grant Commander of the Western Theater. The Battle of Chattanooga occurred on November 23–25, 1863, and consisted of several battles aimed at breaking the siege of Chattanooga. The Battle of Lookout Mountain on November 24 and the Battle of Missionary Ridge on November 25 secured the high ground for the US and broke the siege. In December of 1863, the 16th US Colored Troop (USCT) Infantry Regiment began recruiting black men in Clarksville, Tennessee. In April 1864, this unit moved to Chattanooga for occupation duty. On March 9, 1864, President Lincoln appointed General Grant commander of all the armies of the United States. Union General William Tecumseh Sherman assumed command of the Western Theater.

Clarksville August 19th, 1863

My Dear Husband:

I wrote you on the 16th and now avail another opportunity of writing again. I mentioned that I had received yours of 1st and 28th July and I assure you that they were a great pleasure to me. I also mentioned that Phil and Fanny had left for Yankeedom. Fanny has been gone three weeks today, and I learn this morning that John, her husband, followed her last Monday night. For two weeks after Fanny left, Aunt Lucy and I got along pretty well. I did all the housework and she the cooking and out door work. Hiring a woman to wash and iron. Last week I hired a free girl for the cooking and washing[1] after finding that Aunt Lucy and myself would breakdown. We are getting along a great deal better and happier since Fanny left, for she had become so quarrelsome and disagreeable that the whole family hated the sight of her. I do hope that we will be able to get pay for them all. Aunt Lucy seems glad that they are gone. She says that she spent half her time cleaning up after Fanny and her children. Phil did nothing but cut the wood for some time before he left. Worked out all the time but made nothing for me. He was a dead expense.

My health is good. I have gotten entirely rid of neuralgia and am never sick enough to go to bed. The exercise of housecleaning is good for me unless I do too much, and when it is all done, I sit down contentedly to my sewing for the rest of the day. Jimmy has been complaining for a day or two with torpid liver[2] and deranged bowels. He is better today. The other children are well. Mary has been absent for some time at Trenton.[3] I look for her at home today. The southerners here are low spirited, and if you cannot get home before winter sets in, I think now that I shall give right up. Some times I have the blues terribly, and again, I am more cheerful than many would be under the circumstances. Every body says that I meet difficulties with more fortitude than could be expected. I feel grateful for the health and strength of body that enables me to lay my hand to any kind of work that has to be done, and I would rather do all the work than be worried with a houseful of servants that do what, how, and when they please. I do not think Aunt Lucy will leave or give me any trouble, but there is no dependence to be put in any of them. They have all been turned into fools by the circumstances that surround them, and if we could be compensated for their value, are better off without them. I feel that if poor little Newty could get well, I would be willing to submit to all the other Providences that have befallen, and I am more anxious about him every day. Mrs. Munford has just told me that she sent a letter to the post office to be sent to City Point[4] and old Wynes[5] sent her word that an order has been issued that no more letters could go that way. He is being malicious and tries every way to cut us off from all privileges and therefore I do not believe his statement. Mrs. M. desires me to say that you must excuse her for troubling you so much with letters, but as she has no idea where Will & Bud are, she sends them to you to be forwarded to them. I learned on Monday that the shoes I sent you in April are not lost, only failed to get through and you will [be] likely to get them yet. I shall try to send you the clothes you desired. I sent you six collars and four handkerchiefs by Mr. L. I mention this that I may learn whether he delivered them. I wrote you that Mrs. Clayton[6] arrived here on the first of August and that Mr. Barker had desired me to write to you to acquaint Mr. C. of her safety. We are now having real hot summer weather, and mosquitoes are getting plenty. We spent a pleasant social day two weeks since at W. Macrae's. He sent his buggy in for us. Sam Kennedy sent me word a few weeks ago that if I needed any thing in his power to make me comfortable that I must not hesitate to call on him, and that if I desired it, he would come down to see me. Ben was here last week looking same as ever. Mrs. Barker was grateful to you for mentioning Walton. She has since received a letter from him informing her he has joined Forrest's command.[7] Remember me affectionately to Cousin James[8] and wife. Tell them that Robb[9] is now on a visit to Trenton with Aunt and Cousin Lucy. His health is much improved. The children send a great deal of love to Father. Hoping that you may receive my letters and praying for your preservation and safe return. I remain your devoted wife

S. Kennedy

Clarksville September 19th, 1863

My Dear Husband:

I have received yours of 12th August and having an opportunity to write, I embrace it but feel that I have nothing of interest to communicate. My spirits of late have been at so low an ebb as such a degree to affect my health. I have not felt well for some time. My liver is torpid and last night I commenced taking some pills which I hope will relieve me. The great responsibility and care that rests upon me is quite a burden to bear especially with the high price of everything. I try to live with little expense but fear that my expenses will not meet with your approbation. After having a girl for a month, I have concluded to try to get along with only Aunt Lucy's assistance until the cold weather sets in, and then perhaps I will be able to get a suitable servant for the winter. It is now impossible to get help except that which is more trouble than it is worth. I have felt lately that if I could get a suitable person to take the house, and board me and the children that it would be more suitable, and I see but one objection that is the wear to the house and place for no one will keep it in order as I will. I am so lonely and have so much care. I would like to board some school girls but cannot do so without servants.

The children are all well. Newty has improved totally, and I am trying every remedy that I can hear of. Mary goes to school to Dr. McMullen and continues music with Miss Ring. Jimmy and Sally stay at home to assist me in the housekeeping and tending the children, and I hear their lessons every day. Clara has recovered her health almost entirely, and little Ellen is as fat as a pig and is as sweet as ever. All the southerners here wear countenances of gloom with the exception of those who are making fortunes. They wear high looks and are looked upon as no better than Lincolnites. Col. Bruce has been removed from this command, and Col. Givens[10] of the 102nd Ohio takes his place for the present. Many persons regret this as Col. Bruce was considered very accommodating to the citizens, but I have never found his accommodations to extend further than promises which were never fulfilled.

I have felt great anxiety about your fate since hearing of the troubles at Chattanooga[11] and hope that you have found a quiet and safe retreat from the foe. My hatred for them increases every day, and I feel there is little hope that we will soon be from under their rule. Cousin Sally Copeland[12] is now on a visit to Aunt. Dr. G's family have returned to Nashville. I wrote to you of the death of Mr. Glenn's child, Thornton,[13] of flux. Let his mother know of it. Miss Sally Poindexter[14] died week before last. We have had a cool wet summer with very little fruit. Our peach crop an entire failure. The grapes finer than usual, have not been disturbed by the birds and bees at all. I often wish you could enjoy them with us. Aunt has had a return of chills in the last few days, the family as well as usual. I received a note from our friend, J. B., today announcing the death of Mollie's infant son, Walton.[15] They are having a great deal of sickness, have buried three servants and two more are not expected to recover. The old man is suffering a great deal from rheumatism. I have not seen any of the family for a long while. They never come in, and it is impossible for me to visit them with all my children. The bearer is waiting. I can only say that Miss Carrie sends her love, and all your friends make many kind inquires after you. All the children send love and kisses. Newty goes to your picture and says Father, they all won't let me alone. Hoping to hear from you soon. I remain your devoted wife

S. Kennedy

Clarksville October 6th, 1863

My Dear Husband:

I seize a hasty and uncertain opportunity of sending you some word from home. I wrote you three or four weeks since, but learned last week that my letter had not left the neighborhood. I am deeply grieved that so few opportunities offer [to] send letters. Often and sometimes I feel as if all communication will be cut off. The last from you was dated 12th August. I have heard from you twice since by persons who saw you at Chattanooga as late as the last of August. They give glowing accounts of your healthy appearance, and fine spirits. We are all in excellent health, no complaints at all with the exception of slight colds occasioned by the change of seasons. For a month past, Newty has very perceptibly improved, but for several days past he has had a severe attack of his spasms. They seem to come on him now monthly and are not so severe as formerly. We have become quite accustomed to getting along without servants. I hired one for a month after Fanny left, but was glad when her time was out, and have gotten along with only Aunt Lucy since. The old lady keeps up astonishingly and is a great comfort to me. The children and myself perform all the housework and have nothing to complain of, only if we have company, then the cooking troubles me as Aunt Lucy is not a fancy cook. I feel perfectly reconciled to my lot in this respect. You know the old adage misery loves company, and I have plenty of it. Every day or two we hear of several leaving. Mrs. Robb has not one on her place except one man. Mrs. J. Jones[16] has one old woman left and Mrs. Warfield,[17] our neighbor, has lost every one. Mrs. Elder[18] lost two house maids last week and I understand that this command says that they intend to sweep this whole country of them. I feel that I am more able to get along without them than any, I have mentioned and as long as I am blessed with health can ably bear it, and if sickness should visit us, I trust that we will be provided with friends to assist us. Fanny and her husband have set up a regular establishment in Nashville. John is in a fine business house and Fanny is mistress of her own home. Phil is there also, hobbling about as he was wont to do here. Nashville seems to be the Paradise and to get there the height of their aspirations.

I am afraid I shall have no opportunity of sending you the clothing you desired. When I received my cedar chest from B. I found seven pretty good shirts in it which I wish you had with you. I am trying to arrange for as much comfort as possible for the winter. Am having a supply of wood cut and stored away in the cellar, and Mr. Glenn has had a hundred and seventy-five bushels of coal hauled from the bank cellar which I have snug under the porch. So you see I will be well warmed this winter. I have fitted up the dining room for the family sleeping and living and have the kitchen stove in the servant's room and intend eating with my family by the kitchen stove. You will find me considerably of a yankee woman[19] when you come home. Jimmy brings up the coal and kindling every evening and is my man of all work. Sally minds the little children. Mary goes to school, but makes all the beds every morning before she leaves. They fret sometimes because they have so much to do, but I find that they are every day improving with the experience.

Cousins Sally Copeland and Lucy & Charley Bryan[20] are here on a visit. Aunt's family are in usual health. Cousin Will is very much concerned about her Charley and it is affecting her health. Mr. Barker's family have all been sick this fall with Bilious fever. Mollie's health is very bad. She has lost her infant and her eldest child has been very ill. I have not seen Mrs. Clayton. I find it impossible to go there to see her, having no one to take care of my family in my absence. There is very little visiting. Every one stays at home to attend to their own and to brood over their sorrows. Mr. McGehen from Winchester[21] arrived here with his wife two weeks since. He has returned but his wife is still here. I called to see her, but she has not been to see me yet. I feel very anxious to learn where you are keeping yourself, and how you are prospering and oh how anxious I am day and night for a favorable result to the southern causes in the {indecipherable} sense transpiring in your vicinity, and I pray that the god of Battles will bring us a glorious victory.

Mr. Van Culin's family have been quite sick. First Cousin Lucy White had Bilious fever, then the youngest child had Diphtheria. Then Cousin Bene was very sick. They are all recovering. Mrs. Wardlaw's health is still very feeble, and she is looking very badly. The rest of our friends are well and inquire after you whenever I meet them. Mr. Glenn and Mr. M. are being very kind and attentive to my wants and comfort. We have heard that Cousin James has rejoined the Army but do not know where or in what capacity he is serving.[22] Have you heard anything from Woodville lately? I feel so anxious to hear from Sister and family. Oh, my husband, how I do long and pray for your speedy return to us. My heart sometimes is almost hopeless of ever meeting you again in this world. I shed very bitter tears at the idea and spend sleepless nights pondering the prospect before us. I cannot write more. The bearer is waiting. The children join me in love. They never tire of talking of you and desire so much to see you. Little Newty has his face washed and hair combed every day, to see Father. Remember me affectionately to all our friends. Hoping that I shall soon receive an affectionate letter from you. I remain ever, your devoted wife

S. K.


Clarksville October 22nd, 1863

My Dear Husband:

I wrote you on the 11th of this month by this route. Since that time, no change has taken place in our home affairs. We all perform our accustomed daily routine with nothing to change its monotony. We are all in good health, for which I thank a kind Providence and pray for a continuance of this greatest of all blessings. I am in receipt of yours of 11th & 23rd Sept. and 1st Oct., the sending of which gives me both pleasure and pain. Pleasure that I can hear from you that you are well and comfortably situated, and pain, that you cannot hear from us, and seem so unhappy on account of it. We are comfortably situated. I have every thing necessary except a servant and get along remarkably well without that. There are many worse off in this respect than I am. Lucy is willing and faithful, kind, and sympathizing, and as long as she is able to walk, I feel that I will have no cause for complaint. Tell the kind gentleman and Lady, with whom you abide, that they must take great care of you for the sake of your wife and children, for you are the only source of comfort we have in the world. There are no local items of interest. Our immediate friends are in usual health and are now enjoying the company of cousins S. Copeland[23] & Lucy Bryan. Mrs. M. sends her thanks for your interest in Will.[24] Many friends inquire with interest of your welfare and send kindest regards. Remember me affectionately to Cousin James & wife. The children send bushels of love and kisses to father. Hoping that you are well and happy, I remain as ever, your devoted wife.

S. Kennedy

Clarksville October 24th, 1863

My Dear Husband:

I wrote you on the 6th & 11th and avail a plausible opportunity of writing again. Since my last, I have received your welcome letter of 15th Sept. by old Point Comfer.[25] I am in such distress that my numerous letters do not reach you. Since my letter of 17th June, I have started five others giving you the particulars of home affairs, and am at a loss how to account for your not receiving them. It is now three months since Phil left, and two since Fanny made her departure. I succeeded in getting a free negro girl to stay one month with me thinking I might in the mean time get a permanent servant, but as there is no chance of procuring help of any kind, suitable, I have been getting along with only Aunt Lucy, who keeps up astonishingly and gets through with the cooking, churning, and out door work generally with ease. I perform all the house work with the assistance of Jimmy and Sally. Mary goes to school to Dr. McMullen, and her time is fully occupied with her studies and music. I have fitted up the dining room for a family room, the cooking stove is in the cabin, and we sat by the stove. I hire the washing and have had all the winter wood cut and housed. The cellar and under the porches are filled up with wood ready for any emergency. If Lucy should be sick and the cooking devolves on me, I will not be at all exposed to the weather. Jimmy has housed all the chips and has prepared sufficient kindling wood for the winter.

Beside the wood, I have 175 bushels coal from the bank cellar which is amply sufficient for the winter's supply, and I think some to spare. If my health and strength is spared, I shall get on famously though as you may imagine, I have but little idle time and am sometimes quite worn out with fatigue. The children are all in good health usually though just now they have colds and some sore throat with swollen glands, the latter being quite prevalent. My own health is pretty good. I have gotten entirely rid of neuralgia and feel well whenever I can get a good nights rest which I frequently fail to do on account of the restlessness of the children. After a sleepless night, I find it hard to drag myself out of bed at daylight, kindle the fire, and go to the kitchen to make up the biscuits which I have to do all the time as Aunt Lucy knows nothing about it, though she can bake them nicely after they are made. I have had some hopes that you would be able to come home soon, but that hope has been banished from my mind lately. I have a late letter from Mr. J. W. B.[26] offering any needed assistance. The family have been very much afflicted. Cousins S. Copeland, Lucy, & Charley Bryan are now here. Charley's health seems to be much better than I had expected. They desire me to give their love to you. Cousin Lucy is in much distress. Aunt's family are in usual health. They are all gratified to hear, through you, of their loved ones. Cousin Lucy White has been quite sick with Bilious fever. Bene Vanculin's youngest child has had a severe case of Diphtheria, and Bene has been very sick, but they are now quite well. I feel sorry that you have lost the companionship of Mr. McClure's family but hope that their place may be supplied by other kind friends. My Dear Husband, you must not despair because you do not receive my letters for rest assured that I write whenever an opportunity offers. I am as comfortable as I could be under the circumstances, and you have friends that are as attentive to me as you could wish. Mr. J. L. G. and B. W. M.[27] are as kind and attentive as brothers and not many days pass that one or the other does not come to see after my comfort. Mr. Wardlaw comes often with friendly offers of help, such as he can render. I feel that I am in the midst of friends. Remember me in Love to Cousin James & wife and all friends who you may think interested in me. The children join me in much love to father. Your name is continually on their lips, and they look forward with pleasure to your return. I do hope I may have the gratification of another of your welcome and much prized letters soon. Praying that God will comfort and sustain you and preserve your health and life and enable you to return to us soon in safety. I remain your devoted wife

S. Kennedy

Clarksville November 2nd, 1863

My Dear Husband:

Since my last letter to you by this route, nothing new, strange, or interesting has transpired to interrupt the monotony of our lonely life at home. Every day is the same. An occasional letter from you is the only enlivening circumstance in our life. I have received yours of 8th Sept. which though old of date was read and reread with interest and pleasure. I hope that ere this you have received one, at least, if not more of my letters to you. You do not imagine how miserable I am that you do not hear from me, or how anxious the days, or how sleepless the nights on this account. Indeed, it causes me more trouble than all my other troubles together. This is my fortieth birthday and I have celebrated it by lying on the bed with rheumatism in my back from sitting yesterday in a cold church. I feel much relieved this evening. Our weather is very changeable. Yesterday was freezing cold and today we sit without fires. We are all well except Newty. He is still quite bad, has not had a respite for two weeks, and I am quite worn from worrying with him. Aunt Lucy is not well today, and I suspect she will be in bed soon. In that event, I will have my hands full. I sometimes wish I could be with you in your quiet country home for a little while, but there is no place but this suitable for our children, and I feel that here we must remain separated from you until present difficulties are settled. Our friends are well and send kind regards to you. The children join me in love and kisses to father. Ever your devoted wife,

S. Kennedy

Clarksville November 9th, 1863

My Dear Husband:

An opportunity offers and I embrace it to write you a few lines to let you know how we are all getting on at home. Every thing is going on in about the same way as when I last wrote, but each day is gloomier than the last. From what is passing in our midst, I feel that our day of trial has not yet come, that the dim shadowings are assuming {the next line seems to have been on a fold and is unreadable} has commenced and we are threatened with being burned completely out. It was Saturday night, Frank Beaumont's home[28] was fired and burned to the ground. Whilst it was burning, a stable back of the Masonic Hall[29] was fired which communicated to the Hall which was burned together with Mrs. Winston's house,[30] Landrums,[31] and William Shackleford's.[32] At daylight Sunday morning, Mr. Wardlaw's stable[33] was fired and burned to the ground and his buggy burned in it. They burned Mr.

W's stable through mistake for B. Stewarts.[34] They have a spite at him and say they will burn him out yet.[35] I feel that this is the worst thing that can happen to me, to be burnt out of house and home, and we but hope and trust that it will not be. I hold myself in readiness for such an event, keeping every thing that is entirely necessary ready packed and in a convenient movable place. It was frightful to witness the fire on Saturday night and miraculous that it extended no further, for there was a terrific north wind blowing all the while. The people are in great excitement. I wrote you on the 2nd via Fort Monroe. I have written frequently by that route, and if you do not receive my letters, it is all owing to their being sent wrong. I have always had a gentleman who professed to know all about it to divest them for me, but until I received your last, I did not know that it was necessary to enclose the five cents extra. If my letters do not go through, this can be the only reason.

We are all usually in good health. Mary has headaches a great deal. I think from confinement at school. I expect I shall have to stop her for a while. They all look well. Newty is about the same, sometimes pretty well and again very bad and more trouble than everything else.

We get on famously in household affairs and live with a great deal more comfort and happiness since Fanny and her troop left. She made a perfect Babel here for some weeks before her departure. All negrodom is in a fluster here on account of the opening of a recruiting office for male niggers.[36] The women are howling and wringing their hands in a ludicrous manner. I have received yours of 21st October in which you mention having received mine of 13nth Sept. which was so low spirited. I felt that I had done wrong in giving way to my feelings and was sorry that I had sent it, and determined that I would in the future write more cheerfully. I am so glad that you have such a nice quiet home where you are so comfortable. I am afraid though, that your quiet life will unfit you for the noise and bustle in our home, occasioned by so many noisy, frolicking children. Aunt's family are as well as usual, and send their love to you. Cousin Lucy Bryan is with them. Charley is in New Orleans traveling for his health which is greatly improved since he set out. Mrs. Copeland has returned to Nashville. Dr. Garth's negro Jim and Susan, his wife, have left them for freedom. Miss Carrie says thank Mr. K. for the love he sent me in his letter and says it is doubly returned. The gossips have it that Dr. Cooper[37] and Mrs. Galbreath[38] will be married soon. I wrote you that the Dr. had asked Miss Carrie to marry him and that she had declined to the great indignation of Lady Annie B. who though violently opposed to her father's marrying Miss C. was highly insulted at her refusing him. Lady Annie is not so much opposed to Mrs. G. whose character is more in accordance with her views of a perfect woman.

I hear frequently from Mr. Barker. The old gentleman and lady are both very complaining with Rheumatism and Dyspepsia.[39] Mrs. Clayton has received her letter sent by you to me. Mollie is now here on a visit. She is looking very badly. I wrote you that she had lost her youngest child. Mrs. Munford sends her thanks for the trouble you [have] taken in letting her hear from Will and hopes some day to be able to return your kindness. There is very little of interest here in the social world. Every body stays at home and every body thinks theirs the hardest lot of any, and the women that have their husbands at home with them to cheer and provide for them are so selfish as to think that they feel the hard times as much as those who are left to take care of themselves. I told a lot of them the other day that I would never think of going to them for sympathy for they did not know the meaning of the words. The widows and unprotected gang together and breathe their sorrows only into sympathizing ears. Prices are going up every day, and Bank of Tennessee money worth forty cents on the dollar. Planters and Union Bank fifty-five.[40] Tell cousins James & Lizzy that Robb is well and a late letter from Miss Mary Lusk reports Maud & Jimmy well. I felt very fearful that the fire Saturday night would reach them and had rooms prepared for their reception. They were greatly frightened and packed all their clothes ready for moving. I must close. The messenger is waiting. The children all send heaps of love and kisses. Many friends desire to be remembered. Hoping to continue receiving your welcome and consoling letters. I am ever your Devoted wife

S. Kennedy

Mr. Van Culin's family are well. He is now in Memphis, and it is probable they will move there soon. They are always glad to hear from Mr. McClure's family through their letters. Mrs. Lurton says do you ever hear from her brother Dr. Harman of Enterprise, Miss.?[41]

Clarksville, November 15th, 1863

My Dear Husband:

I wrote you on the 9th ult. which I trust you will receive. I have yours of 21st Oct. in which you acknowledge mine of 19th Aug. & 13th Sept. I have been very unhappy because so few of my letters have reached you, and at the effect this fact seems to have on your spirits. I have written several times by this route, and I do not see why they should fail to go through when others do not sent by the same direction. My health is better now than for some time past. Mary has not been well for three weeks. I think I shall take her from school, as studying and confinement does not agree with her. Jimmy had a chill on Thursday, but as there was no return of it, I hope he will not be troubled with any more. Newty has been very bad for four weeks, and I find that he gives me more trouble every day. He is a great terror to Clara & Ellen and slips off and is gone for hours before he can be found. Indeed, he is more trouble & care to me than every thing else. Sally, Clara, & Ellen are very well. I saw Aunt's family today. All are well. Ellen Hughes says do you hear ever from her husband. If so, do let her know, she is here with a young infant and no nurse. The latter having left her. We are yet getting along with one servant and I see no prospect of changing our mode of life. Our citizens are long visaged since the fire a week since which destroyed Frank Beaumont's house, then the Masonic Hall, Mrs. Winston's, Landon's & William Shackelford's houses. Cousin James's house was on fire five times and Charley's was several times, but by almost super human efforts theirs and Sterling Beaumont's[42] were saved. Mrs. G. has jilted Dr. C. and is using her wiles to catch Mr. H. on the hill, at the Henry house.[43] Miss Carry sends her love. I saw her at church to day, and she inquired very affectionately about you. All the children join me in love. Hoping to hear from you very soon. I am ever your devoted wife.

S. Kennedy

Clarksville December 9th, 1863

My Dear Husband:

I have no letter from you later than 21st Oct. You can imagine my anxiety to read once more one of your comforting epistles and to learn from yourself that you are well, hopeful, and happy. I learn from parties who have lately seen you that you are well and looking stout. Jimmy goes to the post office every day to inquire for a letter and is as often disappointed. I have written you numerous times by this route and have complied with all the rules required for getting them through, but have no assurance that you have received one of them. We are all just recovering from severe colds and are pretty well and comfortable and as happy as the circumstances will admit. We still have no servant but Lucy and no prospect of getting another. Our friends here are all well. I saw Aunt's family to day. We have warm, damp weather. In consequence bad colds are prevalent and severe. We have not had a snow this winter. Local news is scarce. Business as well as every thing else is dull, dull. I am confined almost entirely at home with the care of the children. Mary seemed to be drooping from over study and I stopped her from school a month since. She has improved. Mrs. Dunlop[44] died suddenly two weeks since. I suppose you have heard of Mrs. Fort's sudden death. Our old friend Mr. J. B. wrote me that he would furnish me my porks, which proposal, I have accepted. He is very kind and thoughtful of my comfort. Mr. G. speaks of hoarding in the county on account of the expense of living here. James Macrae[45] has been here and called to see me. He desired to be remembered to you. Newty has been much better for two weeks past. All the children send love. Remember me to Cousins James & Lizzy and other friends. Your devoted wife

S. Kennedy

Cousin Lucy Bryan has a letter from Charlie at N. Orleans. He had been to Bro. Willies. They were well and comfortable.

Clarksville January 18th, 1864

My Dear Husband:

I am just in receipt of your kind favors of 5th & 11 Dec and I need not assure you that they rendered great source of comfort and consolation to me. I feel thankful that some of my letters have reached you for the thought of your not being able to receive my letters is a source of great sorrow to me. I have not written so often of late on account of the multitude of cares devolving upon me. Aunt Lucy has been confined to bed more frequently than normal and sometimes for two weeks, and the whole of the work devolved upon me. For two weeks before Christmas, she was very sick, and Newty in the mean time had one of his severe spasms, of four hours duration, just such a one as you saw upon him two years since. He was very ill for a week. The labor of nursing him was so great that by the time he was well enough to run about, I was completely broken down and in bed for several days. Mary and Jimmy did the cooking and house cleaning as it was utterly impossible to hire assistance. I now have a house girl and a cook and am trying to rest myself. We have had unusually cold weather since New Year and have done nothing but sit by the fire and try to keep warm. Such a long cold spell has not been known here for a number of years. It is now breaking up with a steady, hard rain. I am now suffering with a severe cold contracted by getting up two and three times in the night during the cold weather (with Newty). My health is not so good as it was during the summer and fall, and I am quite thin. My spirits lately have been quite depressed, but I strive to be cheerful under all circumstances of which Newty is the greatest. I have lost all hope of his ever being better, and he will be a greater trouble as he grows older. I do not wish to bother your mind with any sorrows, therefore, I have always written as cheerfully as possible as I am willing and anxious to bear all for your sake and for the children. Mr. Macrae says that I take too much upon

myself and that my strength will fail me if I keep it up. The expense of hired servants is a vain quest again and I hesitate to employ them. We have been living with very little expense without them, and the difference with them is very perceptible. Mary, Jimmy, Sally, Clara, and Ellen are in unusual good health. I shall send Mary & Jimmy to school as soon as the bad weather is over. I think Sally will learn as much with me as she would a school. I find it too great a tax on my strength and time to teach the younger children. They do not take the interest in their studies necessary for them to learn much. I have had an old lady and her two daughters boarding with us since the 1st Jan by the name of Lloyd. The husband and sons are in the south. They left Louisville last summer to go through the lines to join them in the south but failing to do so, the oldest young lady opened a music school for their support. I took them for a month out of compassion for their situation. They are making arrangements to take a school in the country. The old lady has written to her son and directed to your care and your well being doing a good act and confer a great favor by forwarding the letter to its destination. Her husband and sons do not know where she is and she has not heard from them directly for six months. There was an amateur concert and tableaux at Fowler's Hall[46] last Thursday night for the benefit of the poor. The hall was crowded and the whole affair a complete success. All our nicest young ladies were engaged for it.[47] One of the scenes was the Empress Eugenia and her train. Mrs. Galbraith personating the Empress. I would like to tell you more about it, but cannot for want of space. Aunt's family are as well as usual. They all say tell Mr. Kennedy that we enjoy his letters. They give us more comfort than any we receive, but you must be mum on this subject, of course. I hear seldom from Mr. Barker's family and never see them. The old man has lost nearly all his male servants even old uncle Stephen. I wrote him two letters in Dec, but have no assurance that he received either. Lizzy Lewis and family have moved to Elkton.[48] They lost Justin & Paulina, their man and woman two weeks ago. They both died of pneumonia. They will occupy brother Thompson's house.[49] He has purchased the old Dr. Given's and moved into it. All our friends inquire after your health and spirits and always glad to hear from you and many send love. My dear husband, my heart yearns for your society, and it grieves my heart to think it, if the children should be deprived of a father's counsels and examples for how long a time no one can tell and it may be forever. I'm concerned what will become of us? The children all send bushels of love to father. Hoping to hear from you again very soon. I remain
Your devoted wife

S. Kennedy

Clarksville February 11, 1864

My Dear Husband:

Your kind and affectionate letters are a soothing balm to my lonely heart. Yours of the 15th January, I received to day. I have in previous letters acknowledged those of 5th, 9th, 11th, & 16th December. Mary wrote to you the 6th this month in answer to yours of 29th Dec. She was quite sick when she wrote and regretted that she did not write a more lively letter. Her health is quite poor again and I have feared that she would have a serious spell. The other children are well. Jimmy is at an excellent school and is interested in his studies. Sally is learning music from her sister and is making fine progress. Clara is my little seamstress [and] takes great delight in making doll clothes and displays a remarkable talent for needle work. Ellen shifts about here, there, and everywhere. Helps every body and doing a great deal of mischief. Poor Newty's health is no better though his mind has improved and he is a great deal more manageable than he has been. We are more comfortable for two months past having procured the services of a kind black woman in the kitchen. I dismissed my housegirl after one month's trial as she did not suit, but will get another if possible. Servants are in great demand as almost every family have been deprived of everyone they had. Lucy is still at her post performing her duties faithfully. She says thank Master for his kind remembrance of me and tell him that I will die with you all unless they take me by force. I have had very bad health for two months and weigh 123 pounds, 43 pounds less than two years ago. Clarksville would scarcely be recognized by those who left it three years since, business dull, very little social intercourse, and every man for himself seems to be the motto. You seem to be lucky in getting nice boarding houses, and I am gratified that you keep in good health & spirits. The shoes I sent you last April have found their way back home after a long journey. I hope you may have the pleasure of wearing them at home next summer. I try to keep in good cheer, but do not always succeed. I heard today from Bro. Willie's family through Charley Bryan. He writes that Br. W. has made a fortune and that the family are in a more comfortable condition than he has ever known them to be. Charley's health is greatly improved. I saw Mollie Barker to day. The old gentleman has been more complaining than usual with rheumatism. He sent me last week two barrels flour. Aunt is in dreadful health and I fear that she is failing. She looks badly and is low spirited. Miss Carrie was here to day well and sends her love. They all seem sad since the death of Willie Dearing.[50] I could write you about every body and every thing if I had space. Cousin Lucy Bryan, Letty Donoho and the family send love. Ever your devoted wife

S. Kennedy

Clarksville March 7th, 1864

My Dear Husband:

The mail to night brings your welcome favors of 15th & 20th Feb. I was administering a hot foot bath and one of Father's stews to four of the children, Jimmy, Sally, Clara, & Ellen who are all quite sick with a prevailing influenza; when the door bell rang and a neighbor handed in your letters. Mary wrote you on the 5th, and I wrote on 11th Feb. by Flag Truce[51] and on the 2nd of this month I wrote by a different route, all of which I do sincerely hope you may receive.

In my last I acknowledged yours of 10th & 15th Jan. a few days since I received yours of 2nd Feb. I need not assure you of their welcome or of the great comfort and consolation they afford me under this trying separation. You seem to think me very heroic, I do try to feel so but am often ready to give up to despondency, the cause for which seems to increase every day. There is no change in our family arrangements, the monotonous routine of which cannot interest you. My health is much improved in the last week. Mary is still at home, and Jimmy very much interested in his school. My attention will soon be turned to gardening as the winter seems to be breaking up. The birds are already heralding Spring by their songs in the leafless trees, and the Crocus & violets are blooming in the garden. The children brought me a bouquet of violets & hearts ease to day, and little Ellen said Mama don't you wish Father tould smell it, its so fat, and so pitty. She is a sweet little thing and very interesting. There is no gossip or local news of interest I have heard. Aunts health is no better, and I fear that she may never be well again. The rest of the family as well as usual. I have delivered your messages to Miss Carrie & cousin L. Bryan, about writing to you and have urged them to do so. They can give you more news than I because they have greater facilities for news gathering. Mrs. H. who with her daughters have been occupying cousin James' house, have been notified to leave to make room for another occupant. You may guess who. I have a letter of 15th Jan. from Sister via N. Y. I never see any of Mr. J. W. B.'s family and seldom hear from them. I sent ten Postage Stamps in my letter of 11th Feb. and send some in this. I received those sent by you. The children join me in love & kisses to Father. Your Devoted Wife

S. Kennedy

I have not written as frequently of late, as formerly. I shall write oftener hereafter. We had heard of the death of cousin Sue Marr[52] through Misses Quarles & Davie who arrived here two weeks since.

Clarksville March 18th, 1864

My Dear Husband:

In my last to you on the 5th inst. I had the pleasure acknowledging the receipt of yours of 8 and 11 March. I wrote you on the 2nd, 7th, 19th & 29 March, all of which I do hope you received as you seem despondent at receiving so few letters from me. From various causes, I am hindered from writing sometimes. My strength of late has been broken by the frequent sickness of the children and household cares, and I write as often as I possibly can. Clara has recovered from her severe illness. Jimmy was kept at home all last week quite sick, but is now at his studies again. Mary is now suffering with inflammatory rheumatism in her left foot, and I have had great uneasiness fearing that it may extend farther into her system. I sometimes feel almost worn out with anxiety and fatigue. We have such unfavorable weather, first rain, then wintry cold with rain and damp atmosphere that sickness prevails to an unusual extent. Typhoid pneumonia[53] is very prevalent, several deaths having occurred from it. Day before yesterday we had snow, hail, and rain after a few days of balmy weather. The sudden changes are very trying. Mary has been too unwell to answer your letter. Ellen has a severe cold with inflamed sore eyes. Newty is as usual. Sally is the most healthy of the family. I have had a rising[54] on my right cheek for several days which has pained me considerably. Aunt Lucy is just up from one of her spells. I don't see how I could get along without the help of the girl I have hired to help me. I feel grateful to a kind providence for the good health you are permitted to enjoy and my constant prayer is that your health and life may be spared to us. The children are becoming very anxious to see their father and I need not assure you that I grow daily more anxious to see my husband. Your devoted wife

S. Kennedy

I send four postage stamps.

Clarksville March 19th, 1864

My Dear Husband:

On the 7th I received yours of 15th & 20th Feb. and acknowledged them immediately. I also wrote you on the 2nd which I hope you will receive. I yesterday had the pleasure of reading yours of the 10th Feb. which although of older date, was as gratifying as any. It affords me great pleasure to know that your health continues good. My health has improved very much in the last few weeks, and I expect soon to be as well as ever. The children have been quite afflicted with colds during this month, and little Clara has been very ill for ten days with Typhoid pneumonia. She is a little better today. I think she is very sick though the doctor does not consider her dangerous. Newty continues about the same as when I last wrote. His nervous system does not seem to improve, and he has frequent spasms. He is shedding his teeth rapidly, and I still hope that his health will improve when he gets through with this process. Little Ellen, the angel of the household, is very healthy and very attractive. Sally's health is very good. She is taking music lessons and learns rapidly. Mary has improved and is becoming a little more settled, but I fear will never have much constitution. Jimmy is still at school, and I am very much pleased with his progress. I miss his services at home a great deal, but I think it time that he should be learning his books. We are getting on pretty comfortably at home, have one hired servant who though not a number one catch, is a pleasant, kind woman, a good washer and ironer, and assists Aunt Lucy with Newty. I clean all the house except the dining room, in that department, Aunt Lucy reigns (as ever) supreme. Gardening season has arrived and I am at a great loss what to do. The uncertainty of affairs makes me unwilling to go to the expense and trouble of planting it, and if I am permitted to remain at home, it will be very uncomfortable not to have plenty of home vegetables. The authorities have called and taken a list of our personal effects preparatory to confiscation.[55] This together with Clara's illness has caused me great anxiety until today, I received a message from your old and well-tried friend ten miles in the country[56] which has relieved my mind of a great burden, and I hope will be the means of dispelling your fears and anxiety on the subject. As this is a public matter,[57] I venture to mention it to you through this channel knowing that you will hear of it from others and that it will be best and a relief to your anxiety to know that we have the sympathy and help of so able a friend.

MARCH 20: Being hindered by Clara's sickness and other cares I did not finish my letter yesterday and resume it to day. Clara is a great deal better and in a fair way to recover though very feeble. This month has been unusually cold and unpleasant, a chilliness in the atmosphere as if an immense iceberg were near us with sudden changes causing a great deal of sickness. You will be surprised to hear that Mr. Glenn has gone to N. Orleans to live as agent for Sawyer Wallace & Co.[58] B. W. M.[59] has been for three weeks in N. York, and I would not be surprised if his visit will be followed by his removal to that place, though I have not been advised of his intention that way. His brother William is in business there. Mrs. M. wishes you to advise them of Wythe's[60] whereabouts as they never hear from him. I shall miss the friendship and advice of the two first named. James also has frequently offered me any assistance in his power to render me and urges me to call upon him if necessary. Aunt's health is improving and the family are hopeful that she will be restored. They are very anxious about cousin James' health thinking that he keeps from them his true state. All who have seen him give doleful accounts of his appearance. Write to me what you think of him and if not prudent, I will not advise them. Col S.[61] has taken his house for a residence. Gloom reigns in the hearts and homes of most of our people. The widows and widowers are the only ones who are having a gay time. They are styled the rejuvenating club. The club met at Mrs. Munford's last week, had an oyster supper. The next day she sent me word that she was sorry that she had nothing left to send me as the table was cleaned of all refreshments. I sent her word back that Juveniles always cleared the table. Don't let it be known that you learn these things from me. I only mean a little fun. Miss Carrie says that she almost wishes she had been born a widow. They are so fascinating and irresistible. I owe an apology for this blotted letter but know that you will excuse it as you know the many hindrances I have. The children send much love and many sweet kisses to Father. May the lord preserve and bring you back to us, is my constant petition.

Your devoted wife,

S. Kennedy

# 4

## MARCH 29, 1864–
## FEBRUARY 20, 1865

On April 12, 1864, the Battle of Fort Pillow, Tennessee, took place. Confederate General Nathan Bedford Forrest's troops massacred 300 US Colored Troops after they surrendered. On May 7, 1864, Union General William Tecumseh Sherman began his Atlanta Campaign, which was a series of nine battles that resulted in the capture of Atlanta, Georgia, on September 2, 1864. Two of the most famous of these battles were the Battle of Resaca, Georgia, on May 13 and 14 and the Battle of Kennesaw Mountain on June 27. Nathan Bedford Forrest achieved a Confederate victory at the Battle of Brice's Cross Roads, Mississippi, on June 10, 1864, but the US was victorious at the Battle of Tupelo, Mississippi, on July 14 and 15. On August 21, 1864, Forrest made an unsuccessful raid on Memphis, Tennessee. He had planned to capture four US generals who were in the city, but they eluded him. In November 1864, Union General Sherman started his March to the Sea. Before he left Atlanta, he commanded that all military supplies be burned. The fire went out of control and the whole city burned. Sherman headed for Savannah, Georgia, burning and destroying the countryside as he went. He took Savannah on December 21, 1864. Confederate General John Bell Hood removed his Army of Tennessee from Atlanta before it fell and proceeded to invade US-held Tennessee. He hoped to lure Sherman out of Georgia and back to Tennessee. On November 29, 1864, Hood and his army fought at Spring Hill, Tennessee. The aim was to cut off the Federal army there, but US troops managed to sneak by the Confederates in the middle of the night and succeeded in getting to Franklin, Tennessee. Hood attacked Franklin unsuccessfully on November 30, 1864. Despite his defeat, Hood moved on to attack Nashville, Tennessee, on December 15 and 16, 1864. The Federal *victory at Nashville was so complete that Hood's army, in all practicality, had ceased to exist. This was the last battle fought in the Western Theater. Four months later on April 9, 1865, Confederate General Robert E. Lee surrendered to Union General Ulysses S. Grant at Appomattox, Virginia. The last Confederate combat troops under General Joe Johnston surrendered to Union General Sherman at Durham, North Carolina, on April 26, 1865. Fighting had ceased; now reconstruction began.*

Clarksville March 29th, 1864

My Dear Husband:

My last to you was dated 19th in which I mentioned Clara's illness of Typhoid Pneumonia. She has continued to improve daily since, and if the weather permits, will soon be able to go out. The rest of us are very well with the exception of Newty. I see no improvement in him. Winter still lingers with us, and we have had a day of snow. Vegetation is very backward and all tender shrubbery is killed to the roots. I have had all my roses cut off even with the ground. Our Deodar cedar[1] is entirely dead, and the other evergreens are looking badly. We are getting on comfortably. I have succeeded in getting a good well raised white girl to assist me with the house & children, and if she will be contented to remain, will I think be a great comfort to me. I wrote you fully in my last of affairs as they exist with us which I hope was permitted to pass although I mentioned facts which I feared would prevent its going through. My mind has been relieved of all anxiety about having to vacate our house, and you must not let rumors make you unhappy. I have sent you thirty stamps, ten at a time, twice by this and once by another route. I hope you have received them all. We had a scare yesterday. The kitchen chimney burned out with a blaze that frightened the town, and I was waited upon by an officer who asked if I had fired the house intentionally. This is the first insult that has been offered me. Our friends are well. Aunt is recovering fast. We have heard that cousin Lizzy has a son.[2] Aunt's family send a great deal of love. Miss Carrie sends love and says she will write to you. The children send love and kisses to Father. Miss Mary McDaniel[3] and Miss Fannie Balthrop[4] were married this morning. The first to a Mr. Phillips and the last to Dr. Williams. Will write you very soon.

Your Devoted wife,

S. Kennedy

I send three U. S. postage stamps.

Clarksville May 1st, 1864

My Dear Husband:

Since my last to you on the 18th, I have had the exquisite pleasure of reading your very interesting favors of 7th, 18th, & 26 March & 2nd April, and my efforts, which of late, have been more depressed than usual have been so buoyed up that I scarcely recognize myself. Yours for 7th & 26th are particularly interesting, and many others besides myself have enjoyed them. The fun, in which you fully indulge, and the happy bits at a certain class of individuals, have created a great deal of merriment. There are numbers here who look upon this class in the same light that you do, often in a worse, if possible. There are men whom I once respected that pass me on the street unnoticed, though they bow ever so low, and they have learned to keep their bows for others. Since I wrote you last, I have scarcely been able to be up all day and frequently confined to bed three & four days at a time. I have not consulted a physician and am not really sick. I have a tired worn out feeling, as if I needed rest, and for two weeks past, have freely indulged myself by keeping my bed when I did not feel like fatiguing with household affairs. I am now experiencing the good effects of this course. My health and spirits are much improved as also my personal appearance. The children are in better health now than at any time since last fall, Newty excepted, there is no change in him. Jimmy is the only one at school, he thinks he is learning faster than any one ever did before. I attended his school last Friday to hear the boys speak and was highly entertained. I have enjoyed a long talk with a lady who saw you during a late trip through Dixie. She arrived on the 23rd. Tell Dr. Bemiss that he has a patriotic wife, she says (in her inimitable way) that if her husband were to return now, she would feel like beating him back with a broomstick. Mrs. McMullen is in feeble health. Aunt's health is very little better than when I last wrote. She has been confined to her room nearly three months. The troubles that younger persons can stem, have nearly overwhelmed her. I sent your message about Judge Clayton to Mrs. C. Her daughter is in very bad health. I wish very much to make them a visit but consider it imprudent to leave home. B. Stewart has resumed the building of his palace on the hill.[5] I have a nice white girl living with me who is a great comfort as well as assistance. Charley Bryan arrived here last Friday. He came via N. York, his health not much improved, he brings good news from bro Willie's family. I fear that my letters prove stale as I have to be so circumspect in my communications. Many friends send love. The children send bushels of love & kisses to their dear Father. Your devoted wife

S.A. Kennedy

I have enclosed four postage stamps.

Clarksville May 8th, 1864

My Dear Husband:

I wrote you on the 1st acknowledging your kind favors of 18th & 26th March and 2nd April. I am to day in receipt of yours of 11th & 23rd inst. How it rejoices my heart to know that you enjoy such good health and spirits. Without this assurance, my life would be indeed miserable. I truly wish that some of your abundant leisure which seems a bore could be transported to me for I scarcely know what rest is. I have become habituated to toil of mind and body. Your affectionate, cheerful, hopeful letters give me more comfort than any thing else in the world, and I am thankful that this source of pleasant communication with loved ones so widely separated is still granted to us. Spring has opened with its nanal[6] beauty and with it perfect health to all our household, except Newty who I have ceased to hope will ever be well. Clara has not entirely recovered her usual flesh since her spell but is improving daily. Ellen is healthy & lively. Sally has been puny but is getting fat and is learning to spell and read rapidly. She is now reading the First Book of History and thinks she is very smart. Mary's health is a great deal better, and I hope will now be permanently good. Jimmy is still at school and learning fast. I have urged many of your friends, lady & gentleman, to write to you, and a good many have promised me they would, but it seems that none of them have complied with this promise. Time seems to hang heavily on the hands of almost all of our gentlemen citizens, but the ladies have plenty to do at home. I know we are not an isolated case. Since I have succeeded in procuring help, there are many much worse situations than myself. If this situation were solitary, it would be unbearable. As it is, we can all sympathize with each other and bear our burdens with cheerfulness looking to more prosperous circumstances. I find there is nothing that acts as potently as a firm resolve to meet difficulties with boldness and determination to do my duty let the circumstances be what they may. There is nothing of interest occurring here. I have just received a box of dry goods[7] purchased for me in New York by J. Macrae,[8] a great deal cheaper than I could get them here. All the ladies at Aunt's send much love. Miss Carrie also. The children all send love & kisses to Father. Hoping soon to enjoy more of your interesting letters. I remain as ever, your devoted wife

S. A. Kennedy

Enclosed you will find two postage stamps.

Clarksville May 13th, 1864

My Dear Husband:

I wrote you on the 2nd March by this route but again you have not acknowledged its reception. I suppose it has not reached you, this I regret exceedingly as these opportunities so seldom offer. I wrote you also by flag of truce on the 7th, 19, & 29th March, on 5th & 18th April & 1st & 8th inst. I have your interesting favors by a lady friend as also yours by flag truce as late as 11th & 23rd inst. There is nothing in the world as comforting to me as your affectionate, cheerful, hopeful letters. I often am ready to despair of competency to perform the duties and responsibilities that necessarily devolve upon me but having set a firm resolve to sustain my husband in his patriotic devotion to his country and to set an example of heroism and self-sacrifice to our children, I am determined by the help of heaven to let nothing swerve me from this purpose. It was evidently (two months since) the purpose of the Feds to occupy our houses, and I was for a time, fearful that we would be turned out, but my mind is now relieved of that load. On the 9th March, the authorities came and took an inventory of our personal property preparatory (they said) to confiscation. At the suggestion of my business adviser, the property was attached for a debt of C: P & Cs. Mr. W. kindly offered to go to see our friend J. W. B. who sent me word not to be unhappy, that if the property was sold, he would buy it, but 'twas best if debts could be found to save it in that way.[9] If it be possible to send a letter, write me your news of what has been done and advise me for future action. I am determined not to go out of the house, until I am thrust out. Col. Smith occupies cousin James's & the Provost Capt. Morgan,[10] G. B. Fleece's residence,[11] Mrs. Howard & Mrs. King being turned out for the purpose. Two days after the listing of our furniture, a woman professing to have a husband in the southern army and a loud crying rebel, but of doubtful character, called and after saying that she heard that I had been notified to leave my house and expressing sorrow for my situation, she told me that she came to see if I wished to dispose of anything privately. It occurred to me in a moment that she was sent on purpose to try me, and I merely said to her that the Feds would find every thing as they left it. I learned afterward that this same woman was very recently married to a federal soldier. That same night, my smoke house was broken open and everything abstracted. Fortunately, there was very little in it as I did not lay in a supply Pork last fall for fear of accident. I had arranged with Mr. Barker for a year's supply of bacon & lard and was to have sent a wagon the next day for it. After this occurrence I wrote to him that I would take a few pieces at a time as I would not venture so great a risk. I now keep all my supplies in the closet and little stone room at the end of the porch. Spring has opened with its usual beauty and gladness and with it perfect health to all the household.

The peach crop was a failure owing to the severity of the winter. All my gooseberry bushes are killed, but there is a fine prospect for strawberries and raspberries. I find it so expensive to keep the garden in order that I have nothing done except what is entirely necessary. I shall try to have plenty of vegetables dispensing with the ornamental. We are living with more domestic comfort now than since we came home. The hired woman, though not an extra hand at cooking or washing, is quiet and peaceable, and the white girl relieves me of the labor and fatigue of house cleaning beside assisting me with the children, and it is comforting to know that there is some one in the house that I can call on at any time day or night to assist me and to take charge of the housekeeping when I am sick. I pay each of them eight dollars a month. I have many warm and sympathizing friends, and these are times that test friendship as well as patriotism, and the two are invariably linked together. Henry Wisdom[12] has gone with his family to N. York and B. W. Macrae[13] & family will soon leave for the same place. Mr. Glenn is in business in Louisville & Ben Coulter[14] and family left for the same place this morning. Mr. G. leaves his family with his wife's father (characteristic). You wish to know the cause of my bad health. It was attributable, first to care and fatigue, secondly to severe cold taken during the severe weather in January at a time when I had a monthly visitor[15] from getting up in the night with Newty who had a severe diarrhea for eight days and nights. During this time, I was up from two to four times every night having to change his clothing and sheets every time and not a soul to assist me. I am gradually improving from the irregularity occasioned by this exposure and hope soon to be entirely well. This period which has been affecting Mary's health so seriously for a year, she has experienced for two months past, and her health is now more settled. It was this that caused her so much pain in her shoulder & spine and of which she now seems entirely relieved. I shall not send her to school until her health is entirely established. Jimmy is progressing finely in his studies and is highly interested in his school. Sally is spelling and reading the first book of history with me, and to day commenced geography. She is so anxious to learn that I think of sending her to Miss Sallie Howard next session. Newty is about the same. Clara has not entirely recovered her flesh since her severe spell but is improving rapidly. Ellen is fat and rosy and is almost as large as Clara. Mary grows so rapidly that I can scarcely keep her in clothing. I have to alter her dresses and let out tucks two and three times in a season. I have despaired of an opportunity of sending you any clothing but hope that you will have the pleasure of wearing what I have on hand before very long at home.

The gossiping world have had their time fully occupied for several months with the case of Mrs. Munford & Capt. Brown. The widow has been unmercifully handled but is as far from an alliance matrimonial with the

Capt. now as she was before her acquaintance with him. Her difficulties
with the U. S. government have been very great, and she has been compelled
to sign the amnesty oath or have her property confiscated for violation of
Parole of honor, letters and clothing that she sent to Will having been captured. She has not yet received full pardon for her sins but expects soon
to be relieved of all trouble from this source. The Capt. [Brown] has been
removed from this place because he was too kind to the citizens, as was Col.
Bruce. Through her [Mrs. Munford] eloquence in my behalf as her friend,
he [Capt. Brown] made a big speech for me, when Col. S. spoke of taking
our house for a residence, but he [Capt. Brown] told her not to let it be
known that he took a particular interest in the case. Mrs. Galbraith has
failed to catch Mr. Hillman.[16] He is devoted to Miss Tennie Moore, and I
expect it will be a match. Mr. McKeage is contemplating a European tour
for his health which has been very low for several months, and Mrs. G. will
accompany him, and perhaps fish up a titled husband as well as a rich one.
Mrs. Bryce Stewart is thought to be in a decline.[17] They are having their fine
house finished. Miss Marion[18] has recently returned from a northern trip
of several months with a two-thousand-dollar piano and everything else to
match. Charley Bryan arrived three weeks since from N. Y., his health not
much better, he reports the good health and spirits of all our friends in Miss.
Aunt's health is improving slowly. She has not been out of her room for three
months. The rest of the family are as usual. Miss Copeland,[19] cousin Lucy
Bryan, and Lettie Donoho are here. I have a letter from Mr. Barker to day in
which he says that he is almost deprived of locomotion by rheumatism. I so
hope that he may be spared for I should lose one of my best friends if he were
taken.

I heard from Elkton a few days since. Lizzy Lewis has another daughter
and Laura is living with her father. The union men are turning sesech because all their darkies are leaving them, and brother Thompson[20] is almost
deranged on the nigger question. I never hear from brother Donald's family.[21] Ben has not been here for several months. If I possessed the enviable
faculty of transworking my thoughts and feelings on paper as you do, I could
write you an interesting & entertaining letter, but my letters, I know, must
fail of interest, devoid of style or flourish as they are. You know that it is my
character to do every thing in a plain, strait forward manner and to the purpose, and if there is any thing in the world that I envy in another, it is fluency
of speech and writing.

I have urged your friends to write to you that you may be acquainted
with what is going on in our midst, but they excuse themselves by saying
that they do not know what to write by flag truce. Miss Carrie, like the rest

of us, is her own chamber maid. Harvey has left them, and they have but one servant in the place, a woman. Mrs. McMullen is in very delicate health, and the {indecipherable} complaining. I was there a few days since and saw him chopping wood and heard him asking the old lady if that was plenty of wood for morning. High prices for every necessary rule, and after I read your letter advising us to look ahead, I bought sugar, coffee, salt, etc. enough to supply us for more than a year. I have been afraid to keep a great deal on hand but being certain that I would not have to give it up to others. I never had my eyes so fully opened in regard to expenses as I now have. I paid 150 dollars for a barrel sugar, barrel salt, and sack of coffee. Spring chickens the size of a partridge 17 cents apiece, butter 50 cents a pound, and every thing else equally high. These are the prices in green backs,[22] and we must pay a great deal more if in Tennessee money. It is now one o'clock at night, and my burning eyes admonish me that I had better go to bed. This will be called for early tomorrow morning, and I was only advised of the opportunity late this evening. The children send love and kisses and all bade you good night before retiring. I wishing heavens richest blessings upon my husband and imploring for his speedy return to his home. I must retire to rest my body and mind for the duties of the morrow. Aunt's family always send their love to you. I hope I may be able to receive your thrice welcome letters of love and hope, as heretofore.

Ever your devoted wife

S. A. Kennedy


Clarksville June 2nd, 1864

My Dear Husband:

I last wrote you on the 13th May. I also wrote on 1st & 8th same. I have no letter from you of later date than 23rd April, and as there has been none received of later date than 29th, we have concluded that letters by Fortress Monroe have been stopped, the fact though has not been officially announced. In all of my letters up to this time, I have enclosed a few stamps stating the number sent. I have received yours of 18th & 20th April both a source of the greatest pleasure and comfort, and I am now anxiously looking for another of your welcome and deeply appreciated favors. My anxiety to see and hear from you increases every day. Indeed, the time seems so long, that I have almost despaired of seeing you at any time soon. I have hoped that the time for your return to us was not very distant, but my hope is almost exhausted. We are very comfortably situated at home and there is so much to occupy my time that I cannot be idle. Indeed, I never have a spare moment. My health is much better than it was though I am thinner than I have been for a number of years. Mary's health is improved. Jimmy has not been well for three weeks owing, I think, to confinement to the school room. I shall send him (in vacation) to Mr. Ferguson's to rusticate. The other children are in perfect health. Ellen is a beautiful little sprite and a darling treasure to us. Newty has improved within a month, but I dare not think that it will prove permanent. Our home is perfectly beautiful and is the admiration of all who behold it. The flower garden is now very gay, and soldiers come in frequently and ask for a bouquet. The vegetable garden is in a fine state of cultivation, and I am trying to prepare plenty of vegetables for winter use, hoping that you may be permitted to enjoy them. There is no news of interest. I seldom go out unless on business and visiting is rare, everyone finding plenty of employment at home. Aunt's health is improving though she is looking very much worsted from her long sickness. The rest as usual. A severe form of scarlet fever is now raging here. Charley Bryan is in a feeble state. The children send love and kisses to father. Remember me kindly to cousin James & wife and to your kind landlady, and I shall always remember her, love her for her kindness to you. May heaven preserve you is my constant prayer. Your devoted wife

S. A. Kennedy

Clarksville June 9th, 1864

My Dear Husband:

I wrote you on the 2nd inst., and to day. I take great pleasure in acknowledging your kind favors of 2nd, 10th & 17th May. This mail brings the first letters received here for over a month by this route (Fortress Monroe),[23] and we had ceased sending them, fearing they would be lost. I feared that my letter of 19th March would make you low spirited, but I considered it my duty to appraise you of the facts therein stated. This excitement has all died away, and I hope will not be again resumed. I hope that you will not suffer yourself to be very unhappy about it. I have borne all my trials with all the heroism that I could possibly command taking every thing quietly, not allowing a certain portion of the world to see that I have any feeling at all. I am dignified and prudent in word and action and strive to elude notice and but for the reputation of a certain prominent Lord of Creation, to whom I fondly own allegiance; I would be a mere speck in the horizon of public notice. I have lately made a change all round in my domestic arrangements. My cook, washer & ironer left because the work was too heavy. I have filled her place with another. I yesterday gave notice to my white house maid that she was not able to perform the duties for which I employed her, too much of the work devolving on myself and her place is filled by a stout contraband[24] able to perform all the drudgery and not feel it. My health is tolerable, as the summer advances, I grow thinner. Every body thinks I am looking badly, but I think that considering the care and labor that have devolved upon me since last August (and no one but myself knows what I have under gone), I am looking as well as I possibly could. Mary had a severe Cholera Morbus[25] last night and is quite feeble today. We are having sultry Cholera weather and bowel disease is common. The other children are pretty well. Aunt Lucy is failing very fast, suffers with rheumatism. There is no news of interest. I have no late news from Mr. J. W. B's family except that nearly all his servants have left him. Aunt's health is improving. The rest as well as usual except Charley Bryan, his leg is rising and will have to be opened. The children join me in love to Father. May heaven protect, preserve, and restore to us is my constant prayer.

Your devoted wife

S. A. Kennedy


Clarksville August 8th, 1864

My Dear Husband:

I wrote you on the 27th acknowledging yours of 14th June and 4th July. I now have the pleasure to acknowledge yours of 29th June. I was truly gratified at the receipt of news from you as nearly two months had elapsed since I had enjoyed that pleasure. You can imagine how wearily drag the hours to me since the suspension of the flag truce civilities.[26] I have written you to the same old address hoping that the letters would go through after these were resumed, but fearing they would be lost. My anxiety about you has increased with the distance between us, but I am consoled with the knowledge that you are with such good friends and cousin James & Lizzie. I wonder where your next resting place will be. The children are all in perfect health as fat as pigs and as gay as good health can make them. Lettie & Clemy Donoho have been with us for ten days. Lettie is very poorly and my time is fully occupied in nursing her. Mary, Jimmy & Clara went out to Mr. Barkers day before yesterday for a visit of ten days. I have no local news of interest. The great drought that has fallen upon the land seems to have extended to this department. We have had rain almost every day for two weeks, but it is too late to do the crops much good. I have sufficient wood cut and housed for winter. All the chips stored away and kindling wood split and ready for use. We will live in the dining room by a big wood fire. I am thinking seriously of

sending Mary to Miss Mollie Ward[27] in October. She is too fast to be easily controlled in town. I feel confident that it will be the best place for her. I wrote you a long letter on the 1st, but the warning being too short, failed to send it. No news yet of gains of the 2nd July.[28] All our friends as well as usual. Remember me affectionately to cousin James & Lizzie. I heard yesterday from their children. All were well. I will write again very soon.
Your Devoted wife

S. A. Kennedy

Enclosed are three U. S. Postage stamps.

Clarksville, September 2nd, 1864

My Dear Husband:

   Three weeks since I received your first letter advising me of your change of address which I answered immediately. Since which, I have been too unwell to dictate a letter in consequence of a severe cold and rising on my head. You can imagine my condition having witnessed my sufferings from this cause in times past. I have written you regularly up to that time to your old address. Your letter of 1st August mentions the receipt of but few letters from me, and the above is the only reason I can give that you have not gotten them. I hope you will not think me negligent of my duty in this respect, for I assure you, I have written you very often. I have also sent you a number of U. S. stamps. I suppose 60 in all. I sent 10 at a time in three letters as you requested, and 3 & 4 in a number. The children, with the exception of Newty, are pretty well. Newty is no better and frequently worse. I did not sleep at all with him last night, and he is being nervous & restless to day. He gives me more concern than all the others, and I sometimes think his condition will almost craze me. When I last wrote you, Mary & Jimmy were on a visit to Mr. Barker. They both returned well pleased with their visit. Mary started to school to Dr. Ring last Monday. Jimmy will start next Monday to Mr. Blain. Sally will say her lessons at home. Tuition has advanced with every thing else, and our expenses are a source of vast trouble to me. Dr. McMullen is very undetermined whether he will teach. He has to conform to the requirements to do so unless he is so fortunate as to be let off, which I do not think is possible. He's not well, and his wife, I fear, will never be off a sick bed again. I have made several attempts to get the children's pictures but have failed as yet. I shall try again when I am well enough. I fear that it will be impossible to get Ellen's. She is too restless and refuses to sit a second time, says she is too tired. She said today, I wish my Father would come home, every body is so mean to me. She is disposed to have her own way. Aunt Lucy has been in bed for a week, and I have a green house girl. All are as usual at Aunt's. Lucy Donoho is now here. I have been such a perfect recluse lately that I have no news or gossip on hand. The children send love & kisses to Father. I shall write again very soon. Ever your devoted wife

S. A. Kennedy

I enclose six postage stamps which I hope will be allowed to pass.

Clarksville September 2nd, 1864

I wrote you last on the 20th enclosing Ellen's picture. I do hope you will receive it. It is a sweet picture and will do you good to look at it. She says tell Father I do love to talk about him, and when he comes home, I will jump into his arms and he will say, O my sweet little daughter. I have no letter from you later than 25 Aug. Sam Kennedy wrote me last week that he had one from you of 30th, and you were unusually well. This news gave me great pleasure. I wrote you on the 2nd, 10th, & 20th Mary & Jimmy on the 3rd and Mary on 24th, mine of the 12th a long letter. My health has steadily improved of late. All the little ones are well, except Jimmy who has been quite complaining. Going to school does not agree with him. He lost two months last session and had not been at school two weeks before he was taken sick, not dangerously, but is puny all the time. There is no news. The approaching marriage of Mr. Dunlop & Miss Mattie Williams,[29] which I suppose is not news to you, is all that we have to talk about now. They will make a tour to Scotland. I hope she may not repent her passion for his gold. The doors of our church were yesterday closed by Military order. I hope to see them open again before long. Aunt's family are in tolerable health. Cousin Lucy Bryan, Charley & Hallie are on a visit to Rutherford. I hope soon to receive a sweet letter from you. I enclose a picture of Jimmy in this hoping that you may receive it. All the children send love & kisses. Your devoted wife

S. A. Kennedy

I enclose two U. S. Postage stamps. Newty is as usual and a very great care to me and a terror to the children.

Clarksville September 10th, 1864

My Dear Husband:

I wrote you on the 2nd and the children on the 3rd inst. Yours of 2nd July and 11th August have been received. Mary acknowledged the one to herself of 2nd July. Accept my gratitude for your numerous, affectionate letters. They come with a healing balm to my poor lonely heart, and although mine to you have not been as numerous, let me assure you that I have written of-

80

tener than you seem to think. My latest letters, addressed to Atlanta, before I was advised of the change, have, I suppose, been lost.[30] I have not frequent opportunities of writing by other routes, and besides, I have many cares that consume my time and strength from which you are free. Since I last wrote, I have almost recovered from my cold, and my health is much improved. The children are quite well with the exception of Newty who has been very bad for several days requiring all my time day & night. He is now getting over it and will not be so troublesome for a week, the intervals between his spells, and never longer. The charge devolves almost entirely upon me. Aunt Lucy is failing very fast. The rheumatism in her feet frequently depriving her of locomotion for two weeks at a time. My cook is now sick with neuralgia in the head occasioned, she says, by being overheated in the kitchen. She has given notice that she can cook no longer, and I will have to look for another. I have no other servant. The girls that I hire for the house are so trifling that I do not keep them many days. I would rather do all the work myself than be troubled with them, and a month is the longest time they will stay with any one. This makes me miss the children when they are at school. Jimmy especially as he did nearly all my shopping and marketing and even collected money for me. I would send Sally to school but for the need of her help in attending to the children. We have had very hot weather lately. The weather now is like Autumn, cool nights making a blanket comfortable and a little fire acceptable in the morning. Our vegetables are ceasing, and every thing indicates that cold weather is not very far off. I sent you Mr. Glenn's address, but as you may not have received it, I send it again in this. It is simply, J. L. Glenn, Louisville, Ky. B. W. Macrae has not gone to N. Y. yet. Ben C__r[31] has gone to Canada, you may guess why. His family are in Elkton with his mother. Lizzie Lewis is declining with heart disease. She has been relieved of the care of her three youngest children by her friends. Her youngest is a boy.[32] I never hear a word from brother Donald's family. They moved to Russellville some time since. I have made enquiries about John's family, but have failed, as yet, to learn any thing. Will write as soon as I can hear from them. I learn from a highly creditable source that you have an extensive correspondence with ladies of distinguished literary attainments. All I ask of you is not to compare my poor compositions (produced by a person jaded by drudgery and family cares) too closely with theirs lest the contrast should make you dissatisfied with your choice. Our friends are as well as usual. The children send love and kisses. I am unhappy that you have not heard more frequently from me. Your Devoted wife

S. A. Kennedy

I enclose two U. S. Postage stamps.

Clarksville September 21st, 1864

My Dear Husband:

Your kind and affectionate letter of 25th August came by last night's mail, those of 18th & 20th which you mention have not been received. My last to you by this route was on 10th, and I wrote you a long letter on the 12th. Mary and Jimmy wrote on the 3rd. I have nothing of interest to write you except the continued good health of all the family. My own health is much improved. The three eldest children are at school and much interested. Clara, Ellen & I enjoy the quiet very much. Aunt Lucy takes Newty off to walk, and we three have the whole house to ourselves. I go out so seldom that I have no chance to pick up the gossip. Indeed, there is great dearth of the article as all the ladies are closely confined at home attending to their own business. We have had cold nights reminding us that frost is not far away, but there is no premonition that the absent one will be with us soon, and my heart sickens at the thought.

I have succeeded in getting good pictures of all the children and enclose one of Ellen in this. I do hope it will go safely, and that you may be pleasured with it. I will not send the others until I know the result of this. I am glad to hear once in a while of the good health of Sister's family. Present my kind regards to E. J. Mc & family, & cousin James & Lizzy. The children send a bushel of kisses & love to Father. Your Devoted wife

S. A. Kennedy

Ellen was four years old on the 13th of this month.
Enclosed find two postage stamps.

Clarksville October 16th, 1864

My Dear Husband:

I am to day in receipt of your welcome and highly interesting favors of 15th & 22nd Sept. My last to you was on the 3rd containing Jimmy's picture. I have many reasons for allowing two weeks to pass without having written. I have not been very well. Newty has had a serious time. Aunt Lucy in bed. Letty Donoho is here quite sick, and three days ago dear little Ellen fell off the steps injuring her arm very seriously. She has had but little rest from pain, and I fear it will be several weeks before she is over it. This addition to my cares has well nigh crazed me. It is heart rending to witness the suffering of the sweet little thing as she lies with her arm bandaged and splintered. The bone is fractured between the elbow & shoulder. Your letters so laden with sweet love and affection are a healing balm to my lonely life, and I thank you more than I can express. Lucy Donoho says you write so loving, it puts her in mind of trying to get a husband for herself. We have taken up winter quarters in the dining room by a huge wood fire, room enough for us all to sit round and some to spare. We came so near freezing last winter, that it induced me to try this means of keeping warm. We are all well. My health is steadily improving. My weight is 124 pounds, 40 pounds less than it was three years ago. Mary's weight is 98, Jimmy's 65. I enclose Sally's picture which I hope will reach you. Aunt's family are well. She is now in Nashville. Went up with cousin James' children who have been here on a visit. The children were well when they left. All friends well except Mrs. McMullen who does not improve. Mrs. Elder has a baby two weeks old, a boy, and the most unwelcome baby I ever heard of.[33] Mrs. William Erwin died in Hospital in Louisville a short time since. E. P. Fort has gone to marry him a wife in Danville, Ky.,[34] the daughter of a Federal Captain Williams, some kin of Mrs. Ewin Gardner. She rejoices in the poetical name of Parthenia.[35] The match was made by her father without Mr. Fort's having seen her. He visited her twice only. Dr. Lurton's son Charly[36] was shot and killed ten miles from town last Thursday night by a union man. His remains were buried here. I have been luxuriating on the idea of living economically next winter in all of us snug around a good warm fire, taking our meals by the kitchen stove with scarcely an occasion for another fire in the house, when Letty, Lucy, & Jimmy[37] come bag & baggage and took up lodgings with us. I hear others say that they expect to stay with me the whole winter. They increase my table expenses vastly besides a constant fire in their room and other expenses too numerous to be thought of at once. It is another trial of my time and strength which is so much needed for my own family without mentioning the trial of my purse. I told Mr. Glenn when I last saw him that I felt like a beggar whenever I had to ask for money. John's family are all near Dover[38] with a Mr. O'Neil doing well. B. W. Mc is in N. Y. to see James[39] who was expected to die from repeated Hemorrhage of the lungs. Give my best love to cousin Lizzie, also E. J. Mc & family. Thank cousin Lizzy for me for her kindness to you. Ellen says write to Father about my poor little arm. The children send love & kisses. Your devoted wife

S. A. Kennedy

Newty blotted this while I stopped to attend to Ellen. Sally was nine years old 13th Aug last.

I enclose three Postage stamps. Send me some of yours.

Clarksville November 1st, 1864

My Dear Husband:

Since my last to you on the 23rd, I have received yours of 28th Sept. and 7th Oct. which I need not assure you are a great treat to me. I am gratified

that you have had letters from home as I have been not a little troubled that you have been so worried in this respect. You need not be uneasy about my wanting for funds sufficient for our comfort. The demand is always promptly met. I only hesitate to ask for it sometimes. Mr. G. commissioned B. W. Mc. to attend to all my wants, and he is faithful to his trust. On last Friday 28th, Sam Johnson called and paid to me twenty-five dollars in gold. The sum advanced by you to his brother, James.[40] I hesitated to take it without advice from you. I wrote to Mr. G. to tell me what to do with it. The whole Johnson family desire me to express their thankfulness to you for the favor. They also request me to say to you that they would like to make an arrangement with you to furnish their boys as they have no way of sending it to them. I mention this only because they requested me to do it, and will ask me what you have to say about it. In my last on 23rd, I sent Clara's picture, sent Ellen's on 20th Sept., Jimmy's on 3rd Oct., & Sally's on 16th. I do hope you will receive them all in good order. Letty and Lucy leave us to day. They will go to Rutherford in a short time. Aunt's family [is] pretty well. Charley Bryan more complaining than usual. Mrs. McMullen no better, but rapidly declining from Hemorrhage of the bowels. We are all very well. Ellen's arm is rapidly improving though not yet unbandaged, and her spirits as buoyant as if her arm had never been hurt. November has set in raw with an appearance of snow, and I shudder to think of the many cold, gloomy days in store for us, but am grateful to a kind Providence for the means of comfort with which we are favored and try to render praise to him for all the blessings which he has so abundantly bestowed upon us when we are so undeserving. Newty is about the same. I slept none last night. He was so nervous; he could not stay in bed but was running round the room all night and to day had a severe spasm. Mary desires me to say that she will write very soon. We learn that Mrs. Galbraith is a great Belle in Richmond.[41] I told you in a former letter that she had gone there to see her son who was dying from a wound. Aunt's family send love. Letty & Lucy also. I had a message from Mr. Barker who wished to know if he should furnish me with Pork. The children join me in Love.
Your Devoted wife

S. A. Kennedy

Enclosed find two postage stamps.


Clarksville February 6th, 1865

My Dear Husband:

Since my last to you on 31st, I am in receipt of yours from 18th Oct & 1st Jan. Two from the Carolinas and the rest from Augusta. They are a rich treat. I assure you, and one of my daily employments is the reperusal of them all. Every day of our separation I feel more keenly the loss of your society, and my mind ever dwells on the priceless jewel that I possess in an excellent husband. We are all in reasonable health. I cannot say perfect. The severe weather has produced colds from which one and another of us are frequently quite sick. Though at no time has it proved very serious. Newty has been more unwell for two months past and in consequence of Aunt Lucy's having all the kitchen work to perform. I have the entire charge of him to the great neglect of almost every other duty. He is becoming daily a greater charge. He needs some one stout enough to go about with him every day as he is getting too old to submit to constant confinement even in bad weather. If Aunt Lucy could devote her whole time to him, she is too feeble for exposure to all kinds of weather, and it tasks her utmost strength to hold him in one of his spells. If it were possible to procure a nurse for him, one who would perform his or her duty, I would consider no [un]reasonable expense, but this under existing circumstances is impossible. I have determined to take all the care of him upon myself feeling certain that it will prove for his good and for the comfort of us all. After one of his long nervous spells, my own nervous system is almost prostrated. My great anxiety about other matters has a powerful effect upon my nerves. I try to drive all fears for our future abode from my mind and resolve to bear the worst that can come with fortitude. I know that I can bear more than many women in our midst for they who have their husbands with them say to me, I don't see how you can get along so well. I would be willing for my husband to come home and take the oath. I answer them in your own words in one of your letters, "He has maintained his Honor & integrity thus far and I hope will be able to do so to the end." I strive to act upon your advice and am as cheerful as circumstances will allow. Mary calls me a go ahead woman. I am confident that if I do not go ahead that all of us and all we have will go to ruin. Our premises are fast dilapidating. The fences are rotten and falling piece by piece, and I fear that if the peace commissioners[42] do not soon come to a favorable understanding there will not be a piece left. Lucy & Letty have gone home. I never felt so sorry for any one as for them. They are noble girls and have been shamefully treated by professed friends (the C's across the way). It was from Mrs. Anna B. that I had the information that I wrote you and which proved to be false. I am glad that I had it in my power to render them aid and comfort in an hour of need. Aunt is again in feeble health confined to bed and looking badly. Eli Lockert[43] died yesterday evening of small pox supposed contracted at Dr. McMullen's. He was sick only two days. As in Dr. McM's case, the disease did not appear on the skin hence the sudden death of both. All the cases at present at Dr. McM recovering. Mrs. Tompkins is going about the house. Mr. Lockert's remains were accompanied to the grave by his own family only which was a mournful spectacle. I made a mistake in my last in the date of Mrs. McM's death. She died on the 4th Jan and the Dr. on the 14th, just ten days after.[44] I think the manner in which you administered the rebuke to your friends (if you have any) will cause you to hear from some of them. Cousins Will and Lucy threaten to write. They are quite amused at the pen and ink sketch of you, at your darning old socks by the light of a tallow candle. It is no fun to me though. Cousin Lizzie writes that I would be astonished to see how you do without me. I cannot be reconciled to have you perform such work. You would not seem so much out of place cutting wood, working the garden or ploughing the fields. I am not at all disappointed that you should get along as well without me as your good looks, agreeable manners, and noble qualities of mind and heart cannot fail to gain you friends wherever you may go. If cousins W. & L. write that I am looking well and youthful (as they threaten to do), don't believe a word of it for I do not believe you would recognize me, and it is contrary to the opinion of every one else. I am troubled to know what course to pursue with Mary. There is no school for her. I had intended her to study French with Mrs. Bemiss[45] but their school will be broken up for a time on account of small pox in the house. She practices her music at home and would be interested in reading if I had the time to attend to her. The children send bushels of love and kisses and say tell uncle John[46] howdy. Your devoted wife

S. A. Kennedy

I owe an apology for so many blots. Tis mean paper[47] and I have to write amid tumult.

Clarksville February 20th, 1865

My Dear Husband:

I have not been able to write to you since the 6th owing to the severe illness of Clara. She was taken sick on the 7th, and I have spent weary days and sleepless nights. At first the physician thought it pneumonia, but it proved to be a low form of fever caused Gastric. There was considerable inflammation of the stomach with dreadful sore mouth and swollen glands of the throat. She is now able to be up but not to go out. During this time Newty has been very troublesome at night frequently not being able to sleep or even to be in bed before two o'clock at night. I have never felt so worn from fatigue and am suffering with my old pain in my shoulders. You wish to know Newty's condition. It will be hard for me to explain it to you. His nervous system does not improve at all, and when he has one of his spells which sometimes lasts three and four weeks, he is like one distracted, never still, never easy, whining all the time never in the same place two moments at a time unless I am rocking him on my lap or lying with my arm round him on the bed. At such times, he is unmanageable. During his lucid moments, I can manage him pretty well. He seems to understand every thing as well as any one, learns to talk, waits on me, carries messages to the kitchen, hands me any thing I ask him for, brings me a stick of wood. The noise of the rest of the children confuses and excites him. I notice when they are all away, and he is alone with me, he is a great deal better, and the only comfort he has (when in one of his nervous ways) is for Aunt Lucy to walk with him on the most quiet streets, and to continue this until he wishes to go home to see mama. If she says anything about going back until he is satisfied he resists. We have to watch him continually to keep him from going off. He cannot play like other children, does not enjoy toys except to break or throw away, loves a book better than anything else, but does not have one long before tearing it to pieces. I have consulted Dr. Lurton about the seatone.[48] He thinks it would prove a counter irritant, but says it will do no harm to try it. I will have it attended to as soon as Clara is well as I am not willing or able to have this extra tax on my strength. Sally has had the jaw ache for several days from cold in an aching tooth. Her jaw is very much swollen. Jimmy has been vaxinated, and he is whining around quite sick from it. I had some matter put in my arm but see no effects from it at all. Mary & Ellen are perfectly well. Ellen is the brightest little thing you ever saw. She says Mother what is the reason I don't get sick like Tare, as she calls Clara. In the fall, I purchased four hogs for the purpose of making a supply of lard and sausage. I used all for this purpose excepting the shoulders and jolls.[49] Hung these to smoke. Last night the smoke house was broken open and all except three jolls abstracted. There is a perfect settlement of contrabands back of us, all the vacant ground being filled up with shanties. The occupants supplying themselves with something to eat by this means. I told the children that they would have to do without as I am not able to feed both them and the free niggers. I have had a new cook for two weeks. How much longer she will stay is not known as they soon tire of the confinement at one place and seek a new house. Mrs. Munford is now doing her own cooking being entirely out done with hired cooks. She cannot hold out at it as I know from my own experience. Mary & Sally are becoming every day a greater help to me and Mary seems really interested and thoughtful of my comfort. She has done all the housekeeping since Clara's sickness and I rest contented with her inexperience knowing that she will not learn if I am too particular to allow her to do it. She hears

Sally's lessons, practices her music and is learning to sew very neatly. I have been shopping to day at a store selling off at cost. Bought our summer shoes for three dollars and a half. Two and three dollars cheaper than they could be bought elsewhere. Goods are so enormously high that it frightens one to have to buy a supply for such a family as ours. The ladies say they have to carry their money in a basket and bring the goods home in their pocket. I have a letter from Lizzy Lewis in which she says cousin Gordon H. says I need not fear being turned U C & C as he has seen the proper Authorities, but as he is rather windy, she did not know whether to believe him or not. A daughter of George Stacker[50] died of Typhoid fever at Miss Mollie Ward's[51] school. This will decide me not to send Mary there. Mrs. Copeland is now on a visit to Aunt. Aunt has been confined to bed quite sick for three weeks, better today. Emma Dearing has relapsed and is quite sick. Miss Carrie has not taken smallpox. We cannot visit her. I wish I had room to say more. Will resume the thread of my discourse soon. Children all send love & kisses. Your Devoted wife.

S. A. Kennedy

This is miserable paper. Will blot spite of care.

# EPILOGUE

These surviving letters are the only record of Sarah's life written in her own hand in her own words. Late nineteenth- and early twentieth-century society was divided into what historians call public and private spheres. The community and business aspects of society were reported in newspapers and the private domestic women's world was not. While articles focused overwhelmingly on men's public activities, women's marriages and deaths were reported. News of the Kennedy family generally mirrors this pattern, but because of their prominence in Clarksville, important private social activities were reported in the paper. On occasion, we learn of the activities of Kennedy women in their own right, usually through women's organizations such as a prestigious college alumna meeting or the news about the United Daughters of the Confederacy. Because D. N. was a prominent public figure, there are numerous newspaper articles about his community, business, and civic activities and later articles about his son and sons-in-law. There are also articles that give us valuable information about their personal and family lives. The family home was center for all the happiest and saddest events in their lives. It was the venue for extravagant wedding receptions for their children. As family members died, their remains returned to the ancestral home for the last days before interment.

Through the decades, news of deaths, weddings, visits to family members, and church parties were published along with local news that D. N. was a part of, related especially to the Northern Bank, Constitutional Convention, Southwestern College, and national insurance conventions. Social notices tell us of some happy and tragic times, such as Jimmy's wedding followed by the sorrow of his young bride's death after childbirth. D. N.'s public ventures must have been the subject of the couple's daily conversations as he prepared for meetings and returned to tell Sarah how things went. She would have celebrated his triumphs such as the creation of Greenwood Cemetery, preventing Southwestern Presbyterian University (formerly Stewart College) from leaving Clarksville, his trips to insurance conventions (perhaps Sarah even went with him, we just do not know), laying a cornerstone on a large public building, and finally his retirement after four decades at the Northern Bank. Sarah continued to rear her family and attend First Presbyterian Church. We catch glimpses of how she ran her household by the census records which show Black employees living in her home. The African Americans who worked as paid help would have replaced the enslaved. Slavery ended but poor African Americans continued to cook, clean, and wash for the Kennedys.

D. N. returned to Clarksville after General Joseph E. Johnston's surrender in April of 1865. He soon received a pardon from President Andrew Johnson and reopened the Northern Bank.[1] Passions were intense after the Confederate defeat. A committee of leading Clarksvillians, from both sides of the conflict called a meeting to build a consensus on moving toward the future. Former Confederate officers General William A. Quarles and Colonel John F. House were joined by Unionist leaders Col. Smith[2] and William Guy Wines, the wartime postmaster and Stewart College professor. Cave Johnson presided and stated, "All questions growing out of the war have been settled by the sword," yet he continued with a full-throated denunciation of the end of slavery, the confiscation of property, the possibility of distributing land to newly freed African Americans, and the promises of Black suffrage and equal rights.[3]

Kennedy served on a resolution committee that wrote of "abolition of slavery as an accomplished fact" and "We, therefore, deem it the duty of every good citizen to exercise all the offices of a kindly sympathy in ameliorating his condition."[4] Despite the resolution of reconciliation, many in the region remained unreconstructed Southerners.

Churches reopened fully, including First Presbyterian where Kennedy served as an elder. The community saw the need for a home for children orphaned during the war. Kennedy helped establish and served as a trustee for the Tennessee Orphan Society. The organization purchased a mansion above the Red River for $25,000 and the home was supported by subscription. Women's groups supported the orphanage and merchants supplied food and clothing. Almost one hundred children were cared for and received education and religious training.[5]

In 1869, Kennedy was unanimously elected as the Montgomery County delegate to the Tennessee State Convention of 1870.[6] The convention met in January and John C. Brown, former Confederate general and member of the Ku Klux Klan, was elected chair. Tennessee's 1870 constitution preserved the basic structure of state government but restricted the power of the governor. It instituted universal manhood suffrage but also established a poll tax, which was used to disenfranchise African American men.[7]

In the 1870 census, Newty was still in the home, listed as David N. Jr., age 13. Mary was 18; James (Jimmy), 17; Sallie, 14; Clara, 11; and the youngest, Ellen, was 9. Also listed were two African Americans who lived and worked for the family. G. Coleman, a woman, who was 46, was listed as a cook. A teenager, George Smith, was listed as a waiter. There was also a woman listed as a boarder, Mollie Sinclair, age 32.[8] By 1880, Newty was no longer in the household.

By 1873, D. N. was spearheading the development of Greenwood Cemetery, and the paper announced people could view the map and purchase lots. "The establishment of this beautiful resting place for the sleeping dead must commend itself to all those who retain in their hearts a loving memory of those dear to them in life."[9] Greenwood became the resting place for most of the Kennedy family in a large family plot with a large Kennedy monument surrounded by individual headstones. Daughters Ellen and Mary are not buried in Greenwood.

As the Kennedy children married, their announcements were in the paper. Mary, James, and Clara remained in Clarksville. Sally and Ellen married and moved away. Newty was institutionalized. He was not listed in the 1880 census with his family; the 1880 Franklin County, Ohio, Census lists Newton Kennedy as "idiotic" in the Columbus Hospital for the Insane[10] (the hospital had several names over the years). The hospital would have been at the forefront of treatment for mentally ill and for people with disabilities in the late nineteenth century. It was a massive facility covering thirty acres with over eight hundred rooms. It is unclear when the Kennedys committed him, if or how often they visited. He died there in April 1888 and his remains were brought to his parents' house to be interred in the family plot at Greenwood Cemetery.[11]

Mary graduated from Clarksville Female Academy,[12] and in 1870 she wed local pharmacist and businessman, B. H. Owen, and they had six children. Sadly, one of Mary's children died from an accident when his clothes caught on fire in 1894. Surely this must have conjured up painful memories for D. N. and Sarah as they had lost one of their children when that child's clothes caught fire. Owen's professional and civic life emulated that of his father-in-law. He owned a drug store and was an officer in the Knights of Pythias and the Bible Society. He served on the board of the state's professional pharmacist organization and attended conferences. After D. N. Kennedy died, Owen was elected to replace him on the Southwestern Presbyterian University Board of Trustees and served as a moderator for the Presbytery.

Owen even became a banker like his father-in-law and was president of the National Bank. In 1908, he defended Greenwood Cemetery as a board member in a legal dispute.[13] D. N. Kennedy must have respected his judgment because he chose Owen to be the executor of his will.

A year before her older sister married, Sally also graduated from Clarksville Female Academy and married Presbyterian minister, John T. Plunkett, who graduated from Southwestern Presbyterian University and Union Theological Seminary in Columbia, South Carolina.[14] J. T. and Sally had five children and lived in several cities where he served as minister. In 1875, Plunkett was asked to give several talks in Clarksville, at First Presbyterian Church and a literary organization called the Washington Irving Society, followed the next week by giving the commencement address at Clarksville Female Academy. In 1901, newspaper readers learned "Mrs. Dr. Plunkett" had traveled from her home in Augusta, Georgia, to visit her widowed father.

In 1880, the Kennedys had only two children remaining at home, Jimmy and Ellen. Sarah referred to James as Jimmy in her letters but he is known only as James in all the other surviving documents. Also, in the household were two young Black women who could not read or write. Mata Raimey, 21, was listed as a cook and Julia Frasier, 22, worked as a wash woman.[15]

James had graduated from Stewart College, probably just before it was chartered as Southwestern Presbyterian University in 1875. In December of 1885, he married Lois Viser, who was from a well-connected family that included a US Supreme Court justice.[16] D. N. and Sarah hosted a family gathering to celebrate the following day at their Second Street home, attended by their daughters, Ellen Clapp from Memphis, and Sallie Plunkett from Covington, Kentucky.[17] The bride's sisters also attended. Sadly, the marriage ended with the tragic death of Lois a year later from puerperal fever[18] at the same home they had so happily celebrated the wedding in the previous December. The infant baby was named David Newton after his grandfather and uncle. The same minister who performed the marriage ceremony performed the funeral. Lois was buried in Greenwood Cemetery.[19] James' youngest sister, Ellen Kennedy Clapp, may have taken the infant Newton to Memphis to raise in her family. The 1890 census does not exist, but Newton was in the Clapp household in 1900.[20]

When James died, his obituaries mentioned his longtime poor health. It seems that he visited several hot springs in attempts to heal; the paper listed stays at Pyland Springs,[21] Tate Springs,[22] and Hot Springs. Eight years after his first wife died, he married Virginia Vaughn of Hot Springs and they had a daughter in 1894. He was a tobacconist and owned, along with partners, the Cumberland and the Elephant tobacco warehouses. He also was in partnership with his father in D. N. Kennedy and Son Insurance. James worked with D. N. to secure a branch of the L & N Railroad in Clarksville.[23] Earlier in the 1880s, D. N. had been involved in the Mobile, Clarksville, & Evansville Railroad, serving as president. At that point a fifty-mile railroad was built from Princeton, Kentucky, to Clarksville.[24] About 1907, James and his son, David Newton, moved to Knoxville where the younger man worked in the furniture business. They lived in the Imperial Hotel. In 1909, David found his father dead in his bed in his hotel room. The Knoxville obituary said that he had been sick for some years suffering from "nervous trouble."[25] The Clarksville obituary said that despite having ill health for years, James' death was a shock. His remains were returned to the home of his sister, Clara, and interred at the family plot.

Clara attended Mary Baldwin Seminary,[26] a girl's school in Staunton, Virginia, that was affiliated with the Presbyterian Church. In 1880, Clara had married B. H. Burney, a Clarksville lawyer who was the Montgomery County Attorney General,[27] in an elaborate ceremony followed by a large reception at her parents' home. Burney represented Montgomery County in the Tennessee General Assembly in 1887–89. They had four children. In 1890, the family lived a couple of houses down from her ancestral home on South Second Street. B. H. Burney died at age 45 in 1899 and Clara lived another four decades, dying in 1939.[28]

D. N. and Sarah held a large wedding for their youngest daughter, Ellen, who married J. W. Clapp of Memphis in 1881. The Memphis *Public Ledger* said the "church was brilliantly lighted and thronged with the elite of the city."[29] Her parents once again held a reception at the home. Ellen and J. W. had two children, James and Kennedy Newton Clapp. Ellen graduated from Mary Baldwin Seminary and became an officer in their alumnae association.[30]

D. N. Kennedy was instrumental in creating Greenwood Cemetery and later erecting a Confederate monument at the entrance. The monument unveiling ceremony in 1893 was a massive event, complete with a parade, and speeches by dignitaries. It was attended by five thousand people including many, now aged, Confederate veterans. D. N. was the primary organizer of the creation and erection of the Lost Cause monument. The large statue still stands at the cemetery entrance and while most Confederate monuments were erected by the United Daughters of the Confederacy, the Greenwood Cemetery monument predates the founding of the UDC. Enthusiasm ran so high that the number of people who attended the dedication ceremony of "The Heroic Dead Remembered by Patriotic People"[31] equalled the population of Clarksville in 1862. Presumably they were patriotic to the Confederacy, although Southerners became ardent US government supporters as time went along.[32]

Sarah died in June of 1899 at age seventy-six. All her surviving children attended the funeral and her obituary praised her "as an earnest, practical Christian woman who did good and shunned all parade." She was a "model wife and mother."[33] Her husband lived five more years and his social visits sometimes appeared in the paper, visits with his daughters or friends and family in Elkton, Kentucky, a place he had left to strike out on his own as a very young man.

In 1897, Clarksville held an elaborate ceremony of the laying of the cornerstone of what was called then simply the Public Building. A cornerstone box was filled with what leaders and organizers thought were important documents. Kennedy placed the charter and rules of Greenwood Cemetery, a copy of the "Manual of Clarksville Presbyterian Church" and a Tennessee Constitution of 1870, with proceedings of the convention written by none other than D. N. Kennedy.[34] The building has been one of the most iconic features in Clarksville's landscape because of its unique architecture featuring gargoyles, serving as the US Post Office, Customs House, Department of Electricity and now the Clarksville Customs House Museum and Cultural Center. Kennedy retired from Northern Bank in 1898 and, at the time, was the oldest banker in Tennessee.

In 1903, a short announcement said that the widowed D. N., along with his daughter, "Mrs. J. W. Clapp" (Ellen), returned from Augusta where they visited "Dr. and Mrs. Plunkett" (Sallie). It added that "Mrs. Clapp is a delegate from Memphis to the UDC."[35] Clarksville held the Tennessee Division of the United Daughters of the Confederacy conference that year. D. N. Kennedy also made the paper for that conference. During one session, the Reverend J. H. Lacy presented a Confederate flag that Kennedy gave to the Clarksville Caroline Meriwether Goodlett Chapter. It was "three by five feet" with red, white, and blue ribbons on which they would print the chapter name. Elite women, literal daughters of Confederates, formed the backbone of the early UDC. The Daughters had the ardent support of their elite male family members. The Kennedy family took great interest not only in the creation and erection of the Confederate monument in Greenwood Cemetery but also the successful promoting of Lost Cause ideology. At Ellen Kennedy Clapp's death in 1947 the *Nashville Banner* and the *Bristol News* stated that Clapp was president of the Tennessee Division of the UDC,[36] but the official history does not list her as state president.[37] She, following in her father's footsteps, served as recording secretary for the large Memphis chapter and later was elected president.[38] Clapp also served as recording secretary for the 1907 state convention.[39]

In his early eighties, D. N. took on his last big public role. In 1875, Stewart College became Southwestern Presbyterian University. Kennedy served as the superintendent of First Presbyterian Church's Sunday School, as an elder of the church, and on Southwestern Presbyterian University's Board of Trustees. In 1901, the Presbyterian Synod of Atlanta wanted to establish a Presbyterian University in Atlanta by merging Clarksville's Southwestern Presbyterian University with South Carolina's Columbia Theological Seminary and moving the new combined college to Atlanta.[40] Immediately, Clarksvillians protested and began legal action to prevent relocation. Kennedy became the spokesman for the opposition and pointed out the charter required that the university remain in Clarksville. Eventually, the court decided the outcome. The Tennessee Supreme Court ruled in favor of Southwestern in 1905. Although this fight to stave off a move was successful, the university was eventually relocated to Memphis in 1925 and is now named Rhodes College. Austin Peay State University, established in 1927, is currently on the site occupied by Southwestern in Clarksville. Kennedy did not live to see the success of his efforts to keep Southwestern in Clarksville. He died the previous year.[41]

On April 22, 1904, Clarksvillians read a short notice in the paper, "Mr. Kennedy's Condition Very Precarious," noting he was "quite low" and given his advanced age, "he may not possibly rally."[42] He died the next day. D. N. and Sarah are interred in Greenwood Cemetery; a large monument marks their grave. The paper carried several tributes to Kennedy, a long obituary,[43] a tribute from the Northern Bank,[44] and one from Forbes Bivouac.[45] The minutes of First Presbyterian Church stated that "A Prince in Israel has fallen."[46]

D. N. Kennedy left a thorough, detailed, handwritten will[47] in which he divided his assets. He left the family home to be held in trust for his grandson David Newton and named his son-in-law, B. H. Owen, as executor. Kennedy made provisions for the grandchildren's education. He requested no public sale of his estate after his death but did stipulate how the furniture would be divided among his children, with James receiving his office furniture. He bequeathed an oil painting of Sarah and him, along with a clock, to his daughter Mary. Sadly, this portrait has been lost to history. Kennedy left to Laura Clardy,[48] his live-in hired help, the furniture in her room and made provision for the children to give her whatever they did not themselves want. He wrote that Laura had been a "faithful servant to me."[49]

Local historians have recognized the immense influence D. N. Kennedy had in Clarksville history, yet his legacy did not survive in public memory. Perhaps the bureaucratic nature of his historical significance is not appealing to the public's imagination. He is often listed at the bottom of newspaper articles, which he probably submitted, as "D. N. Kennedy, Sec'y." In contrast, Sarah's Civil War letters evoke great interest and have been studied by Civil

War historians for decades. It is ironic that interest in letters detailing war experiences of Sarah, who lived in the private sphere of society, will lead to her very public husband, D. N., receiving some long-neglected historical attention. During her life, Sarah would have been seen as the perfect help-meet: loving wife, devoted mother, efficient housewife (really household manager), and faithful church attendee. She bore, reared, and buried children. She kept the metaphorical and literal home-front fire burning, caring for their family while her husband was away at war, apparently working a nondescript bureaucratic job for the failed Confederate state.

In October 1968, the *Clarksville Leaf Chronicle* carried a story about the demolition of the Kennedy home, razed to make room for a modern office building. Through the decades after the house had left the Kennedy family possession, the property had several owners, including the sister of Governor Austin Peay. Over the years, the large house was divided and rented as several apartments. The newspaper account by local historian Ursula Beach was imbued with a Lost Cause interpretation of Sarah's Civil War years. Beach wrote the family was forced to leave the home and were treated harshly by Federal troops in retribution of D. N.'s removing the bank's gold before occupation. Beach also claimed the Federal authorities only allowed Sarah to light one fire for the whole house in an upstairs room. The letters do not indicate being forced to leave and do not describe harassment by troops nor forcing her to limit her fires. By her own account, Sarah was conserving coal because of the uncertainty of war.

The beautiful antebellum home, the physical and emotional center of the large and loving Kennedy family, has disappeared from the Clarksville landscape. Numerous Kennedy family members are buried in Greenwood Cemetery. Newspaper archives are now digitized and articles and information on the Kennedy family is more accessible than ever. Sarah's wartime letters are preserved at the Tennessee State Library and Archives.

Sarah's private letters to her husband chronicle hardship and turmoil of turbulent years of war, military occupation, and the end of slavery. Through the public record, the family story can be recreated, giving us valuable insight into an elite white Southern family. Despite the advantages of wealth and privilege, the family suffered with incredible sorrows, the death of young children, a daughter-in-law dying in childbirth, and the uncertainty of caring for a special needs child. Yet, Sarah and D. N. celebrated many joys and triumphs of business successes, marriages of children, and many loving grandchildren. Knowing the story of Sarah Bailey Kennedy and her family enriches our understanding of late nineteenth-century history.

# NOTES

## Introduction

1. D. N. Kennedy had a lengthy and detailed biography in William S. Speer, *Sketches of Prominent Tennesseans: Containing Biographies and Records of Many of the Families who Have Attained Prominence in Tennessee* (Nashville: A.B. Tavel, 1888), 429–31. Reprinted by Southern Historical Press by Silas Emmit Lucus Jr., 1978.

2. Sarah Kennedy's letters are housed at the Tennessee State Library and Archives, Civil War Collection Confederate and Federal 1861–1865, Confederate Collection, Box 9, Folders 6–8. Unpublished letters and journals from the Civil War include John Nicholas Barker's Civil War journal housed in the Genealogy Room, Clarksville–Montgomery County Public Library, Clarksville, and the Margaretta Lewis letters housed at the Montgomery County, Tennessee, Archives in Clarksville.

3. Ursula Smith Beach, *Along the Warioto: A History of Montgomery County, Tennessee* (Nashville: McQuiddy Press, 1964), iv.

4. Amy L. Wink, *She Left Nothing in Particular: The Autobiographical Legacy of Nineteenth-Century Women's Diaries* (Knoxville: Univ. of Tennessee Press, 2001), xxv.

5. Wink, *She Left Nothing in Particular*, xv.

6. Wink, *She Left Nothing in Particular*, xxv–xxvii.

7. Candice Shy Hooper, *Lincoln's General's Wives: Four Women Who Influenced the Civil War—for Better or Worse* (Kent, Ohio: Kent State Univ. Press, 2016). Hooper explores the relationships of John and Jessie Frémont, George and Nelly McClellan, William and Ellen Sherman, and Ulysses and Julia Grant.

8. Drew Gilpin Faust, "We Little Knew: Husbands and Wives," *Mothers of Invention: Women of the Slaveholding South in the American Civil War* (Chapel Hill: UNC Press, 1996), 114–38. Faust refers to Sarah Kennedy on pages 73, 120, 121, 130 and 149.

9. Minoa D. Uffelman et al., eds., *The Diary of Nannie Haskins Williams: A Southern Woman's Story of Rebellion and Reconstruction, 1863–1890* (Knoxville: Univ. of Tennessee Press, 2014).

10. Minoa D. Uffelman et al., eds., *The Diary of Serepta Jordan: A Southern Woman's Struggle with War and Family, 1857–1864* (Knoxville: Univ. of Tennessee Press, 2020).

11. Stephen V. Ash, "A Community at War: Montgomery County, 1861–65," *Tennessee Historical Quarterly* 36, no. 1 (Spring 1977): 161–76; Stephen V. Ash, *Middle Tennessee Society Transformed, 1860–1870: War and Peace in the Upper South* (Knoxville: Univ. of Tennessee Press, 2006), 18, 25; Richard P. Gildrie, "Dilemmas and Opportunities, 1860–1900," in *Historic Clarksville: The Bicentennial Story, 1784–2004,* second edition, eds. Charles M. Waters and John L. Butler (Clarksville, TN: Historic Clarksville Publishing Company, 2004), 63–95.

12. Ursula S. Beach and Eleanor Williams, *Nineteenth Century Heritage: Clarksville, Tennessee* (Oxford, MS: The Guild Bindery Press, 1989), 175.

13. *Leaf-Chronicle*, April 23, 1904, 1.

14. These training camps were Camp Boone, Camp Burnett, Camp Forbes/Duncan/Humphries (most common name Duncan), and Camp Quarles/Breckinridge, *Nannie Haskins Williams Diary*, 206–7.

15. The fort on the Cumberland River in New Providence was one of three forts built in Clarksville by Confederates to deny use of the rivers to the Federal Army. Initially known as Fort Sevier it was later named Fort Bruce during occupation, named after Colonel Sanders D. Bruce, commander of Clarksville from December 1862 to late 1863. Today the fort is known as Fort Defiance, the name Flag Officer Andrew Foote used in his report of the capture of Clarksville. Fort Defiance Civil War Park and Interpretive Center is located at 120 Duncan Street, Clarksville, Tennessee.

16. Founded in 1854 by David N. Kennedy and James L. Glenn, Northern Bank first opened its doors in a building still standing on Public Square. It moved to the current location of Second and Main in 1885. The bank survived the Civil War largely because Kennedy rode on horseback with the bank's assets to New Orleans, where he shipped the money with a blockade runner to a friend and business associate in London. After the war the assets were returned. W. P. Titus, *Picturesque Clarksville, Past and Present: A History of the City of the Hills* (Clarksville, TN: W. P. Titus, 1887, repr. Ann Alley and Ursula Beach, 1973), 236–39. Northern Bank emerged from the Civil War as the oldest bank in the state, and before it merged with First American Bank (now Regions Bank) in 1988, it was the oldest bank operating under the original name and charter south of the Mason-Dixon.

17. Gildrie, "Dilemmas and Opportunities," 65.

18. Beach, *Along the Warioto*, 226. Waters, *Historic Clarksville*, 208–9.

19. W. Daniel Harrison, "Southern Presbyterians in the Confederacy," *The North Carolina Historical Review* 44, no. 3 (1967): 231–55.

20. Minutes of the General Assembly of the Presbyterian Church of the Confederate States of America, Augusta, Georgia, Steam Power Press Chronicle & Sentinel, December 4, 1861; Minutes of the General Assembly of the Presbyterian Church, Confederate States of America, Montgomery, Alabama, May 1, 1862.

21. Minutes of the General Assembly, Presbyterian Church, Confederate States of America, Southern Guardian Steam-Power Press, Columbia, South Carolina, May 7, 1863, 131–32.

22. Minutes of the General Assembly, Presbyterian Church in the United States, 1868, Office of the Southern Presbyterian Review, Columbia, South Carolina.

23. "History of the Church," Presbyterian Historical Society: The National Archives of the PC(USA), https://www.history.pcusa.org/history-online/presbyterian-history/history-church, accessed October 7, 2021.

24. Sarah Kennedy Letters, December 6, 1862.

25. Sarah Kennedy Letters, December 6, 1862.

26. C. Wallace Cross, *Cry Havoc: A History of the 49th Tennessee Volunteer Infantry Regiment 1861–1865* (Franklin, TN: Hillsboro Press, 2004), 30.

27. See Cross, *Cry Havoc*, for a detailed account of movement of the 49th Infantry during the war.

28. Sarah Kennedy Letters, June 17, 1863.

29. Sarah Kennedy Letters, September 2, 1864.

30. D. N. Kennedy Pardon Vertical File, Brown Harvey, Sr. Genealogy Room, Clarksville-Montgomery County Public Library, Clarksville, Tennessee.

31. Ernest A. Smith, "The History of the Confederate Treasury," *Southern History Association* 5. no. 1 (1901): 117.

32. Letters Received by the Confederate Secretary of the Treasury, 1861–1865, Pamphlet Accompanying Microcopy 499, National Archives Microfilm Publications, The National Archives, National Archives and Records Service General Services Administration Washington, 1967, 7.

33. Charles Bailey was born in North Carolina on February 9, 1791. His father, David Bailey, died in 1794, and his mother, Mary Williamson, brought her children and her niece Elizabeth White to Montgomery County, Tennessee, upon his death. Charles married Mary Bryan on May 29, 1817. Together they had five sons and one daughter. He was an elder in the Clarksville Presbyterian Church, longtime clerk of the Circuit Court, and also served as a justice of the peace. Charles Bailey died in his home on March 15, 1863. Titus, *Picturesque Clarksville*, 269.

34. US Marriage Records, Tennessee State Library and Archives, Tennessee, 1780–2002. Microfilm.

35. *Clarksville Chronicle*, July 20, 1860, 2.

36. *Clarksville Chronicle*, April 19, 1861, 2.

37. *Clarksville Chronicle*, August 5, 1859, 3.

38. *Clarksville Chronicle*, September 6, 1861, 3.

39. Gildrie, "Dilemmas and Opportunities," 64–65.

40. Beach, *Along the Warioto*, 182–83.

41. *Clarksville Jeffersonian*, November 20, 1849, 2.

42. *Clarksville Jeffersonian*, September 11, 1850, 3.

43. See Civil War Philatelic Society, https://www.civilwarphilatelicsociety.org/, accessed August 30, 2021; Trish Kaufman, https://www.trishkaufmann.com/files /Knowles1.pdf, accessed August 30, 2021.

44. Smithsonian Postal Museum, https://postalmuseum.si.edu/exhibition/about -philately-covers-and-letters-in-times-of-trouble-conflict-mail/civil-war-1861-1865, accessed October 29, 2020.

45. Winifred Gallagher, *How the Post Office Created America: A History* (New York: Penguin Books, 2016), 141–58.

46. Smithsonian Postal Museum, https://postalmuseum.si.edu/exhibition/about -philately-covers-and-letters-in-times-of-trouble-conflict-mail-civil-war-1861-1865, accessed October 29, 2020.

47. Smithsonian Postal Museum, https://postalmuseum.si.edu/exhibition/about -philately-covers-and-letters-in-times-of-trouble-conflict-mail/civil-war-1861 -1865, accessed October 29, 2020.

48. Trish Kaufman, https://www.trishkaufmann.com/files/Knowles1.pdf, accessed August 30, 2021.

49. The war brought reform and improvements to the USPS. Without the opposition of conservative Southern politicians, US Postmaster Montgomery Blair implemented changes. He eliminated the long-distance charge for letters, allowing for all letters to be mailed for three cents. Additionally, he instituted a money order system, eliminating the dangerous act of mailing money, which could be targeted by thieves. Blair hired permanent letter carriers for free home delivery in cities. People no longer had to pick up the mail at the post office. Some cities even had twice-a-day delivery. This popular feature was implemented for rural free delivery in 1893. Devin Leonard, *Neither Snow nor Rain: A History of the United States Postal Service* (New York: Grove Press, 2016), 47–51.

50. Sarah Kennedy Letters, December 6, 1862.

51. Lisa C. Tolbert, *Constructing Townscapes: Space and Society in Antebellum Tennessee* (Chapel Hill: Univ. of North Carolina Press, 1999), 127.

52. Tolbert, *Constructing Townscapes*, 128–29, 143–51.

53. Clarksville Female Academy was the city's premier girls' private school from 1846 to 1882. Instruction ceased with the impending Civil War. During the war, the school served as a Federal hospital. In the fall of 1866, the school reopened. It was located on Madison Street between Fifth and Sixth Streets. See Beach and Williams, *Nineteenth Century Heritage*, 44–45.

54. Nannie Haskins, *The History of Clarksville Female Academy* (Clarksville, Tennessee Library Committee, Women's Building, Tennessee Centennial, 1896; repr. Montgomery County Historical Society, 1896).

55. Nashville Female Academy was founded in 1816 and continued until Nashville fell to the Federals in 1862. Metro Historical Commission Foundation, "Nash-

ville Female Academy," Nashville Sites, https://nashvillesites.org/records/01ae3439
-3b8e-4ca7-b9ed-d568538a6321, accessed July 29, 2021.

56. Sarah Kennedy Letters, December 29, 1862.

57. Sarah Kennedy Letters, December 29, 1862.

58. Sarah Kennedy Letters, December 29, 1862.

59. Sarah Kennedy Letters, December 29, 1862.

60. Sarah Kennedy Letters, December 29, 1862.

61. Sarah Kennedy Letters, February 2, 1863.

62. Sarah Kennedy Letters, May 5, 1863.

63. Sarah Kennedy Letters, February 6, 1865.

64. Sarah Kennedy Letters, January 7, 1863. Aunt Lucy was the only enslaved
person who opted to stay with the family after emancipation.

65. Tolbert, *Constructing Townscapes*, 187–94.

66. Sarah Kennedy Letters, December 22, 1862.

67. Sarah Kennedy Letters, November 9, 1863.

68. It is difficult to say exactly how many African Americans from Clarksville
served in the USCT. When the Federal Army initially garrisoned the town, they
impressed Black men for labor on the fortifications without regard to status (free
or slave). Many of these laborers were sent on to Nashville and other nearby areas
to work on fortifications where they were recruited into the Army. The 16th USCT
had a recruiting station in Clarksville for five or six months and recruited between
300 and 800 men. The 101st USCT had their regimental headquarters in Clarksville and recruited quite a number of men from Clarksville's contraband camp,
which attracted escaping slaves from surrounding counties.

69. Sarah Kennedy Letters, April 24, 1863.

70. Sarah Kennedy Letters, June 17, 1863.

71. In African American oral tradition, Brer Rabbit was the main character who
succeeded by his wits over authority figures. The stories draw on African trickster
stories. Joel Chandler Harris wrote popular Brer Rabbit stories in the late nineteenth century and early twentieth century. Many people know of Brer Rabbit
because Walt Disney made a popular movie, *Song of the South*, in 1946.

72. Faust, "Enemies in Our Household: Confederate Women and Slavery," *Mothers of Invention*, 53–79.

73. Sarah Kennedy Letters, October 6, 1863.

74. Sarah Kennedy Letters, March 19, 1864.

75. Sarah Kennedy Letters, February 11, 1864.

76. Sarah Kennedy Letters, March 19, 1864.

77. *Clarksville Tobacco Leaf*, May 17, 1877, 3.

78. *Daily Tobacco Leaf-Chronicle*, November 23, 1893, 1.

79. *Daily Tobacco Leaf-Chronicle*, June 26, 1899, 3.

80. Serepta Jordan also expressed affection for her enslaved young girl, Inez, early

in her diary, but as Inez exerted her independence and eventually left, Serepta was bitter, angry, resentful and expressed that she never wanted to see her again. Faust, in *Mothers of Invention*, discusses White women's anger about enslaved people leaving for freedom, 74–79.

## Chapter 1

1. Cloverlands was the home of John Walton Barker (see note 51 below). Completed in 1820, Cloverlands is still in existence and is located in Montgomery County about a mile from the Kentucky/Tennessee state line. The Kennedys were renting their Clarksville house to a Union family named Parker, and Sarah was living at Cloverlands. Information on the Barker Family and Cloverlands is available in unpublished research at Montgomery County Archives.

2. Mr. G. was James Lyle Glenn, D. N. Kennedy's partner in the formation of the Northern Bank of Tennessee. The 1860 Montgomery County, Tennessee, Census lists J. L. Glenn, 31, banker, with household members Ella, 25, and Thornton, 1.

3. Sarah and D. N. Kennedy's daughter, Clara S. Kennedy, was born in 1859.

4. Newty was a nickname for their son, David Newton Kennedy, born in 1857.

5. Ellen was D. N. and Sarah Kennedy's youngest child, born in 1861.

6. Sarah was referring to Ellen Watson Morris Carr Barker, John Walton Barker's second wife.

7. John J. Hickman married Elizabeth Hollingsworth on May 11, 1859, in Todd County, Kentucky. Kentucky Compiled Marriages, 1851–1900. The 1850 Todd County, Kentucky, Census lists Elizabeth T. Hollingworth [sic], 10, in the household of Thomas K., 52, and Amanda Hollingworth, 42, with other children Mary A., 20; Nancy J., 14; and Cornelia, 4. The Hickmans lived in Trenton, Todd County, Kentucky, at the time of this entry. The 1870 Jefferson County, Kentucky, Census lists J. J. Hickman, 30; Elizabeth, 29; John, 10; and Newton, 9, living in Ward 5, Louisville, Kentucky. John Hickman was working as an insurance agent.

8. A rockaway was a light, four-wheeled, horse-drawn carriage first introduced in Rockaway, New Jersey. The back was enclosed and the roof projected over the driver's bench.

9. Patty Hollingsworth may have been Martha "Patty" Gray Hollingsworth (1831–1904). She was the widow of Samuel Newton Hollingsworth (1825–1861) and had five living children under the age of ten at this time: William, Frances (Fanny), Lucy, Samuel Jr., and Alberta (Birtie). "Candace Ricks Family Tree," http://www.ancestry.com, accessed October 14, 2020.

10. The 1850 Todd County, Kentucky, Census lists Mary A. Clark, 22, in the household of Nancy Kennedy, 47, with Samuel W. Kennedy, 26; Settitia (Lettitia) Kennedy, 16; Octavia Kennedy, 12; and James D. Clark, 25. The 1870 Todd County, Kentucky, Census lists Mary A. Clark, 42, school teacher, in a household with

Nancy Kennicy (Kennedy), 64; Lettitia J. Kennicy (Kennedy), 38; Willie K. Clark, 15; John W. Lewis, 40; Odaria Lewis, 33; John L. Lewis, 3; and Charles K. Lewis. Nancy Kennedy was the widow of D. N. Kennedy's brother, James Newton Kennedy (1803–1844).

11. Tishy K. was probably Lettitia Kennedy, listed as age 16 in 1850 and 38 in 1870.

12. Sarah and D. N. Kennedy's daughter, Mary B. Kennedy, was born in 1851.

13. The Confederacy had established its own Post Office Department on February 21, 1861. The United States Government banned mail exchange between the US and Confederacy on August 26, 1861. Sarah was residing in an area controlled by Federal troops. In order to get letters to her husband, who was in an area controlled by the Confederacy, someone had to carry the letter out of the Federal area and into the Confederacy in order to put it in the Confederate mail system.

14. Sarah and D. N. Kennedy's daughter, Sally G. Kennedy, was born in 1855.

15. Sarah and D. N. Kennedy's son, James T. Kennedy, was born in 1853.

16. Mrs. B. was Ellen Watson Morris Carr Barker, John Walton Barker's second wife.

17. Mr. Ferguson was probably Robert French Ferguson, son-in-law of John Walton Barker. Robert French Ferguson married Ann "Nannie" Minor Barker in 1842. Ann was John Walton Barker's youngest daughter by his first wife, Mary Minor Meriwether Barker. The 1860 Montgomery County, Tennessee, Census lists the household of R. F. Ferguson, 45, farmer, with N. M. (Nannie Minor), 39; M. M., 15, female; E. M., 13, female; T. B., 12, male; S. A., 11, female; Jesse, 8, female; B. A., 6, female; R. T., 4, male; J .B., 2, female; G. W. Butler, 24 , male, overseer; and M. T. Brockman, 44, female, teacher.

18. These lines are from the song "Home Again." Thomas G. Doyle. Bookseller, Stationer and Song Publisher, No. 297 N. Gay Street, Baltimore, Library of Congress website, https://www.loc.gov/resource/amss.as105400.0/?st=text, accessed September 3, 2020.

19. It is obvious from the letters that Miss Carrie is a close friend. Without another indication of who she is, it is impossible to identify her.

20. Lucy Bryan is listed as age 28 in the 1850 Montgomery County, Tennessee, Census, in the household of her sisters, Sarah B. Copeland, 45, and Elizabeth Bryan, 55. Interestingly, Sarah, D. N., and a son, William D., 2, were living there as well. William died later that year. Sarah's aunt, Mary (Polly) Bryan Bailey, married to her uncle, Charles Bailey Sr., may have been aunt to these Bryan siblings as well.

21. In 1858 Dr. Robert Burns McMullen, a former chemistry professor from Knoxville, became president of Stewart College and professor of Mental and Moral Sciences. He excelled at fundraising, which allowed the construction of the first dormitory, Robb Hall, named after Colonel Alfred Robb, local lawyer and college benefactor. During the winter of 1861–1862, Confederate forces commandeered

the entire campus to convert the president's house into a military hospital. Many Stewart College students joined the 14th Tennessee Infantry. After the fall of Fort Donelson, US troops looted and damaged the campus. McMullen said the damages equaled $10,000. In 1924 Congress reimbursed the college $25,000. Richard P. Gildrie and Thomas H. Winn, *A History of Austin Peay State University, 1927–2002* (Clarksville, TN: Austin Peay State Univ., 2002), 11–12.

22. Dr. R. B. McMullen used rooms at First Presbyterian Church to keep the preparatory school operating. Some of the girls who attended classes at the church with Dr. McMullen called themselves the Mullen Stalks.

23. As was common with enslavers, Sarah used the word "servant" to refer to enslaved people. The Kennedy slaves stayed with the Clarksville house that the Parkers rented while Sarah lived at Cloverlands. She was letting D. N. know why she would not take the slaves from the Parkers as he had suggested and at the same time asking his advice on how to handle the situation.

24. Parker was the name of the Unionist who rented D. N. and Sarah's house in Clarksville.

25. It is difficult to know exactly what Sarah meant by "close yankee fashion"; however, one might guess she was suggesting the Parkers did little entertaining and therefore and did not require enslaved labor. This understanding is bolstered by a quote in James M. McPherson's *For Cause & Comrades.* "In June 1863, a lieutenant in the 2nd North Carolina stopped for a meal at the home of a Pennsylvania farmer during the Gettysburg Campaign. 'They live in real Yankee style wife & daughters . . . doing all the work,' he wrote his mother. 'It makes me more than ever devoted to our own Southern institutions.'" James M. McPherson, *For Cause & Comrades: Why Men Fought in the Civil War,* (New York: Oxford Univ. Press, 1997), 107.

26. Phil was one of the Kennedys' enslaved men.

27. The 1860 Montgomery County, Tennessee, Census lists H. M. Acree, dentist, 29, with Caroline Acree, 29, and Sue Acree, 2 months. Horace M. Acree (1828–1923) married Caroline Allen on September 12, 1859, in Montgomery County, Tennessee.

28. Joshua Cobb (1809–1879) was born in Eddyville, Kentucky. He came to Clarksville in 1851. He was a graduate of West Point and a medical doctor, who was reported to have followed the 14th Tennessee Infantry, serving as a doctor. He was a member of Montgomery County Court, mayor of Clarksville twice (1865, 1867–1868), and on the board of Clarksville Female Academy for twenty-five years. His first wife was Julia Mims, and when she died he married Marina Turner Dortch and had seven children and two stepchildren. Sarah's comment about Dr. Cobb's not being "a southern rights man" is interesting. His two sons, Edwin and Robert, died fighting in the Confederate Army. His daughter, Nina, married Lieutenant H. C. Jessup of the US Army in December 1865. Jessup was the son of Judge William Jessup, who introduced Abraham Lincoln at the Republican National Convention in 1860.

29. Lucy Catherine Bailey (1820–1867) was the daughter of Charles Bailey Sr. and Mary (Polly) Bryan Bailey, Sarah's uncle and aunt. "John McQuaide Family Tree," http:www.ancestry.com, accessed October 13, 2020.

30. Because Sarah was sending letters to her husband in Confederate territory, she had to rely on acquaintances going south to carry them. Federal authorities were particularly concerned about preventing the flow of any information that might aid Confederates and numerous guerrillas operating in Middle Tennessee. Policing the mail often turned into a cat-and-mouse game. Networks of Confederate loyalists secretly delivered letters under the noses of Federal officials.

31. Ben was D. N.'s nephew, the son of Aaron Donald Kennedy, D. N. Kennedy's brother. The 1860 Montgomery County, Tennessee, Census lists B. N. Kennedy, 24, merchant, living with D. N. and Sarah and the children.

32. Patsy was an enslaved woman hired from her owners for a set period of time.

33. According to "Rudy's List of Archaic Medical Terms," the term "bilious" described diseases causing a secretion of bile. Bilious remittent fever describes a relapsing fever characterized by bilious vomiting and diarrhea. It was also used to describe cases we now know as yellow fever. https://glossarissimo.wordpress.com /2016/05/26/en-rudys-list-of-archaic-medical-terms-antiquus-morbus-home/, accessed September 12, 2020.

34. Quinine is commonly used to treat malaria, a disease spread by mosquitoes with typical symptoms of high fever, shaking chills, and flu-like symptoms. In the nineteenth century, malaria was prevalent and was one of this country's leading causes of death.

35. At this point Newty was five years old; therefore this comment indicates his language development was delayed.

36. Sarah was referring to Confederate success in Stonewall Jackson's Shenandoah Valley campaign and the success of the Confederate army in turning back the Federal army during McClellan's Seven Days' Battles. Also, in the month before this entry, the Confederate army achieved a victory at the Second Battle of Bull Run.

37. "Rubbins" seems to be a colloquialism for a difficult time, given the context. Clarksville was initially captured by US forces on February 23, 1862. It suffered under a succession of commanders who passed through with troops. A more permanent occupation force of about 300 soldiers from the 71st Ohio under Colonel Rodney Mason was established after the Battle of Shiloh. On August 18, 1862, Mason was bluffed into surrendering by partisan ranger commanders Colonel Thomas Woodward and Colonel Adam Rankin Johnson. Johnson and his troops left to confront Federal troops in Kentucky. Woodward unsuccessfully attacked Federal troops at Fort Donelson and was pursued back to Hopkinsville, Kentucky. Federal troops recaptured Clarksville on September 6 or 7, 1862. Their reoccupation was harsh since Clarksville citizens had aided the Confederate forces. On December 24, 1862, a permanent occupation force was established under Colonel Sanders Bruce.

38. This would have been Union Colonel William Lowe and the 5th Iowa Cavalry, who were chasing Thomas Woodward and his unit after a failed attempt by Woodward to retake Fort Donelson.

39. Throughout the war, Southerners traded rumors back and forth of extreme crimes and conduct of the Federal army. Confederate civilians truly believed that Federal soldiers would rape, murder, and pillage wherever they went. In this case, Sarah was talking about Lowe's Cavalry, which was intent on making Clarksville sorry that the city had supported Colonel Thomas G. Woodward and Colonel Adam Rankin Johnson in briefly retaking the town from Federal occupation. They upset the city so much that a letter of complaint was sent to Confederate President Jefferson Davis. Davis declared Lowe and the 5th Iowa Cavalry criminals so that, if caught, they did not have to be treated as prisoners of war. Benjamin Franklin Cooling, *Fort Donelson's Legacy* (Knoxville: Univ. of Tennessee Press, 1997), 107.

40. M. T. Brockman was listed in the 1860 Montgomery County, Tennessee, Census as a 44-year-old teacher living in the household of Robert French Ferguson.

41. Dr. Charles William Bailey (1826–1897) was a physician in Elkton, Kentucky, a town in Todd County about 25 miles from Clarksville. He was Sarah's first cousin, son of Charles Bailey Sr. and Mary (Polly) Bryan Bailey.

42. Her renter, Mr. Parker, wanted to make a deal to keep the house rent free and have a room for storage while he was in Louisville.

43. Sarah was referring to her Uncle Charles Bailey Sr., listed in the 1860 Montgomery County, Tennessee, Census as a 69-year-old circuit clerk with a personal estate valued at $4,200. In his household were M. B. (Mary "Polly" Bryan Bailey), 61; Lucy, 39; and C. D. (Charles Duncan), 24. Major Charles Bailey Sr. (1791–1863) was born in North Carolina and moved to Clarksville in 1808. He served as clerk of the circuit court from 1836 to his death, with a break from 1852 to 1856, when he was defeated in the election to that office. Titus, *Picturesque Clarksville*, 269.

44. Fanny was one of the Kennedy enslaved women. The Kennedys also owned Fanny's husband.

45. A bone felon is a deep abscess in a fingertip on the palm side, usually caused by Staphylococcus aureus bacteria or herpetic whitlow virus. It causes extreme pain at the fingertip and if left untreated can spread to the bone and cause permanent damage

46. The 1859 Clarksville City Directory lists a Dr. James F. Johnson as a partner with Dr. Edward Branch Haskins. Their office was on the southwest corner of Second and College Streets, where the Haskins residence was also located. The September 15, 1877, *Clarksville Weekly Chronicle* (3), reported that Johnson died on September 12 in Guthrie, Kentucky, of an overdose of morphine. His obituary noted he had served in the Confederate army as a surgeon with the 14th Tennessee Infantry. *Williams' Clarksville Directory City Guide and Business Mirror*, vol. 1, 1859–60 (Clarksville, TN: C. O. Faxon, 1859; repr. Ursula Beach, privately published, 1976).

47. Mollie Meriwether Barker was the eldest child of John Walton and his second wife, Ellen Watson Morris Carr Barker.

48. Cal Meriwether was mentioned in Nannie Haskins Williams' diary on December 9, 1864. The Meriwether family was numerous in Montgomery and surrounding counties but census records did not indicate a Cal or a variation that Cal could have been a common diminutive form of. Cal could have been a nickname.

49. The 1860 Todd County, Kentucky, Census lists Virginia Carney Bailey, 29, and husband Charles William Bailey, 35, physician, with a post office of Elkton, Kentucky. Dr. Bailey was Sarah's cousin, son of Charles Sr. and Mary (Polly) Bryan Bailey.

50. Sarah was referring to herself as Mrs. K.

51. Sarah Kennedy was referring to John Walton Barker, owner of Cloverlands. J. W. Barker was one of the wealthiest landowners in Montgomery County and had a vast tobacco plantation that included land in both Tennessee and Kentucky. The 1860 Montgomery County, Tennessee, Census lists him as 69 years old with real estate valued at $124,000 and a personal estate value of $60,000.

52. C. B. would be Chiles Terrell Barker, born in 1816 to John Walton Barker and his first wife, Mary Minor Meriwether Barker.

53. At the beginning of the war, more than 300 US military officers, along with numerous clerks and officials, resigned to join the Confederacy. Concerned about disloyalty among those who remained, President Abraham Lincoln on April 30, 1861, ordered all military personnel to retake an oath of allegiance. Major General Benjamin Butler as military governor of New Orleans required after October 12, 1861, anyone who wanted to do business in the city or with the US government to take an oath of allegiance to the United States. As the war continued, an oath of allegiance became a test of loyalty for common citizens, particularly in Border States and occupied territory. Jim O'Neal, "Oaths of Loyalty to the U.S. were Common at Time of Civil War," The IC Blog, http://intelligentcollector.com/blog/oaths-of-loyalty-to-the-u-s-were -common-at-time-of-civil-war/, accessed September 12, 2020.

54. On September 22, 1862, President Abraham Lincoln issued a preliminary Emancipation Proclamation which proclaimed that as of January 1, 1863, all the slaves in states that were still in rebellion would be free. Because Tennessee was occupied by the US, it was excluded from the proclamation, but enslaved people still took advantage of Federal occupation and left their owners.

55. *Biddy* was a nineteenth-century slang term for an Irish maid.

56. William T. Dortch, 26, is listed in the 1860 Montgomery County, Tennessee, Census with an occupation of merchant. He had a real estate value of $25,000 and a personal estate value of $6,000. His business was listed in the 1859 Clarksville City Directory as Dortch, Atwell & Co.

57. The Breckinridge Cannel Coal Company was chartered by the Kentucky legislature in 1854. Hancock County had large deposits and Cloverton in Breckinridge County on the Ohio River allowed for cheap shipping to markets.

58. Joseph E. Broaddus is listed in the 1859 Clarksville Directory as living on the southeast corner of Franklin Street and Seventh Street, 41.

59. These Federal soldiers were probably part of Colonel Sanders Bruce's 1st Brigade. At the time of this letter, Bruce made his headquarters in Russellville, Kentucky, and was actively trying to disrupt Confederate partisan ranger activities in both Kentucky and Tennessee.

60. Confederate Colonel Thomas G. Woodward was a Hopkinsville, Kentucky, lawyer and teacher who raised the Oak Grove Rangers, a one-year command accepted into the Confederate army on June 25, 1861. This was a partisan ranger unit which mainly attacked US forces behind their lines.

61. *Jayhawkers* is a term that could either mean a unit from Kansas or an undisciplined, amoral unit comprising murderers and thieves.

62. Miss Margaret Ring was the daughter of Dr. Levi D. Ring. Both Miss Ring and her father were prominent school teachers in Clarksville, Tennessee.

63. Woodville, Mississippi, is the county seat of Wilkinson County in the southwest corner of the state. The town has the oldest continuously published newspaper in Mississippi. It is 545 miles southwest of Clarksville.

64. Bro Willie was probably Wylie Blount Bryan (1814–1887), who married Sarah's sister, Mary Williamson Bailey, on November 23, 1837. The Bryans were living in Woodville, Wilkinson County. He is listed as joining the local Confederate Wilkinson County, Mississippi, Minute Men Company F&S as a captain. Wylie Blount Bryan was the brother of Sarah and Mary's aunt-by-marriage, Mary (Polly) Bryan Bailey, wife of Charles Bailey Sr.

65. *Neuralgia* was a catch-all term for nerve pain which follows the path of a specific nerve.

66. The only Jordan listed in C. Wallace Cross's *Cry Havoc: A History of the 49th Tennessee Volunteer Infantry Regiment, 1861–1865* (Franklin, TN: Hillsboro Press, 2004), 147, is Private John Jordan, who enlisted in Company E of the 49th Tennessee Infantry on April 9, 1863, in Grenada, Mississippi. Because he had lived in Missouri since 1857, he transferred to the 1st Missouri Infantry, Company E.

67. By November of 1862 the 49th was ordered to Port Hudson, Louisiana, twenty miles north of Baton Rouge. They remained at Port Hudson until May of 1863. Cross, *Cry Havoc*, 30.

68. Murfreesboro, Tennessee, is the county seat for Rutherford County. It is 75 miles southeast of Clarksville. The Battle of Stones River, also called the Battle of Murfreesboro, was fought near the city between the Union Army of the Cumberland and the Confederate Army of Tennessee from December 31, 1862, through January 2, 1863. The rival armies suffered a combined total of 23,515 casualties. It was the bloodiest battle of the war by percentage of casualties.

69. At this time there were two bridges crossing the Red River, one on the Hopkinsville Pike near the town and Fort Bruce and the other connecting Franklin

Street with the Russellville Pike. The one on Russellville Pike was farther upriver. Sarah would have been able to see a fire from either bridge from her house, but she referred to the "upper" so it was probably the Russellville Pike bridge.

70. Secesh, a derivative of Secessionist, was a derogatory term for Southerners who supported the Confederacy.

71. The 1860 Montgomery County, Tennessee, Census lists Elizabeth Kennedy Lewis, 29, with her husband, G. B. (George Barbee) Lewis, 36, and children, A. B. (Annie), 6; M. C. (Mary Clark), 4; M. P. (Martha Phelps), 2; E. G. (Emma), 6 months; Laura Kennedy, 18; and R. Coleman, 28, male. Lizzie Kennedy Lewis was D. N.'s niece, the daughter of Jane Peden and William Thompson Kennedy, D. N.'s brother. "Campbell Heyn Public Master Tree," http://www.ancestry.com, accessed October 27, 2020.

72. Whooping cough, or pertussis, is a highly contagious respiratory tract infection. The high-pitched intake of breath followed by the severe hacking cough sounds like "whoop." A vaccine for whooping cough was developed in the 1930s.

73. Laura Kennedy was Lizzie Kennedy Lewis's half-sister. "Campbell Heyn Public Master Tree," http://www.ancestry.com, accessed October 27, 2020.

74. In the fall of 1862, Great Britain came close to recognizing the Confederacy as a separate nation. The horrible bloodshed of the Civil War shook both France and Great Britain, and humanitarians were in favor of interceding to stop it. Two things caused them to postpone intervention until it was no longer feasible. The first was Confederate General Robert E. Lee's invasion of Maryland, which led the British to believe that the Federal Government would suffer yet more losses that would predispose the US government to accept mediation to end the war. The second was Lincoln's preliminary Emancipation Proclamation, which shifted the purpose of the war to ending slavery. The US had also threatened war with any country that recognized the Confederacy as an independent nation. https://www.essentialcivilwar curriculum.com/union-and-confederate-diplomacy-during-the-civil-war.html, accessed on September 28, 2020.

75. Enslavers tried to prevent the enslaved from hearing about the Emancipation Proclamation and the possibility of freedom. Enslaved people gathered information by listening secretly and giving no reaction. They would share information with each other clandestinely. White owners constantly tried to ascertain the amount of knowledge and the plans of their human property.

76. The 1860 Montgomery County, Tennessee, Census lists M. M. Keer, 54, tobacconist, born in Scotland, with E., 25, female; Virginia, 20; William, 18; Lucy C., 12; and George, 9.

77. Bill McCall may have been Private William McCall, who enlisted in Company B of the 49th Tennessee Infantry on November 29, 1861, in Charlotte, Tennessee. He deserted from Fort Donelson on February 6, 1862. Cross, *Cry Havoc*, 160.

78. Bob Johnson may have been Robertson Yeatman Johnson, who enlisted in

Company B of the 49th Tennessee Infantry on December 2, 1861, at Clarksville. He was captured at Fort Donelson and exchanged at Vicksburg, Mississippi, on September 27, 1862. He was promoted to captain on September 27, 1862, and assumed command of the consolidated company on October 12, 1862. Cross, *Cry Havoc*, 146.

79. Hopkinsville, Kentucky, is the county seat of Christian County and is about 30 miles northwest of Clarksville. US troops were stationed there. While Kentucky never joined the Confederate States of America, the western part of the state was pro-Confederate and Federal soldiers were garrisoned there. The Hopkinsville Home Guard was Unionist.

80. This is a reference to Stewart College.

81. Mary Elizabeth Brunson Garland Forbes, widow of Stewart College math professor William A. Forbes and stepdaughter of former US Postmaster General Cave Johnson, lived at 607 North Second Street. William A. Forbes was commissioned a colonel in the 14th Tennessee Infantry in Clarksville in 1861. He was re-elected on April 26, 1862, but was killed in action August 31, 1862, at the Second Battle of Manassas.

82. Mrs. Robb was Mary E. Conrad Robb, widow of Alfred Robb. Alfred Robb practiced law in Clarksville and in 1860 he served as a Tennessee delegate to the Democratic National Convention. He enlisted in Company A of the 49th Tennessee Infantry and was promoted from captain to full lieutenant colonel. He was mortally wounded at Fort Donelson and taken home where he died two days later. The couple had five children: Emma V. Robb Johnson, A. C. Robb, Edward Conrad Robb and twins, Clara Lelia Robb Nisbet and Minnie L. Robb. https://www.find agrave.com/memorial/100559269/alfred-a-robb, accessed September 26, 2020.

83. Smallpox is a viral infection. Initial symptoms are fever and vomiting followed by sores in the mouth and a skin rash which will turn into fluid-filled bumps that eventually scab over and fall off, leaving scars. The smallpox vaccine was the first vaccine, developed in 1796 by British doctor Edward Jenner. He demonstrated the relatively mild cowpox virus conferred immunity against the deadly smallpox virus.

84. John McKeage owned one of Clarksville's first tobacco stemmeries, was on the board of trustees for Stewart College in 1855, and was a trustee of the Clarksville Female Academy. John's wife Rebecca died in 1855. The 1860 Montgomery County, Tennessee, Census lists John, 55, with his children: Ellen McKeage Galbraith, 35; Robert, 27; and William, 19; and granddaughter, Ellen Galbraith, 19.

85. Charlotte Road was where Greenwood Avenue is today. Maps show it to be the section of Greenwood starting at Madison Street and ending where Crossland Avenue is today. Crossland and the other end of Greenwood did not exist then.

86. Sam Kennedy was D. N. Kennedy's nephew. He was the son of James Newton Kennedy.

87. Mr. Clark may have been George W. Clark, who was enlisted in the 49th Tennessee Infantry as wagon master by James Edmund Bailey on January 7, 1862,

at Fort Donelson. He was captured as a prisoner of war on February 16, 1862, and sent to Camp Douglas, Illinois. On August 1, 1862, stating he was a citizen, he was discharged and paroled as being a nonconscript, meaning that he was a citizen not a soldier. Cross, *Cry Havoc*, 105.

88. Russellville, Kentucky, is the county seat of Logan County. It is about 45 miles northeast of Clarksville.

89. Mr. Barker was probably John Walton Barker.

90. Mr. Ferguson was probably Robert French Ferguson.

91. Clarksville did have publicly funded schools; in 1858, 10 cents of the $1 per $100 value property tax went to public schools. Ursula Smith Beach, *Along the Warioto: A History of Montgomery County, Tennessee* (Nashville: McQuiddy Press, 1964), 160–61. However, wealthier residents like the Kennedys were more likely to send their children to one of the private schools operating in Clarksville. In later letters, Sarah mentions White Hall School, operated by sisters Lucy Fielding and Mollie Ward; Mrs. Bemiss's school; and L. D. Ring's Clarksville High School.

92. Patrick Henry was the youngest son of Marion and Gustavus Adolphus Henry Sr. He was listed as age 14 in the 1860 Montgomery County, Tennessee, Census. Henry was a graduate of the Virginia Military Institute, class of 1867. He and fellow Clarksvillian Clay Stacker were with the VMI Corps of Cadets who fought as a unit at the Battle of New Market in Virginia on May 15, 1864. At this battle, 257 cadets were on the field; 10 cadets were killed in battle or died later from the effects of their wounds, and 45 were wounded. The cadets ranged in age from 15 to 25. "The Battle of New Market, May 15, 1864," Virginia Military Institute website, https://www.vmi.edu/archives/manuscripts/new-market-vmi-in-the -civil-war/battle-of-new-market/, accessed March 8, 2013.

93. Colonel Sanders Bruce was a Unionist from Lexington, Kentucky. He helped raise the 20th Kentucky Infantry Regiment and commanded the 22nd Brigade of Nelson's Army of the Ohio at the Battle of Shiloh in April 1862. He became ill after the battle and after recovery served as Commander at Bowling Green, Kentucky; Russellville, Kentucky; Clarksville, Tennessee; and finally, Louisville, Kentucky. He resigned from the Army in June 1864.

94. Brigadier General John Hunt Morgan (1825–1864) was nicknamed the "Thunderbolt of the Confederacy" for leading successful raids against US forces in Kentucky and Tennessee.

95. Lieutenant General Nathan Bedford Forrest (1821–1877) was nicknamed the "Wizard of the Saddle" because of his daring and genius use of cavalry tactics. He was perhaps the most successful cavalry commander of the Confederacy. He joined the Confederate army as a private and rose to become the most feared cavalry commander in the war.

96. Seven Mile Ferry operated on the Cumberland River south of Clarksville in Montgomery County.

97. Several Montgomery County diaries and letters commented on the foraging of Federal troops. Serepta Jordan wrote on January 29, 1863: "Col. Bruce continues to send out his forage wagons, the country for miles around has been stripped of everything eatable either for man or beast. Some of the poorest families are left almost without a sufficient amount for the next month much less during the coming year." Uffelman et al., *Diary of Serepta Jordan*, 345. In February 1863, John Nicholas Barker made numerous diary entries like this one: "Links took 9 loads of hay and 7000 lbs. corn by Lt. John B. Brown." (*Links* is short for Lincolnites.) February 20, 1863, entry, John Nicholas Barker, unpublished diaries (1843–1868), microfilm 878, Brown Harvey Sr. Genealogy Room, Clarksville-Montgomery County Public Library, Clarksville, Tennessee. See also note 110 below.

98. Tex was the nickname of Louisa McTyler Barker, born in 1844 to John Walton Barker and his second wife, Ellen Watson Morris Carr.

99. Colonel Sanders Bruce married Isabelle (Labelle) Combs, daughter of General Leslie Combs, on January 27, 1848. They were divorced in Russellville on October 13, 1863, and Bruce was awarded custody of their four children.

100. Thomas McCulloch, listed in the 1860 Montgomery County, Tennessee, Census as a 43-year-old merchant, served as a steward of Madison Street United Methodist Church. Eleanor S. Williams, *Worship along the Warioto: Montgomery County, Tennessee* (Clarksville, TN: First Federal Savings Bank, 1995), 295.

101. Madison Street United Methodist Church was one of the large downtown churches. The other three were First Presbyterian, First Baptist, and Trinity Episcopal.

102. Sarah is commenting that many in the congregation at Madison Street United Methodist Church chose to attend her church, First Presbyterian, rather than listen to the Federal army chaplain.

103. Originally, Clarksville had three forts. The main fort was located on a cliff in New Providence. The Confederates named it Fort Sevier and the Federals renamed it Fort Bruce. Another fort, Fort Clark, was built closer to Clarksville and situated in the flood plain of the Cumberland River. A third fort was built farther up the Red River and called Fort Terry. Since the US was interested in controlling traffic on the Hopkinsville Pike (currently 41A), they expanded Fort Sevier and possibly built a small fortification for cannon across the Pike. When Union Flag Officer A. H. Foote sailed past Fort Sevier to claim Clarksville after the fall of Fort Donelson, he saw a white flag flying in what he called Fort Defiance. That name for Fort Sevier, later Fort Bruce, has stuck and was chosen for the current city-owned Fort Defiance Civil War Park and Interpretive Center.

104. J. E. B. was Sarah's first cousin, James Edmund Bailey, son of Charles and Polly Bailey. The 1860 Montgomery County, Tennessee, Census lists J. E. Bailey, 37, lawyer, in a household with E. (Elizabeth "Lizzie" Margaret Lusk) Bailey, 29; Matilda, 5; and James, 1. Colonel James Edmund Bailey enlisted as a captain in

Company A of the 49th Tennessee Infantry on November 29, 1861, in Clarksville. He was promoted to colonel on December 24, 1861. Captured and arrested with other officers at Fort Donelson, he was sent to Camp Chase, Ohio, transferred to Fort Warren in the Boston Harbor, then to Fort Monroe, Virginia, for exchange on July 31, 1862. He was recommended for promotion to brigadier general by the secretary of war in June 1863. Cross, *Cry Havoc*, 90–91.

105. Mrs. Forbes' house on North Second Street in Clarksville still stands.

106. Nannie Garland and her sister, Bettie, were daughters of Mary Elizabeth Brunson Garland Forbes and her first husband, deceased Clarksville attorney Hudson Garland. The 1860 Montgomery County, Tennessee, Census lists Bettie, 16, with sister, Nannie, 19, in the household of W. A. Forbes. Nannie Garland died on May 6, 1863.

107. The 1860 Montgomery County, Census lists F. S. Beaumont, 27, merchant; L. E. (Laura E. Conrad), 21; Ida H., 5; and Georgia, 1. The Slave Schedule lists four slaves. Captain Frank Beaumont died in 1861 in Virginia of typhoid fever. Sarah Kennedy's letter on November 9, 1863, describes the Beaumont house burning.

108. The 1860 Montgomery County, Tennessee, Census lists James Hunt, 40, farmer, in the household with Mary, 37; Thomas, 12; Penelope, 10; James, 5; and Susan, 1.

109. Johnson's Island is a 300-acre island in Sandusky Bay, three miles from the city of Sandusky, Ohio. Near the southern shore of Lake Erie, the island was fairly isolated, accessible by boat except in winter. The military prison was built to house up to 2,500 Confederate officers. Eventually it held privates, political prisoners, spies and people sentenced by court martial, and civilians arrested as guerrillas. In the final months of the war, its population peaked at 3,200 officers and enlisted men. Nevertheless, Johnson's Island had one of the lowest mortality rates of any Civil War prison. "Johnson's Island," Touring Ohio website, http://touringohio.com /history/johnson-island.html, accessed June 8, 2021.

110. Foraging was the procedure of procuring rations and forage (food for animals) and replacing broken-down animals for the Army. During an active campaign, soldiers procured rations wherever they could find them. The ideal procedure was for an officer to accompany the soldiers tasked to get these provisions and to give receipts for everything taken. If there was lax discipline among the troops or lax enforcement of the rules of war, then soldiers would take anything they wanted from civilians and would engage in wanton destruction with the excuse that they did not want to leave anything for the enemy to use. Colonel Sanders Bruce was intent on winning the civilians back to the Union and strictly enforced rules against pillaging and indiscriminate destruction of property. "Foraging and Looting," Ency-clopedia.com, https://www.encyclopedia.com/history/applied-and-social-sciences -magazines/foraging-and-looting, accessed June 8, 2021.

111. The Reverend T. Delacey Wardlaw, D. D., was born in Ireland and graduated

from King's College in Belfast. He was pastor of First Presbyterian Church in the 1860s. He refused to sign the oath as ordered and was arrested. He left Clarksville in 1863 or 1864 for Canada, but returned by the end of July 1864. Later he left for Philadelphia but was back in Clarksville at First Presbyterian in August 1865. Wardlaw was professor at Southwestern Presbyterian University, which succeeded Stewart College on the same site in 1875. He was also a physician. He died August 22, 1879, in Shelbyville, Tennessee.

112. The 1859 Clarksville Directory lists Bryce Stewart as a tobacco buyer on the northeast corner of Third Street and Main. Born in Scotland in 1811, he was married first to Eliza J. McClure and second to Sallie West Cobb, daughter of Dr. Joshua Cobb and Marina Turner Dortch Cobb. Bryce and Eliza had four children; Bryce and Sallie had a son named Norman Stewart.

113. Aleck Barker may have been John Walton Barker's nephew. He was the son of Alexander Meriwether Barker, John Walton Barker's brother, and Lucy Ann Meriwether Barker.

114. The 1860 Montgomery County, Tennessee, Census lists J. L. Johnson, 40, farmer, in the household with Virginia, 32; B. W., 19, male; and R. T., 16, male.

115. The 1860 Montgomery County, Tennessee, Census lists R. M. Humphreys, 35, lawyer, in the household with M. W., 26, female; Nannie, 9; Elizabeth, 7; and Caroline, 4.

116. The Federal army established headquarters for a military prison on present-day Legion Street, known locally as "Davie's bank" after one of its owners, Ambers Davie. Wentworth Morris in "The Davie Home" wrote: "Some of the offenses for which Southerners were imprisoned were those of being a 'rebel agent,' a 'spy,' a 'guerrilla,' or of 'giving information to guerrillas,' 'capturing a Union man,' or of 'helping a citizen to get a negro outside the Union lines.' In every month one or two persons were charged with violating their oath to support the United States." He noted that the greatest single cause of imprisonment was for stealing horses and mules. Wentworth S. Morris, "The Davie Home and the Register of the Federal Prison at Clarksville," *Tennessee Historical Quarterly* 8, no. 3 (1949), 250–51.

117. The First and Second Confiscation Acts enabled the US Army to "confiscate" Confederate property, including slaves, whether they had been used in the war effort or not. Slaves who had been "pressed" to work for the US usually were not returned to their owners. They formed a vital labor force that facilitated the Federal war effort. In Clarksville, Federal soldiers were concerned about controlling the roads into and out of the town. The fortifications they inherited from the Confederates were built to control river access, so Black men were pressed into service to monitor land routes. At the beginning of the occupation, the US did not differentiate between enslaved and free Black men when gathering their labor force. "The Confiscation Acts of 1861 and 1862," The United States Senate, https://www.senate.gov/artandhistory/history/common/generic/ConfiscationActs.htm, accessed June 8, 2021.

118. Dr. Walter Harding Drane (1824–1865) was a physician and later tobacco farmer in Montgomery County. In 1843 he moved his family from the College Street home to a farm on Hopkinsville Road. Three of his sons fought for the Confederacy, and Drane himself volunteered his services near his sons' units in Virginia and West Virginia. The Drane Family papers are housed in the Tennessee State Library and Archives, Microfilm Accession Number 1143.

119. Drane's Pond was a large pond north of present-day College Street just above the intersection with Third Street. It no longer exists but the area is prone to flooding during heavy rains.

120. This action was part of John Hunt Morgan's Christmas Raid on Kentucky. The purpose of this raid was to disrupt the Federal supply line and provide some relief for Confederate General Braxton Bragg's army. On December 27, 1862, Morgan captured Elizabethtown, Kentucky. The following day, Morgan attacked the stockade guarding the two wooden railroad trestles on Muldraugh's Hill and successfully captured them and burned both trestles. During this raid, Morgan destroyed six railroad bridges and captured 1,877 prisoners. Betty J. Gorin, "Morgan is Coming!" *Confederate Raiders in the Heartland of Kentucky* (Louisville: Harmony House Publishers, 2006), 64–97.

121. This entry is an example of unfounded rumor. John Hunt Morgan terrorized Indiana and Ohio until he and 360 of his men were captured by US forces in Salineville, Ohio, on July 26, 1863.

122. Sara Louisa Fisler married her minister, the reverend Thomas Delacey Wardlaw, nine years her senior, in April 1852 in Port Carbon, Pennsylvania.

123. Colonel James M. Shackelford was commander of the United States 8th Kentucky Cavalry Regiment.

124. Water levels in the Cumberland River vary during a single year. At certain times of year, specific parts of the river are impassable to regular boats. Light draft steamers are boats that measure less from keel (the bottom of the boat) to deck so they displace less water. They are made to operate in shallow water.

125. Dr. Levi D. Ring opened one of the earliest area high schools called the Collegiate Institute in his home on Fifth Street, Clarksville. By 1859 he was listed in Clarksville Directory, 65, as principal of Clarksville High School on the east side of Fifth Street between Franklin and Commerce Streets. His daughter, Margaret, taught music.

126. Aunt Lucy was the oldest of the Kennedy enslaved women. Her age is listed as 60 on the 1860 Montgomery County, Tennessee, Slave Schedule. Slave Schedules listed gender and age only. No enslaved people were listed by name in the census. The only way to know an enslaved person's name is from another source such as this letter.

127. The 1860 Montgomery County, Tennessee, Census lists A. G. (Amanda Green) Munford, 32, housekeeper; W. B., male, 18, law student; A. H., 11; E. H.,

female, 9; L. G., male, 6; E. S., male, 3; and W. H., male, 7 months. It also lists real estate valued at $16,000 and personal estate valued at $27,000.

128. Julia Anderson was the daughter of Thompson Anderson and Mary Shelby Johnson. The 1850 Montgomery County, Tennessee, Census lists Thompson Anderson, 36, merchant with real estate valued at $10,800. Listed with him are Mary S., 34; Julia F, 12; Martha H., 10; Laura M., 6; Thompson Jr., 2; and Mary, 1 month.

129. In a letter dated February 6, 1865, Sarah mentioned that she had planned to send her daughter Mary to school with Mrs. Bemiss to study French.

130. Edward Branch Haskins was a prominent Clarksville physician and the father of Nanny Haskins Williams. Uffelman et al., *Diary of Nannie Haskins Williams*.

131. Balm of Gilead is a small tree that grows from ten to twelve feet high. Its bark is a rich brown and it has wand-like spreading branches with small scanty leaves. This plant does not do well outside of the Middle East and was rare even in 1863.

132. Confederate Cavalry General Joseph Wheeler captured four large transport boats and destroyed three on the Cumberland River near Harpeth Shoals in January 1863.

133. Federal Brigadier General James M. Shackelford was a Kentuckian who fought in the Mexican War and returned home to study law. At the start of the Civil War, Shackelford raised the 25th Kentucky Infantry Regiment, which he commanded during the Battle of Fort Donelson. He was forced, through ill health resulting from exposure during the battle, to resign. At Lincoln's request, he later raised the 8th Kentucky Cavalry, which was part of Bruce's Brigade when he occupied Clarksville in December of 1862. Promoted to brigadier general on January 1, 1863, he was in command of 1st Brigade, 2nd Division, 23rd Corps at the time of this letter.

134. Major Joseph M. Kennedy of the US 8th Kentucky Cavalry was in the area around Clarksville from September 1862 through the spring of 1863. Kennedy led a night march to engage Confederate Colonel Thomas Woodward at Camp Coleman in Todd County, Kentucky, successfully dispersing the whole force. "8th Regiment, Kentucky Cavalry (Union)," https://www.familysearch.org/wiki/en/8th_Regiment ,_Kentucky_Cavalry_(Union), accessed October 15, 2020.

135. D. N. and Major Joseph M. Kennedy almost certainly were related and may very well have known each other, since D. N.'s parents were married in Garrard County where Major Kennedy lived. The Kennedys were a large and successful family in early Madison and Garrard Counties of Kentucky. Popular lore suggests Harriet Beecher Stowe, author of *Uncle Tom's Cabin*, visited the Thomas Kennedy home in the Paint Lick section of Garrard County in her only visit to the South while gathering material for the book. The cabin said to have formed the basis of her novel was an actual structure behind the plantation house. Gerald R. Tudor, "Fiction, Fact, and Embellishment: The Kennedys and Uncle Tom's Cabin," http:// freepages.rootsweb.com/~josephkennedy/genealogy/Source%20Materials /Kennedy/fiction_fact_and_embellishment.htm, accessed October 14, 2020.

136. Garrard County, Kentucky, is in the Bluegrass Region and is about 215 miles northeast of Clarksville.

137. Isabina Parker and her husband had rented the Kennedys' house.

138. Smithland is the county seat of Livingston County, Kentucky, at the confluence of the Ohio and Cumberland Rivers. Smithland is part of the Paducah, Kentucky-Illinois Metropolitan Statistical Area. The goods must have been shipped down the Ohio River to the Cumberland River, which flows past Clarksville.

139. "Co. Bailey" was probably Sarah's cousin Colonel James Edmund Bailey of the 49th Tennessee Infantry.

140. William B. Munford Jr., enlisted on November 29, 1861, at Clarksville. He was captured at Fort Donelson and sent to Camp Douglas, Illinois, and exchanged in Vicksburg, Mississippi, on September 16, 1862. In 1862 his name was on hospital rolls in both Marion and Clinton, Mississippi. He was assigned to Brigadier General William Andrew Quarles' staff as a clerk from September 20 to December 31, 1863, at Brigade Headquarters. He was killed in action at Franklin, Tennessee. Cross, *Cry Havoc*, 167.

141. Mr. Leonard was perhaps T. D. Leonard. The 1860 Montgomery County, Tennessee, Census lists him as a 46-year-old farmer in a household with F. L., 48, female; M. L., 10, female; and Robert Teakman, 32, laborer.

## Chapter 2

1. The 1860 Montgomery County, Tennessee, Census lists B. W. Macrae, 29, merchant, in a household with Alice, 22; Virginia, 2; and Mary, 6 months. Macrae owned real estate valued at $16,000 and had a personal estate value of $16,000. In several letters, Sarah mentioned him as someone she turned to for financial advice.

2. Sarsaparilla is a tropical plant native to South America, Jamaica, Mexico, and the West Indies and found in rain forests. It was used for a wide variety of ailments including joint disease and general infections. If Sarah thought her daughter's illness was caused by her shoulder and spine, this would have been a logical treatment for the time. https://www.healthline.com/health/food-nutrition/sarsaparilla#benefits, accessed February 9, 2021.

3. George Lent Marr was born about 1835 and was the sixth child of Constant Hardin Perkins Marr and Elizabeth Stuart White Marr. He was the younger brother of Duncan Marr, a local businessman and slave trader. George enlisted in the 10th Kentucky Cavalry, Company B, was captured at Smithville Point, Kentucky, on August 20, 1864, and held at Camp Morton, Indiana. He was transferred for exchange on February 19, 1865. Sarah Kennedy, Duncan Marr, and George Marr were second cousins. Their grandmothers were sisters. "Griffin Williams Family Tree," http://www.ancestry.com, accessed June 26, 2021.

4. Henry Allen enlisted as a private in Company A, 14th Tennessee Volunteer Infantry Regiment, on May 14, 1861, in Clarksville. The 1860 Montgomery County, Tennessee, Census lists him as 18 years old in the household of D. L. Allen, 33, laborer, with Mary, 25; Eliza, 22; and Margret, 34, with a post office in Palmyra, Tennessee.

5. "Old Wines" was probably Guy Wines, wartime postmaster. See chapter 3, note 5. To start a business in an occupied town, the owners and anyone working for them had to take the oath of allegiance. Each time people entered or left an area of occupation, they had to receive a pass from the Federal commander. Despite the difficulties, Clarksville was desperate for goods. Businesses may have been short lived in the turmoil of war.

6. In nineteenth-century slang, "mushroom" referred to a person who had suddenly come into wealth; an upstart. The word was an allusion to the fungus that pops up overnight. Candice Hern, "Regency Glossary," https://candicehern.com /regency-world/glossary/, accessed October 14, 2020.

7. This firm was probably a short-lived business. They were not listed in the 1859 Clarksville Business Directory and no mention of them has been found after the war.

8. Sarah was possibly referring to B. R. Peart, who is listed in the 1860 Montgomery County, Tennessee, Census as a 47-year-old stonemason living with Ophelia, 17, and Columbus, 13. Peart's real estate value is listed as $8,500 and his personal estate value as $3,500. His house was listed in a sheriff sale announcement in the *Clarksville Chronicle* on December 8, 1865, as "a large and comfortable two-story brick house."

9. In August 1862, the Confederate army erected earthworks at Port Hudson, Louisiana, in an effort to deny the US control of the Mississippi River. In December 1862 the Federal army sent 31,000 troops commanded by General Nathaniel P. Banks to New Orleans. They arrived on December 14 and immediately moved to reoccupy Baton Rouge. Sometime in late October or early November of 1862, the 49th Tennessee Infantry, CSA, was ordered to Port Hudson where they remained until May 1863. The increase in Federal troops alarmed Confederates, who sent Major General Franklin Gardener to take command of Port Hudson. On May 21, 1863, General Banks moved against Port Hudson in support of General Ulysses S. Grant's fight at Vicksburg. Banks commanded five divisions, including two African American units, the 1st and 3rd Louisiana Native Guards. After frontal assaults were repulsed, the US settled into a siege, which was the longest in US military history up to this point. Vicksburg fell to the US on July 4, 1863. After receiving news of Vicksburg's fall, the Confederate garrison at Port Hudson surrendered on July 9, 1863.

10. In her April 19, 1863, diary entry, Nannie Haskins mentioned on a trip to nearby Oak Grove, Kentucky: "I was astonished to find goods there so much cheaper than they are here. I got beautiful calico for 33 cts. per yard. Everything else is as cheap in proportion." Uffelman et al., *Diary of Nannie Haskins Williams*, 16. For

a more detailed explanation of cost of goods in Clarksville, see Stephen V. Ash, "A Community at War: Montgomery County, 1861–65," *Tennessee Historical Quarterly* 36, no. 1 (Spring 1977): 41–42.

11. E. J. McClure was Eliza Jane White McClure, eldest child of William Stewart White and Lucy Walton Sherman White. She married Warren Clark McClure on May 31, 1846. Her younger sister, Robena (Bene) E. White, married John H. Van Culin. Before the war, Eliza and Warren moved to Memphis. The 1860 Shelby County, Tennessee, Census listed W. C. McClure, 45; Elisa McClure, 37; Lucy McClure, 8; and Noland White, 21, in Memphis in Ward 7. Sarah and E. J. were cousins through the Whites because their grandmothers were sisters. The McClures seem to have been living in or near Woodville, Mississippi, where D. N. was. Whether they had fled Memphis, which was occupied by the Federal army from June 6, 1862, or the family had followed Warren McClure with the Confederate army is unclear.

12. Port Hudson, Louisiana, did not fall until July 9, 1863.

13. E. J. McC. was Eliza Jane White McClure.

14. In the letters Sarah consistently misspelled Van Culin as Van Croylen. The 1860 New Orleans, Ward 1, Census, lists John H. Van Culin, 35, merchant, in the household with Robina E., 23, born in Tennessee, and Lucy W. White, 59, born in Virginia. Van Culin's birthplace is listed as New Jersey and his personal estate was valued at $1,800.

15. Cousin Sue Marr was Susan Perkins Marr McLean, born in 1830, third child of Constant Hardin Perkins Marr and Elizabeth Stuart White. Susan Marr's grandmother, Margaret Williamson, was the sister of Sarah's grandmother, Mary Williamson. "Griffin Williams Family Tree," http://www.ancestry.com, accessed June 26, 2021.

16. George Warfield was probably George W. Warfield, listed in the 1860 Montgomery County, Tennessee, Census as age 17 in the household with G. H., male, 56; E., female, 37; Amanda, 11; Charles, 9; Joseph, 8; Nannie, 7; P. H., female, 5; S. J., male, 2; and Luther, male, 1 month. G. H. Warfield is listed as a farmer with real estate valued at $54,000 and a personal estate valued at $55,000. He served as a sergeant in the 50th Tennessee Infantry Regiment. Bud Warfield could have been one of George's three living brothers: James Harvey Warfield, Samuel D. Warfield, or Jacob Warfield. The 10th Tennessee Infantry Regiment was recruited from Davidson, Humphreys, Giles, and Montgomery Counties. It served at Forts Henry and Donelson, in Mississippi, in engagements from Chickamauga to Atlanta, and moved back to Tennessee with General John Bell Hood.

17. Grenada, Mississippi, is the county seat of Grenada County. It is 300 miles southeast of Clarksville.

18. Brigadier General Lloyd Tilghman, an engineer from Paducah, Kentucky, was in charge of building Fort Henry on the Tennessee River and Fort Donelson on the Cumberland. He was in command of both places but remained at Fort Henry

when it was attacked and surrendered. He was held at Fort Warren in Boston until he was exchanged. He then commanded a brigade in Mansfield Lovell's division of Earl van Dorn's Army of the West. Tilghman was killed at the Battle of Champion's Hill, Mississippi.

19. Matthew McClung was born in Knoxville, Tennessee, on March 11, 1833, to Matthew McClung Sr. and Elizabeth Jane Morgan. He married Julia Frances Anderson on April 27, 1858, in Nashville, Tennessee. The 1860 Davidson County, Tennessee, Census finds Matthew living with his father-in-law and family in Nashville's Ward 5. Matthew, 26, was a merchant with a personal estate of $10,000. Julia, 23, and Mary, 6 months, were also living with him.

20. Cousin Will was probably Wilmoth Boyd Bailey, widow of Charles Sr. and Polly's son, Henry Lewis Bailey (1818–1848).

21. Mr. L was perhaps T. D. Leonard, mentioned as a letter carrier in earlier letters.

22. Pneumonia is an infection of the lungs which causes the alveoli, or air sacs, to fill with fluids. This inflammation interferes with the ability to absorb oxygen into the blood stream or release carbon dioxide. Severe cases are fatal.

23. By the winter of 1862–1863, the Federal blockade began to limit the Confederacy's export of cotton. The price of 92 cents per pound in New York was a good price. D. N. may have been considering using Clarksville's status as occupied territory to sell cotton in New York. But in doing so, he would have been tacitly giving up on the single great advantage the South assumed it had had when the war began—cotton needed by mills in Great Britain. On the other hand, there was the possibility of losing everything by sending cotton to Liverpool if it was stopped by the Federal blockade. Interview with Professor Gregory Zieren, Austin Peay State University History Department, October 12, 2020.

24. Major Joshua Elder is listed in the 1860 Montgomery County, Tennessee, Census as a 55-year-old broker. He is listed with M. M., female, 30; John, 7; and Martin, 4. His real estate value is listed as $102,880 and personal estate value of $75,000.

25. Cousin Lucy White was perhaps Lucy Walton Sherman White, wife of William Stewart White and mother of Eliza Jane White McClure.

26. Puny is colloquial for poor health in this context. Puny can mean slight, thin, or weak.

27. Dr. Lycurgus L. Lurton is listed in the 1870 Montgomery County, Tennessee, Census as a physician, age 49, with a personal estate valued at $5,000 and real estate valued at $3,500. Listed in his household are Sarah A., 46; N. H., 20; Edmond B., 21; Frank L., 19; Fannie, 24; and Kata, 1. Lurton, a practicing medical doctor turned Episcopal priest, moved to Clarksville during the war. One of his sons, Horace Harmon Lurton, fought with Brigadier General John Hunt Morgan's cavalry. After the war, as a successful Clarksville lawyer, Horace Lurton was elected in 1886 to the Tennessee Supreme Court and then in 1910 appointed by President William Howard Taft to the US Supreme Court.

28. The French word "douche" means a shower or a stream of water. While frequently associated with feminine hygiene, that is unlikely to be its prescription here. The Kennedys may have had a tub with a shower, or Sarah may have poured a stream of water over Mary's shoulder and back. Historian Maureen Ogle writes of the "sheer whimsy" of showers that proliferated in homes in the early nineteenth century. Ogle, *All the Modern Conveniences*, cited in Sarah Zhang, "Showering Has a Dark, Violent History," *The Atlantic*, December 11, 2018, https://www.theatlantic .com/health/archive/2018/12/dark-history-of-showering/577636/, accessed September 28, 2020.

29. Sarah used the word *gravel* twice in the letters to describe kidney stones. Email from Civil War historian Glenna Schroeder-Lein, December 7, 2022.

30. The "interesting situation" was her pregnancy. In her May 25, 1863, letter, Sarah noted Mrs. Wardlaw had a three-week-old daughter. From November 20, 1861, for a period of nearly four years nothing was recorded in the First Presbyterian Church session minutes except the baptism of Varina Davis Wardlaw, Thomas and Sara Wardlaw's daughter, on April 4, 1864. Phil Kemmerly, "1862–1881: War, Reconstruction, and Cultural Upheaval: A World Turned Upside Down," in *Following the Faith: A Bicentennial History of First Presbyterian Church, Clarksville*, ed. Ellen Kanervo (Clarksville, TN: Amazon Kindle Direct Publishing, 2022), 64–95.

31. The old Montgomery County fairgrounds was on Dunbar Cave Road in Clarksville. It comprised 43 acres between the rail line and Russellville Pike. Paul Hyatt, Marie Riggins, Ralph Winters, and Thurston L. Lee, "One Hundred Years of County Fair in Montgomery County, Tennessee," Clarksville-Montgomery County Historical Society, 1960.

32. The Battle of Dover, also known as the Second Battle of Fort Donelson, occurred on February 3, 1863. Confederate Generals Joseph Wheeler and Nathan Bedford Forrest attacked Fort Donelson expecting to overwhelm a small, weak Federal garrison. The US troops were prepared for them and repulsed the Confederates, inflicting heavy losses on them. The battle effectively ended when both sides ran out of ammunition. The Confederates retired.

33. Alfred Robb and James Edmund Bailey were law partners. Their office would have been vacant because Colonel Robb had been killed at Fort Donelson in 1862, and Colonel Bailey was serving with the 49th Tennessee Infantry.

34. Enslavers were aware of enslaved persons freeing themselves, how they chose to do it, and where they went. In this case, Sarah thought it newsworthy to tell D. N. that her cousin's enslaved woman, Zillah, left for Nashville.

35. Caroline Pritchett may have been another enslaved person leaving for freedom. No Caroline Pritchett was listed in the 1860 Montgomery County Census. Enslaved people's names were not listed, only the gender and age.

36. Mollie Allen was probably Mary Allen, listed as age twenty-five in the 1860 Montgomery County, Tennessee, Census in the household with D. L., Eliza, Henry,

and Margret. Sarah had written of Henry Allen's arrest in her February 9, 1863, letter, his refusal to take the oath of allegiance and subsequent incarceration, and of his escape from jail in her February 28, 1863, letter.

37. The Clarksville Female Academy was located on Madison Street, Clarksville, Tennessee, and was a prestigious school for young women.

38. Mr. Macrae was probably B. W. Macrae, listed as age 29, merchant, in the 1860 Montgomery County, Tennessee, Census with Alice, 22; Virginia, 2; and Mary, 6 months.

39. Dr. Bailey was probably his son, Dr. Charles William Bailey, who had a medical practice in Elkton, Kentucky.

40. T. F. Munford was listed in the 1859 Clarksville City Directory as Clerk and Master of Chancery Court. The 1860 Montgomery County, Tennessee, Census lists T. F., 51; M. A. (Mary Ann), 44; L. C. (Lucretia), 16; Betty, 12; C. L., male, 10; R. V. B. Killebrew, female, 6. R. V. B. Killebrew lists a real estate value of $5,000 and personal real estate of $5,000. Mary Ann Munford was a Killebrew before marriage.

41. The 1870 Montgomery County, Tennessee, Census lists M. Mattill, male, 53, carpenter, in the household with D. W. Mattill, 30, male; George H. Mattill, 28; Joe C. Mattill, 16; and Jemill B. Mattill, 14, female.

42. The 1859 Clarksville City Directory listed C. H. Roberts with a lumber yard on the wharf between Franklin and Commerce Streets and a Saddle and Harness shop on the south side of Franklin Street between First and Second Streets.

43. The 1859 Clarksville City Directory listed John S. Lay, a butcher, on the southwest corner of Seventh and College Streets.

44. The 1859 Clarksville City Directory listed Stephen M. Woodrum, blacksmith, south side of Commerce Street between 3rd and Hiter Streets.

45. The 1859 Clarksville City Directory listed William Abbott, moulder, working at Whitfield, Bradley & Co. Iron Foundry.

46. Elija Broaddus is listed in the 1860 Montgomery County, Tennessee, Census as a 45-year-old butcher in a household with M. A. Broaddus, female, 42; Edward Broaddus, 19; and J. W. Broaddus, male, 10.

47. G. Lewis was George Lewis, D. N.'s nephew by marriage. His wife, Lizzie Kennedy Lewis, was the daughter of D. N.'s brother, William Thompson Kennedy.

48. The original Tennessee State Penitentiary opened on Church Street in Nashville on January 1, 1831, with 200 cells, a warden's residence, and a hospital. In 1863, the Federal army commandeered the state penitentiary to use as a military prison. Under US occupation, the prison population tripled. Convicts were leased to the federal government by the Occupation Government of Tennessee to help repay their mounting debts.

49. Duncan Marr was listed as a "Slave Trader" on page 79 of the 1859 Clarksville Directory and is listed in the 1860 Montgomery County, Tennessee, Census

as a 33-year-old farmer with a personal estate valued at $39,700 and real estate valued at $42,900. Born about 1827, he was the second child of C. Hardin P. and Elizabeth Marr. His obituary in 1907 was topped with the headline, "An Old Land Mark Dead." Duncan Marr was connected in business with Bryce Stewart. Irene Griffey, *Riverview Cemetery: Looking Back to Those Who've Gone Before* (Clarksville, TN: Montgomery County Historical Society, 2002). In the Federal Writers' Project publication *Slave Narrative: A Folk History of Slavery in the United States from Interviews with Former Slaves,* Mary Wright related the story that "Mr. Dunk Morr's" slave market sold stolen enslaved people who had been promised freedom and instead were resold in Clarksville (vol. 7, p. 64). His slave pen was on Franklin Street off the public square.

50. Lucy Walton Sherman White was the mother of Eliza Jane White McClure and Robena (Bene) White Van Culin.

51. Photography technology had improved so that it was common for people to pose for portraits to send to loved ones. Images from this time are unsmiling and stiff because people had to hold the pose and not move for a long while or the image would be blurred.

52. Edward Walton Barker enlisted as a private in the Confederate 2nd Kentucky Cavalry Regiment (Duke's) on November 1, 1862. "U.S., Civil War Soldier Records and Profiles, 1861–1865," http://www.ancestry.com, accessed September 26, 2020. The 1860 Montgomery County, Tennessee, Census lists E. W. Barker, 23, tobacconist, living in the household of Jacob and Barba Powers.

53. Camp Morton was a prisoner-of-war camp established on the fairgrounds of Indianapolis, Indiana, to house noncommissioned officers and privates. The first Confederate prisoners arrived on February 22, 1862. It was one of the largest prisoner-of-war camps the US operated. The last prisoners left on June 12, 1865.

54. John Van Culin was married to E. J. McClure's sister, Robena.

55. Nannie Haskins wrote of Charles Bailey Sr.'s funeral: "Last Sunday evening Major Bailey, 69, one of the oldest citizens of Clarksville, departed this life. Monday at 3 o'clock p.m. his funeral was preached at the Presbyterian Church by the Reverend T. D. Wardlaw. The house was crowded to overflowing. He was a peaceable citizen, a kind father, and a devoted husband. What more could be said of man!" Uffelman et al., *Diary of Nannie Haskins Williams,* 12.

56. Cousin Margaret was probably Margaret Jane Bryan, daughter of James Hardy Bryan and Margaret Bailey. Margaret Bailey was the sister of Sarah's uncle Charles Bailey Sr., and James Hardy Bryan was the father of Charles Bailey Sr.'s wife Polly Bryan Bailey.

57. The 1860 Montgomery County, Tennessee, Census lists Lucy Donoho, 22, in the household of Dr. Thomas J. Donoho, 55, physician, and Harriet, 47. Other children listed are Lynch, 26; Letty, 24; Charles, 20; Henry, 16; Harriet, 14; Clementine, 10; Sallie, 8; and James, 5.

58. Sarah was referring to the Battle of Brentwood. Brentwood was a station on the Nashville & Decatur Railroad and was used by the US as a supply depot. On March 25, 1863, Confederate General Nathan Bedford Forrest attacked the seven hundred–man Federal garrison with two brigades of cavalry and a field artillery unit. The surrounded Federal garrison surrendered.

59. The 1860 Montgomery County, Tennessee, Census lists T. Roxie Tarwater, 21, in the household of E. A. Tarwater, 50, male, merchant, and Ellison, 46, female. She was probably the sister of E. A. (Gus) Tarwater, who served in the 14th Tennessee Infantry, Company H. He was a prisoner of war in 1863, paroled in 1865, and died in 1867 on the day he was to marry Blanche Lewis.

60. Mr. G. and Mr. Mc. were James Lyle Glenn and B. W. Macrae.

61. Since Tom was D. N.'s property, he would have had to give written consent for Tom to be sold.

62. The Second Confiscation Act permitted the US to seize all the real and personal property of anyone who took up arms against the government, aided the rebellion directly, or offered aid or comfort to the rebellion. The act did not exempt enslaved people from seizure, so as a result, when the Federal army needed laborers, they simply impressed local slaves. Under the act, they did not have to return the enslaved men since the act also provided freedom for all slaves who escaped to Federal lines. Thus, if enslaved people returned, it was their choice.

63. *Dyspeptic* is an outdated term that was used to indicate someone suffering from depression or indigestion.

64. John must have been an enslaved man who accompanied D. N. to Woodville, Mississippi.

65. Cousin Eliza was Eliza J. McClure. Lucy was her daughter, aged eight in 1860.

66. Louisa McTyler "Tex" Barker was the second daughter born to John Walton Barker and his second wife, Ellen Watson Morris Carr Barker. She was born in 1844.

67. The Trice family was large and there were several branches. Serepta Jordan's aunt married a Trice and members of the Trice family were mentioned numerous times throughout her diary. Trice's Landing in New Providence is on the Cumberland River. Uffelman et al., *Diary of Serepta Jordan*.

68. Walton was Edward Walton Barker, who married Mary Meriwether "Mollie" Barker, daughter of John Walton Barker. Walton Barker joined Company F, 2nd Regiment Kentucky Cavalry and was captured at Brandyville, Tennessee, on March 1, 1863, by the 4th Ohio Cavalry. He was sent to Camp Butler, Illinois, on March 11, 1863, and transferred from there to Fort Monroe, Virginia, on May 29, 1863. He was paroled at Fort McHenry, Maryland, on May 29, 1863. His military records have variations of his name and the file is listed with the erroneous middle initial "J." https://www.Fold3.com/image/88481120, accessed September 2, 2021.

69. On June 4, 1863, Nannie Haskins described some of the consequences for those writing letters that were captured: "Yesterday the Yankees (plague take them)

captured a rebel mail which had been fixed up here to send to the 14th Regiment by the negro who came through from the South and brought letters from boys last week. They did not capture the boy {though} they are 'glorifying over it considerably' and 'making a great to-do.'" Miss Haskins may have believed that correspondence between an occupied area and the enemy soldiers they supported should have been protected. Federal authorities, however, understood this as a dangerous form of subversion. The captured mail resulted in harsh consequences for both men and at least one woman. A Dr. Moody was arrested for the information in his letter and "Miss Mollie Ward also wrote a letter very abusive of the Yanks. Coln. Bruce is very angry about it. How I do wish those letters could have gone through." Uffelman et al., *Diary of Nannie Haskins Williams*, 28.

70. Mr. Brunson may have been Isaac Brunson, listed in the 1860 Montgomery County, Tennessee, Census as a 41-year-old plasterer in a household with H. N., 28, female; Belle, 6; A., 3, male; Lacky, 1, female; and Sallie, 1.

71. Bene (Robena) Van Culin and E. J. McClure were sisters whose maiden names were White.

72. The breakdown of slavery meant enslavers lost mastery over their enslaved and the enslaved began to have negotiating power. In US military–occupied territory, enslaved people had more ability to work on their own or leave for contraband camps. Enslavers were hesitant to pay the high cost of purchasing a person when the longevity of ownership and the ability to exploit their labor was in doubt.

73. The 1860 Montgomery County, Tennessee, Census lists D. N.'s niece, Elizabeth Kennedy Lewis, 29, with G. B. Lewis, male, 36; A. B. Lewis, female, 6; M. C. Lewis, female, 4; M. P. Lewis, female, 2; and E. G. Lewis, female, 6 months.

74. The next "scion" may have been Laurah F. Lewis, born in 1863. Laurah is listed in only two of the thirty-four ancestry.com family trees listing children for George and Lizzie Lewis. Neither tree had information for her beyond her birth year. She probably did not survive infancy. A son, George William Lewis, was born in 1864 and died in 1865. The Lewises had one more child (who survived to adulthood) after these two, Herbert Graves Lewis (1871–1940). The child mortality rate in 1860 was 34 percent, meaning a third of all children under the age of 5 could be expected to die. This rate compares to 7 child deaths per 1,000 today, or fewer than one tenth of a percent of all children today may be expected to die before age 5. https://www.statista.com/statistics/1041693/united-states-all-time-child-mortality-rate/, accessed October 27, 2020.

75. W. J. McCormac is listed as a "Photographic Artist" with rooms on the west side of Public Square, Clarksville. See 1859 Clarksville City Directory, 54. McCormac's studio was visited by local citizens and Federal soldiers. In her journal, Serepta Jordan described a September 19, 1863, visit to his gallery: "As usual the gallery was crowded, but 'first come first served' with Mr. MacCormac and so we were fortunate enough to get off rather early." Uffelman et al., *Diary of Serepta Jordan*, 282.

76. Cheney may have been an enslaved woman who labored as a chamber maid.

77. "Last Thursday" was April 30, 1863. On March 30, 1863, President Abraham Lincoln issued the following proclamation declaring April 30, 1863, to be a day of national fasting, repentance and prayer: "I do, by this my proclamation, designate and set apart Thursday, the 30th day of April, 1863, as a day of national humiliation, fasting and prayer. And I do hereby request all the People to abstain, on that day, from their ordinary secular pursuits, and to unite, at their several places of public worship and their respective homes, in keeping the day holy to the Lord, and devoted to the humble discharge of the religious duties proper to that solemn occasion."

78. May 1 has been celebrated as the beginning of spring in northern hemisphere cultures for millennia. Through the centuries May Day celebrations have taken on various forms. Marking the day with the coronation of a May Queen, complete with flower strewers, train bearers, heralds, maids of honor, and other court members was popular in the South into the twentieth century. Nannie Haskins gave a detailed description of the Clarksville May Day festivities in her May 2, 1863, entry. Uffelman et al., *Diary of Nannie Haskins Williams*, 21.

79. John H. Poston built a three-story brick Federal style house near present-day Poston Street and Red River Street. Near the house was a spring which provided crystal clear water. Neither the spring nor the house has survived. Currently, Skyline Bowling Alley on Kraft Street occupies the general area of the spring.

80. Colonel William P. Boone was with the US 28th Kentucky Infantry, Company B, which was garrisoned at Clarksville from December 1862 through August 1863. Boone filed a report on April 4, 1863, from Clarksville signing himself as "Commanding Post." US War Department, *The War of the Rebellion: A Compilation of the Official Records of the Union and Confederate Armies*, 128 vols. (Washington, DC, 1880–1901), series 1, vol. 23, part 2, correspondence 208. Hereinafter referred to as *OR*, followed by series, volume number, and page number. Nannie Haskins referred to him as Adjutant Boone and described him as "a right fine looking man," a "fop," and "a clever Yankee." Uffelman et al., *Diary of Nannie Haskins Williams*, 19, 27.

81. The 1860 Montgomery County, Tennessee, Census lists S. R. Lewis, female, 16, in the household of G. T. Lewis, ironmaster, with M. O. Lewis, female. Sallie Lewis was the daughter of George T. and Margaretta Lewis, and younger sister of Blanche L. Lewis. George was a wealthy merchant involved in the iron industry in Stewart County, Tennessee.

82. The Virginia lithography firm, Hoyer & Ludwig, in Richmond printed the first CSA stamps. The firm had no background in stamp printing. The first official issue was a five-cent green stamp which featured CSA President Jefferson Davis, making him the first living president to appear on a postage stamp. Because of the low quality of their stamps, Hoyer & Ludwig lost their contract. The CSA next contracted with the internationally known London, England, printing firm

of Thomas De La Rue & Co. A Southern firm, Archer & Daly, began producing stamps in 1863. "The Confederate Postal System," Smithsonian National Postal Museum, https://postalmuseum.si.edu/exhibition/a-nation-divided/the-confederate-postal-system, accessed October 22, 2020.

83. The 1859 Clarksville City Directory lists the residence and office of T. J. Donoho, physician, on Second Street between Commerce and Madison Streets. This house was close to the Kennedys' home.

84. Mrs. Elder was probably Melissa Martin Elder, wife of Joshua Elder.

85. General William Rosecrans issued Order 43 on March 8, 1863: "The general commanding finds within his lines many helpless and suffering families, whose natural protectors and supporters are in arms against us—these people need food, clothing, and protection, which it is neither our duty nor our power adequately to provide—many others whose sympathies and connections are such as to surmount all the obligations that arise from their permission to remain within our lines, forbidding them to communicate with the enemy or act as spies against us. . . . It is therefore ordered that, first, all those whose natural supporters are in the rebel service, and, second, all those whose sympathies and connections are such that they cannot give the assurance that they will conduct themselves as peaceable citizens, shall hold themselves in readiness to go south of our lines within ten days from the date of notice" (OR, series 1, vol. 23, chapt. 35, part 2, correspondence 121).

86. Mr. W. may have been the Reverend T. Delacey Wardlaw. He had refused to sign the oath as ordered and was arrested but not jailed. He did not go south but left Clarksville in 1863 or early 1864 for Canada and returned by the end of July 1864.

87. Susan Perkins Marr married John S. McLean on June 29, 1857. McLean was a farmer and he and Susan were listed in the 1860 Carroll County, Mississippi, Census with Martha, 22; Calmet, 11; Mary, 9; Hardin, 2; and William, 1 month.

88. Cousin Lucy was Lucy Catherine Bailey, second child of Charles Bailey and Mary (Polly) Bryan.

89. Cousin Jamie was James Edmund Bailey, third child of Charles Bailey and Mary (Polly) Bryan, serving with the 49th Tennessee.

90. Sarah was probably referring to the Confederate victory at Winchester, Virginia, on June 13, 1863, and the US's failed attempt to take Port Hudson, Louisiana, on June 14, 1863.

91 James O. Shackelford was listed in the 1860 Montgomery County, Tennessee, Census as a 50-year-old lawyer with a personal estate of $12,500 and real estate worth $29,200. Listed in his household were S. M, female, 44; R., male, 20; Mary, 16; J. O. Jr., male, 10; Gertrude, 6; S. H., male, 4; E. H., male, 10 months; W. T., male, 22; S. A., female, 23.

92. The Confiscation Act of 1862 or the Second Confiscation Act allowed the US Army to confiscate and use the property of anyone aiding the rebellion. Since D. N. was working for the Confederate Treasury Department, this applied to the

Kennedy family. The US army was authorized to recompense loyal Unionists for the use of their slaves upon proof of their loyalty. "Chap. CXCV—An act to suppress Insurrection, to punish Treason and Rebellion, to seize and confiscate the Property of Rebels, and for other Purposes," U.S. Congress, pp. 589–92, 17 July 1862. Courtesy of the Library of Congress.

93. Mrs. Lusk was probably the mother of Elizabeth Margaret "Lizzie" Lusk Bailey (1830–1897), wife of Sarah's first cousin, James Edmund Bailey (1822–1885). "John McQuaide Family Tree," http://www.ancestry.com, accessed October 13, 2020. Mrs. Lusk lived in Nashville; James and Lizzie had a home in Clarksville, but Lizzie appears to have left their three children with grandparents while she followed the 49th Infantry with her husband. D. N. must have been staying near the 49th as well. Sarah often asked in her letters for D. N. to greet "cousin James and wife" or "James and Lizzie" for her.

94. Maude, Jimmy Bailey, and Robb were the children of Sarah's cousin James Edmund Bailey and his wife Lizzie: Maude Lusk Bailey (1854–1924), James Edmund Bailey Jr. (1859–1931), and Alfred Robb Bailey (1860–1931). Sarah's aunt was Mary (Polly) Bryan Bailey, wife of Charles Bailey Sr. and grandmother of these children. "John McQuaide Family Tree," http://www.ancestry.com, accessed October 13, 2020.

95. The 1850 Montgomery County, Tennessee, Census lists Harriet (called Hattie), 4, as the daughter of Dr. Thomas J. Donoho, physician, 43, and his wife Harriet, 38. Other children listed are Lynch, 17; Letty, 15; Lucy, 13; Charles, 11; Henry, 6; and Clementine, 1. Hattie was good friends with Nannie Haskins, who mentioned her often in the diary and was in a photo with her when they were students of Dr. R. B. McMullen.

96. W. McC. is probably Warren Clark McClure, Eliza Jane White McClure's husband.

97. Sarah writes the concert was held Sunday night. Nannie Haskins wrote of a concert at the Presbyterian Church on Monday night. Nannie listed the songs individuals sang and gave an account of several songs favored by Confederate patriots. Perhaps they were at the same concert and got the dates off by a day. Uffelman, et al., *Diary of Nannie Haskins Williams*, 30–32.

# Chapter 3

1. Rebecca Sharpless in *Cooking in Other Women's Kitchens: Domestic Workers in the South, 1865–1960* (Chapel Hill: Univ. of North Carolina Press, 2010) examines the lives of African American cooks. Newly freed women had few options for employment other than cooking and cleaning. The relationship between employer and employee could be fraught with tension. Black women would quit a difficult employer if another option was available.

2. In the nineteenth century, vague symptoms like tiredness, depression, gas, and indigestion were often ascribed to a sluggish liver.

3. Trenton, Kentucky, is a town about 17 miles from Clarksville in Todd County.

4. Mail from the North to the South could be sent under a flag of truce through City Point, Virginia. https://postalmuseum.si.edu/exhibition/about-philately -covers-and-letters-in-times-of-trouble-conflict-mail-civil-war-1861-1865, accessed October 29, 2020. Flag of truce letter exchanges were offered principally for prisoners of war but were extended to a limited number of civilians as well. Perhaps there was some temporary break in the civilian exchanges. The flag of truce system ran from September 1861 through June 1865. Harry K. Charles Jr., "American Civil War Postage Due: North and South," Postal History Symposium, Nov. 2012, https:// stamps.org/Portals/0/Symposium/CharlesPaper.pdf, accessed September 28, 2021.

5. William Guy Wines (ca. 1814–1898) served as postmaster at Clarksville from 1862 to April 1865. He was a Unionist. Wines represented Montgomery County in the 34th (Reconstruction) and 35th Tennessee General Assemblies, 1865–1869. A native of New Jersey, he lived in Michigan and Kentucky before coming to Montgomery County about 1857. He is described as a teacher and educator, was head of Stewart College in 1859, and was a delegate to the Union State Convention in Nashville on January 9, 1865. Robert M. McBride and Dan M. Robison, *Biographical Directory of the Tennessee General Assembly 1861–1901*, vol. 2 (Nashville: Tennessee State Library and Archives and Tennessee Historical Commission, 1979), 995–96.

6. Barbra Ann Barker Clayton was John Walton Barker's third daughter by his first wife Mary Minor Meriwether Barker. Barbra Ann married Judge Alexander M. Clayton in 1839.

7. Walton Barker initially served in the 2nd Kentucky Cavalry, was captured in March 1863, and paroled at Fort McHenry, Maryland. He then appears to have joined the cavalry commanded by General Nathan Bedford Forrest. Forrest at this time was commanding the cavalry corps which had belonged to Confederate General Earl Van Dorn. Van Dorn was murdered at Spring Hill, Tennessee, on May 7, 1863, by a jealous husband.

8. Cousin James and wife were James Edmund and Lizzie Lusk Bailey.

9. Alfred Robb Bailey, son of James Edmund and Lizzie Lusk Bailey, was about two years old when this letter was written. He was staying with his paternal grandmother in Clarksville while his older brother and sister, Jimmy and Maude, were with their maternal grandmother in Nashville.

10. The 102nd Ohio Infantry was organized at Mansfield, Ohio, as a three-year regiment and was mustered into service at Covington, Kentucky. The regiment arrived in Clarksville on December 25, 1862, and stayed nine months before moving out to Nashville where they assisted in repelling a cavalry attack by General Joseph Wheeler. They went into winter quarters in Nashville on October 30, 1863, staying there performing guard duty for approximately six months. It is entirely possible that a portion of the unit was at Clarksville during that time. They were commanded by Colonel William Given.

11. The Battle of Chickamauga occurred on September 19–20, 1863, and was a Confederate victory. The US was forced to fall back to Chattanooga where the Confederates occupied the heights surrounding the town cutting off the Federal supply lines. This bloody battle cost the Federals 16,170 casualties and the Confederates 18,454.

12. The 1850 Montgomery County, Tennessee, Census, lists the household of Sarah B. Copeland, 45, with children, Mary, 16, and James, 14. Others in the household were Elizabeth Bryan, 55; Lucy A. Bryan, 28; D. N. Kennedy, 30; Sarah A. Kennedy, 26; William D. Kennedy, 2; and Lucy Bailey, 2. William was Sarah's infant son who died later that year. Sarah B. Copeland, Elizabeth Bryan, and Lucy Bryan may have been Sarah's aunt Mary (Polly) Bryan Bailey's sisters, Sally Bryan (1805–1867), Elizabeth Bryan (1795–1863), and Lucy Ann Bryan (1817–1892). "John McQuaide Family Tree," http://www.ancestry.com, accessed October 13, 2020.

13. The 1860 Montgomery County, Tennessee, Census lists Thornton Glenn, male, 1 year old, in the household of J. L. Glenn, 31, printer, and Ella Glenn, 25. J. L. Glenn had a personal estate of $38,000 and owned real estate worth $8,000. James Glenn and D. N. Kennedy were partners in founding the Northern Bank of Tennessee.

14. Sally was the daughter of John (1793–1877) and Elizabeth Poindexter (1796–1877), who had children, Mary L. (1818–1900), Elizabeth J. (1820–1881), John W. (1822–1877), Lucy Jones Poindexter Quarles (1825–1861), Philip B. (1830–1863), Nicholas (1833–1849), Ella (1835–?), Sallie (1838–1863), and Virginia Ritchie (1844–?). The Meriwether Society, Inc., http://MeriwetherSociety.org and http://www.ancestry.com, "Adoue Family Tree," both accessed February 22, 2013. The 1860 Christian County, Kentucky, Census lists the household of John, 67, and Betsy (Elizabeth), 64, with Mary L., 42; Sally, 22; and Richie, male, 18. Although, Richie was listed as male, she was actually Virginia Ritchie Poindexter, who went by her middle name. She and Nannie Haskins were close friends. Uffelman et al., *Diary of Nannie Haskins Williams*, 16, 83, 108, 115, 119–20, 122 (for Ritchie); and 40, 44 (for Sallie).

15. J. B. was probably John Walton Barker. Mollie Meriwether Barker was the eldest child of John Walton and his second wife, Ellen Watson Morris Carr Barker. She was married to E. Walton Barker, who was serving with General Nathan Bedford Forrest's cavalry.

16. Mrs. J. Jones was possibly the wife of Joseph M. Jones listed in the 1859 Clarksville City Directory as living on the south side of Madison Street between Third and Fifth Streets.

17. The 1860 Montgomery County, Tennessee, Census shows E. Warfield, 37, living with G. H. Warfield, 56, farmer with real estate valued at $54,000 and personal estate of $55,000. Also living with them were George W., 17; Amanda, 11; and Charles, 9. On the census record Warfields are on page 21 and the Kennedys are on page 19, indicating that they were close neighbors.

18. Mrs. Elder was probably M. M. (Melissa Martin) Elder, listed as age 30 in the 1860 Montgomery County, Tennessee, Census in the household with Joshua, 55, broker; John, 7; and Martin, 4. Joshua was the only child of James and Lucinda Wallace Elder. James Elder was the first mayor and first postmaster of Clarksville.

19. Sarah appeared to stereotype Northern women as living simply and conservatively.

20. Charles Bailey Bryan was the son of James Hardy Bryan and his second wife, Margaret Bailey Bryan. He was the half-brother of Sarah's aunt Mary (Polly) Bryan Bailey. "John McQuaide Family Tree,"https://www.ancestry,com, accessed September 8, 2021. The 1850 Montgomery County, Tennessee, Census lists Charles Bryan, 18, clerk, in the household of James E. Bailey, attorney, with real estate worth $10,000. Others listed in the James Edmund Bailey household in 1850 were E. M. (Lizzie), 20; Charles, 60; Mary, 52; Lucy C., 26; C. W., male, 14; Wilmoth, female, 28; Charles Bailey Jr., 5; and Lucinda Bryan, 11. Wilmoth Boyd Bailey may have been the widow of Charles and Polly's son, Henry Lewis Bailey, (1818–1848) and Charles Bailey Jr., may have been their son.

21. Winchester is the county seat of Franklin County, Tennessee. Winchester is 126 miles southeast of Clarksville near Chattanooga.

22. Cousin James was Colonel James E. Bailey. In December 1862 through January 1863, numerous petitioners, including Gustavus Adolphus Henry, Brigadier General John Gregg, and Tennessee Governor Isham Harris (1857–1862), launched a campaign to have Bailey promoted to brigadier general. However, by the spring of 1863, Bailey was suffering from severe, chronic dysentery. He requested and received a thirty-day leave of absence on April 22, 1863, because of his ill health. At the end of his furlough, on May 27, 1863, he requested and received approval to resign from the 49th Tennessee Infantry Regiment because of the chronic diarrhea, fever, and emaciation. No record of Bailey's rejoining the army could be found; however, he may very well have recuperated and rejoined the 49th by October 1863. On May 7, 1864, G. A. Henry wrote President Jefferson Davis, saying that he thought Bailey would make a fine brigadier general, but if promotion was not possible, he believed Bailey would be an outstanding judge in a military court. He was informed no military courts were being organized at the time. Compiled Service Records of Confederate Soldiers Who Served in Organizations from the State of Tennessee, https://www.fold3.com/image/79490889, accessed September 30, 2021.

23. S. Copeland was Sarah (Sallie) Bryan Copeland.

24. Mrs. M. was Amanda Green Munford.

25. Old Point Comfer is probably Old Point Comfort, which is a point of land located at the tip of the Virginia Peninsula at the mouth of Hampton Roads. Fort Monroe was built on this site and was active during the Civil War in routing mail between the North and the South. This was also the site where the first enslaved Africans landed in August 1619 in what became the United States.

26. Mr. J. W. B. was probably John Walton Barker, owner of Cloverlands.

27. J. L. G. was James Lyle Glenn and B. W. M. was B. W. Macrae. Sarah mentioned both men frequently as being helpful to her.

28. Frank Beaumont is listed in the 1859 Clarksville City Directory as living on the southeast corner of Third and Franklin Streets. Captain Frank S. Beaumont died October 6, 1861, at Warm Springs, Virginia, of typhoid fever. During the war he was captain of Company H of the 14th Tennessee Infantry. His wife, Laura E. Conrad Beaumont, died March 26, 1863, according to the April 9, 1863, entry in Nannie Haskins Williams' diary. The couple left three children, Ida (1855–1903), George (1859 -?), and Franklin Summerfield Beaumont Jr. (1861 – 1904); however, it is unlikely they were living in the home. "Larry's Family Tree," http://www.ancestry .com, accessed October 25, 2020; Griffey, *Riverview Cemetery*; Uffelman et al., *Diary of Nannie Haskins Williams*, 17.

29. The Masonic Hall was located on Franklin Street near Trinity Episcopal Church where the parish house now stands. http://clarksvillelodge89.org/index .php/history-of-cl89/, accessed on August 23, 2020.

30. S. J. Winston is listed in the 1859 Clarksville City Directory as living at the northeast corner of Main and Sixth Streets.

31. The Landrums may have been M. M., 51, farmer, and Elizabeth, 61, listed in the 1860 Montgomery County, Tennessee, Census, with Susan, 18; Orian, 15, female; and Ann, 13.

32. William Stamms Shackelford was a portrait painter who moved to Clarksville in the 1850s. He is listed in the 1860 Montgomery County, Tennessee, Census as a 46-year-old artist with a household consisting of Sarah Shackelford, 34; M. L. Shackelford, 13; and Elinor Read, 60. According to the 1859 Clarksville City Directory, 67, he had a studio under the Masonic Hall and a home on Franklin Street between Third and Fourth Streets. It is likely due to its location that his studio burned down as well as his house.

33. Thomas Delacey Wardlaw, pastor of First Presbyterian Church, is listed in the 1859 Clarksville City Directory, 73, as living on Main Street between First and Second Streets.

34. Bryce Stewart was a tobacco buyer who lived on the northeast corner of Third and Main Streets, according to the 1859 Clarksville City Directory.

35. Sarah did not say who "they" were, but Serepta Jordan Homer, writing about these fires in her diary, blamed African Americans: "Up town he [Mr. Homer] learned that a large fire over in Clarksville had destroyed a great many valuable buildings both public and private. It is supposed they were set on fire by the negroes, offended of course because they were refused permission to go in and take possession. We will not be surprised when they order us out of homes—they are getting at such a high pop." Uffelman et al., *Diary of Serepta Jordan*, 291.

36. Sarah was referring to a recruiting station for the 16th US Colored Troops Infantry set up near Fort Bruce, now known as Fort Defiance. This recruiting station was in operation from November 1863 until the unit moved out to Chattanooga in April 1864. Serepta Jordan had Lieutenant Bishop W. Perkins, adjutant of the 16th USCT, as a boarder until the unit left Clarksville. Uffelman et al., *Diary of Serepta Jordan*, 305.

37. Dr. Charles R. Cooper, age 50, is listed in the 1860 Montgomery County, Tennessee, Census with a real estate value of $6,000 and a personal estate value of $2,500. Also listed in his household are M. C. Cooper, 48; L. R. Cooper, 25; C. R. Cooper, 21; W. C. Cooper, 15; and A. B. Cooper, 12. A. B. Cooper may have been Lady Annie B., who opposed her father's match with Miss Carrie but approved of Ellen Galbraith. Sarah seems to be using the term "Lady" sarcastically. Dr. Cooper (1805–1865) was born in Carlyle, Pennsylvania. He came to Clarksville in 1843 after graduating from Jefferson Medical College in Philadelphia. Mary C. Cooper, born in Carlyle, Pennsylvania, died in 1861 at age 53. Her obituary noted she was a leader in forming First Presbyterian Church in Clarksville. See *Clarksville Weekly Chronicle*, September 27, 1861, 3 and 4; October 4, 1861, 3; November 3, 1865, 1. The 1859 Clarksville City Directory lists Dr. Cooper's office at the northeast corner of Madison and Second Streets, 44.

38. Ellen Galbraith is listed in the 1859 Clarksville City Directory as living in the home of her father, John McKeage. Ellen was the widow of Robert W. Galbraith, a partner in Galbraith, Cromwell and Co. in Clarksville. The couple moved to New Orleans where Galbraith was in business with prominent Clarksvillian, Thompson G. Greenfield. Galbraith died in New Orleans, leaving Ellen with a daughter, Ellen, age nineteen in 1860. In her October 2, 1863, diary entry, Nannie Haskins mentioned the same rumor that Ellen Galbraith and Charles Cooper were to be married. Nannie added, "I hope she won't be such a fool." Uffelman et al., *Diary of Nannie Haskins Williams*, 50. They did not marry, as Sarah noted in a letter of May 13, 1864.

39. Dyspepsia, commonly called indigestion, is characterized by pain or discomfort in the upper abdomen.

40. Before the Civil War, states would charter banks that could issue their own paper money. This money would only be as good as the finances of the bank that issued them. Sarah was recording what these particular banks would pay to redeem their script. During the Civil War, national currency issued by the Federal government began to dominate other currency in the economy. By the end of the war, Confederate currency was virtually worthless.

41. Enterprise is a town in Clarke County, Mississippi. It is 315 miles south of Clarksville.

42. Sterling Beaumont's home was on the south side of Franklin Street between Third and Hiter Streets.

43. Dr. Charles R. Cooper's courtship of Ellen Galbraith did not work out. She appeared to be more interested in one of the Hillman brothers, whom she met at the home of Marion and Gustavus Adolphus Henry Sr.

44. Mrs. Dunlop may have been Hugh Dunlop's first wife. The 1860 Montgomery County, Tennessee, Census lists Hugh Dunlop, 45, farmer, born in Scotland, in a household with R. P., 28, female; W. B., 8, male; and James Logan, 21, clerk. Hugh Dunlop was a wealthy tobacconist.

45. James William Frederick Macrae was the brother of Bailey Washington Macrae Sr. and was the uncle to Bailey Washington Macrae Jr. The 1860 Prince William, Virginia, Slave Schedule showed that James Macrae owned fourteen slaves.

46. Wells Fowler built Fowler's Hall on Franklin Street between First and Second Streets. He was a silversmith from Connecticut and may have established the first jewelry store in Clarksville circa 1836–1837. Fowler moved to Palmyra, Tennessee, about 1846.

47. *Tableaux* is the plural of *tableau* (from the French diminutive of *table*); a tableau is a representation of a picture, statue, or scene, by one or more people posed in costume. A popular nineteenth-century entertainment was to stage a series of tableaux from literature or history, frequently in conjunction with musical entertainment or short skits and used to raise funds for civic projects. Nannie Haskins mentioned she would be "Lady Jane Grey at her execution" in the next tableaux in her January 31, 1864, diary entry. Uffelman et al., *Diary of Nannie Haskins Williams*, 54.

48. Elkton, Kentucky, is the county seat of Todd County and is about 25 miles north of Clarksville.

49. Thompson was probably D. N. Kennedy's brother, William Thompson Kennedy (1805–1877).

50. The 1860 Montgomery County, Tennessee, Census, lists W. I. Dearing, 21, in the household of Eli Lockert. Eight young men, aged 13 to 21, with different last names, appear to have been boarding with Lockert, his wife and daughter.

51. After August 26, 1861, mail had to be sent by flag of truce with regulations. Mail could only cross the lines at designated exchange points. Mail from the North to the South passed through City Point, Virginia, and from the South to the North at Fort Monroe, Virginia. Smithsonian Postal Museum, https://postalmuseum.si .edu/exhibition/about-philately-covers-and-letters-in-times-of-trouble-conflict -mail-civil-war-1861-1865, accessed October 29, 2020.

52. Numerous family trees have Sue Marr's death as April 29, 1869, in Carroll County, Mississippi. This letter indicates that Marr died in 1864. The editors have not found Sue Marr on Find A Grave.

53. Pneumonia and bronchitis are common secondary complications of typhoid.

54. A "rising" seems to mean a boil.

55. The Second Confiscation Act allowed the confiscation of property from active rebels, which was the classification probably given to D. N. Kennedy.

56. Sarah obviously did not want to name the person in a letter that may have been intercepted or read by a censor if sent by flag of truce. She may have been referring to John Walton Barker, who owned Cloverlands, the home where Sarah and the children lived for several months when they evacuated from their downtown Clarksville home.

57. It is probable that Sarah was referring to the inventory of their property.

58. Sawyer, Wallace & Co. was a tobacco and general commission mercantile which had offices in New York and Louisville. It was established about 1850 by Clarksville native S. A. Sawyer, David L. Wallace, and Thomas Miller. The firm went bankrupt in 1890. "Failure of Sawyer, Wallace & Co." *Daily Tobacco Leaf-Chronicle*, September 5, 1890, newspapers.com, https://go.newspapers.com /welcome, accessed June 8, 2021.

59. B. W. M. was Bailey Washington Macrae. The 1860 Montgomery County, Tennessee, Census, spelled his name as McCrae; it is also sometimes spelled MacCrae. The Census lists B. W., 29, merchant, with real estate valued at $16,000 and personal estate at $16,000, living with Alice, 22; Virginia, 2; and Mary, 6 months. He was partners with Ben F. Coulter in a dry goods business and they lived next door to each other.

60. George Wythe Macrae (1838–1922) was living in Memphis in 1860. He was the brother of William Stewart Macrae (1826–1916) and Bailey Washington Macrae Jr. (1830–1903). "Allingham Family Tree," http://www.ancestry.com, accessed September 6, 2021. The 1860 Memphis, Ward 4, Shelby County, Tennessee, Census, listed G. W. Macrae, 22, merchant, personal estate valued at $9,000, living with S. P. Pugh, 16, male, clerk.

61. Colonel Arthur A. Smith was the commander of the 83rd Illinois Infantry Regiment. The right wing of the 83rd moved to Clarksville on September 20, 1863, and the rest of the regiment was stationed at Fort Donelson.

## Chapter 4

1. Deodar cedars are large evergreen trees that grow quite tall with needle-like leaves. Their color varies from bright green to blue green. They are ornamental trees that originally grew at higher elevations in the Himalayan Mountains. The deodar cedar is the national tree of Pakistan.

2. Lizzie may have been D. N. Kennedy's niece, Elizabeth "Lizzie" Kennedy Lewis. She and her husband, George, had a son, George William Lewis, born in 1864 and died in 1865.

3. The 1860 Montgomery County, Tennessee, Census listed Mary McDaniel, 15, living with J. White, 50, a laborer with real estate valued at $500 and personal estate valued at $300; Mary White, 36; J. S. McDaniel, 59, a laborer and probably her father; and Mahola McDaniel, 54. At the time of this letter, Mary McDaniel would have been 19 years old.

4. Dr. R. B. McMullen joined Fannie Balthrop and Thomas W. Williams in holy matrimony on March 29, 1864, probably at First Presbyterian Church. Tennessee State Library and Archives; Nashville, TN, USA; Tennessee State Marriages, 1780–2002.

5. Bryce Stewart was a tobacconist who was born in Scotland. In 1858–1859, he hired Adolphus Heiman to build a stone castle. It was set on a hill with acres of land around it. Building stopped because of the war and the death of his first wife. In 1864, building resumed but when his new bride didn't want to live in a castle the project was abandoned. A road and subdivision called Castle Heights occupy the area of Stewart's Castle. Beach and Williams, *Nineteenth Century Heritage*, 92–95.

6. *Nanal* is a word of English origin and means beautiful and kind.

7. Although Sarah did not mention specific items, dry goods could have been products such as textiles, ready-to-wear clothing, toiletries, or grocery items that do not contain liquid, such as tobacco, sugar, flour, and coffee. The phrase had largely disappeared from use by the beginning of the twentieth century.

8. J. Macrae was probably James William Frederick Macrae, uncle to Bailey Washington Macrae Jr., George Wythe Macrae, and William Stewart Macrae.

9. Sarah and her advisors came up with a clever scheme to save the house from confiscation. John Walton Barker thought the army would confiscate the house in order to sell it; therefore, it was smart to attach a debt to the house as the debt would have to be paid before any sort of legal transfer could be done, thus making it a much less attractive object for confiscation. The initials "C: P & Cs" are unclear. Perhaps they referred to a business that may have loaned money against the deed for the house.

10. This is possibly Captain John T. Morgan of Company F, 83rd Illinois Infantry Regiment.

11. The 1859 Clarksville City Directory lists George B. Fleece as a Chief Engineer for the Memphis, Clarksville & Louisville Railroad, boarding at Charles M. Hiter's house. Hiter's house was located on the south side of the corner of Franklin and Hiter Streets. The M. C. & L Railroad was charted in 1850 and ran from Paris, Tennessee, to Bowling Green, Kentucky. The 1860 Montgomery County, Tennessee, Census listed Fleece in the home of Mary E. Hall with several other boarders. The directory listed Hall's house on the west side of Telegraph Street between Main and College Streets. It is unclear what residence Sarah was referring to, but it would have been downtown. Both places Fleece boarded were close to Public Square.

12. Henry Wisdom was listed in the 1859 Clarksville City Directory as cashier of the Branch Bank of Tennessee. He resided on the north side of Madison Street between Sixth and Seventh Streets.

13. Bailey W. Macrae of Macrae and Coulter was listed in the 1859 Clarksville City Directory as living on the Nashville Road. Macrae and Coulter was a dry goods store located on the northeast corner of Public Square and Franklin Street.

14. Benjamin F. Coulter was a partner in the dry goods firm of Macrae and Coulter. He was listed in the 1859 Clarksville City Directory as residing on the south side of Franklin Street between Fourth and Fifth Streets. The 1860 Montgomery County, Tennessee, Census lists Benjamin F. Coulter, 27, merchant, personal estate valued at $26,000, with Bell, 24; Frank, 3; W. F., 17, male; J. B., 14, male; F. C., 52, female; and M. D. Moore, 55, female.

15. Sarah was probably referring to menstruation.

16. Poor Ellen Galbraith seems doomed to matrimonial failure. Nannie Haskins wrote on July 25, 1863, about her flirting with Bryce Stewart's brother, Dan, a polite, entertaining, homely gentlemen who had just returned from New York. "It amuses me to see Mrs. Galbraith. How she is trying to catch the rich old bachelor. 'She is making a dead set.'" Uffelman et al., *Diary of Nannie Haskins Williams*, 40. Mr. Hillman may have been a member of the prosperous Hillman family. Four brothers, Daniel Jr., James, George, and Charles, worked in the iron business with their father. If Mr. Hillman was Daniel Jr, both Ellen Galbraith and Tennie Moore were doomed to failure. After the death of his first wife, Nannie Marable Hillman, he married Mary Gentry of Bedford County, Tennessee, in 1865. She was thirty-four years younger than Hillman. Griffey, *Riverview Cemetery*, 22.

17. Eliza J. McClure Stewart died on May 28, 1866. The "fine house" was never completed after her death.

18. Marion Stewart was the daughter of Bryce and Eliza Stewart. The 1850 Montgomery County, Tennessee, Census lists Marion, 5, in the household of Bryce Stewart, 39, tobacconist, with Eliza J., 28. Marion married William Hume, a banker in Louisville, and they had one child, Bryce Stewart Hume.

19. Miss Copeland may have been Sarah Copeland's daughter, Mary, listed as age sixteen in the 1850 Montgomery County, Tennessee, Census.

20. D. N.'s brother Thompson was the father of Elizabeth "Lizzie" Kennedy Lewis and Laura Kennedy.

21. Donald was D. N. Kennedy's brother, Aaron Donald Kennedy (1815–1890). He was Ben Kennedy's father. Donald Kennedy lived in Todd County, Kentucky.

22. On the brink of bankruptcy and pressed to finance the Civil War, Congress for the first time authorized the US Treasury to issue paper money in the form of non-interest-bearing treasury notes, commonly called "greenbacks" because of their ink color. The bill authorized Treasury Secretary Salmon P. Chase to issue $150 million in paper notes as "lawful money and a legal tender in payment of all debts, public and private, within the United States." Because greenbacks were not backed by gold or silver, the standard basis for economic transactions, the bill, signed into law by Abraham Lincoln on February 25, 1862, was challenged in court. The suit went to the US Supreme Court, which ruled it constitutional on December 18, 1863, just three days after hearing arguments. Dawinder S. Sidhu, "Opinionator: The Birth

of the Greenback," *New York Times*, December 31, 2013, https://opinionator.blogs
.nytimes.com/2013/12/31/the-birth-of-the-greenback/, accessed August 14, 2017.

23. In 1862, Fort Monroe began to be used as a transfer point for mail exchange.
Mail that came from Confederate states addressed to Federal locations was sent
by a flag of truce to Fort Monroe. It was opened, inspected, resealed, marked, and
sent on. Since D. N. Kennedy was behind Confederate lines and Sarah was living
in Federal territory, they could have qualified to use this route. This system also
explains why Sarah sent her husband U. S. Postage stamps. The US did not honor
Confederate stamps, and the Confederacy did not honor US postage.

24. Contraband originally referred to smuggled goods. Slaves who sought refuge
in Federal military camps or lived in US-controlled territory were declared "contraband of war." In 1861 Union General Benjamin F. Butler formulated the policy
of not returning slaves and creating contraband camps. Contraband camps at
Clarksville were among the best managed and healthiest of the seventeen camps in
Tennessee. See Paul H. Bergeron, Stephen V. Ash, and Jeanette Keith, *Tennesseans
and Their History* (Knoxville: Univ. of Tennessee Press, 1999), 154. See also Ash,
*Middle Tennessee Society Transformed*, 135–39, for a more detailed account of the contraband camps in Clarksville and Pulaski.

25. *Cholera Morbus* is a historic term for what is known today as gastroenteritis.
It is characterized by abdominal pain, diarrhea, nausea, and vomiting.

26. The US and Confederate mail systems had exchanged letters across enemy
lines. This suspension of "flag truce civilities" must have been a period when the
mail was not allowed to cross Federal-Confederate lines, and Sarah had not received letters from D. N. in a while.

27. Mollie Ward and her sister, Lucy Ward Williams, ran a girls' boarding school
known as White Hall School in Ringgold, just north of Clarksville. White Hall
School was established in 1845 by Lucy Williams, widow of Fielding Williams, a tobacconist and owner of Ringgold Mill. He built the home White Hall in 1839. White
Hall School operated through the Civil War under the guidance of the two sisters.

28. No major battles took place on July 2, 1864. Sarah may have been talking
about the aftermath from the Confederate victory at the Battle of Kennesaw
Mountain on June 27 in the Atlanta Campaign; however, the victory failed to stop
Sherman's advance to Atlanta. The 49th Tennessee would have taken part in that
battle. Alternatively, she may have been hopeful that Confederate General Jubal
Early would capture Washington, DC, as he came within five miles of the capital
city before he was driven back into Virginia on July 13, 1864.

29. Martha (Mattie) Pennington Williams married widower, Hugh Dunlop,
tobacconist, in May 1865, when she was twenty-three and he was fifty-three. Dunlop paid off the heavily mortgaged debt on her family home, Tip Top; afterwards
he and Mattie took up residence there. Her widowed mother, Sarah Williams,
with her nine remaining children, moved downtown into a large brick home

next door to Madison Street United Methodist Church, Clarksville. In her diary, Nannie Haskins described the wedding of Mattie Williams and Hugh Dunlop in her May 21, 1865, entry: "Cousin Mattie Williams and Mr. Dunlop were married last Wednesday evening at five o'clock at Trinity Church by Mr. Ringgold. Mr. Westerfield and I waited together, Mr. Bryan and Lucy Bryarly, Mollie Boyd and Mr. Blain, Millie Williams and Mr. Bryarly. All of the party except Mr. Blain, Mr. Bryan, and I went to Louisville with them. Very, very warm," (114). She mentioned their honeymoon in her November 14, 1865, entry: "Mr. & Mrs. Dunlop have returned to Clarksville after a long bridal tour to Europe. They visited Ireland, England, Scotland, and France, besides a long [stay] in New York," (121–22).

30. Union General William Sherman's Atlanta Campaign consisted of numerous battles including the Battle of Kennesaw Mountain. Not all of these battles were Federal victories, but the goal of the campaign was to destroy the Army of Tennessee under Confederate Generals Joseph E. Johnston and John Bell Hood and capture the city of Atlanta. On September 1, 1864, Hood pulled the Army of Tennessee out of the Atlanta area and turned back to Tennessee hoping to distract Sherman and pull the Federal army to Tennessee. Atlanta fell to Sherman the next day, September 2, 1864, and Sherman started his March to the Sea soon after. Sarah did not express worry for her husband's safety so he must have relocated before Atlanta was attacked and fell.

31. Sarah knew that both sides read and censored the mail. She only wrote the first and last letters of this person's last name to protect his identity. He was either a Confederate deserter, someone who refused to take a loyalty oath or was perhaps going to Canada for business. It seems that D. N. would have had a good idea of the reason. This person was probably Ben Coulter, who was a partner in the dry goods store with Bailey McCrae. See Sarah's May 13, 1864, letter.

32. Elizabeth Kennedy Lewis lived until 1907. At this time she would have had at least six living children under age ten. Her youngest would have been George William Lewis (1864–1865). "Glaser/Lang Family Tree," www.ancestry.com, accessed October 1, 2021.

33. Eamert Elder would have been born the third son of Joshua and Melissa Martin Elder in late 1864. A ten-year gap between the second and third sons suggests Eamert could have been a surprise. The 1870 Montgomery County, Tennessee, Census lists in the household Joshua, 65; M. M., 37; John, 17; Martin, 14; Eamert, 5; John Wesley, 50; Martha Wesley, 29; and Monroe Wesley, 10.

34. Danville, Kentucky, is the county seat of Boyle County. It is 200 miles northeast of Clarksville.

35. Parthenia Williams married Elisha P. Fort on October 19, 1864. Compiled Kentucky Marriages, 1851–1900. The 1880 Brinkley Township Monroe County, Arkansas, Census listed E. P. Fort, 62, farmer; Parthenia, 38. They had two hired laborers living with them.

36. The Reverend Samuel Ringgold conducted the funeral in defiance of occupation rules about Confederate funerals. Nannie Haskins attended the funeral and wrote eloquently of her sorrow on October 15, 1864. Uffelman et al., *Diary of Nannie Haskins Williams*, 79–80.

37. Letty, Lucy, and Jimmy were children of Dr. and Mrs. Thomas J. Donoho. In 1864, Letty would have been about 28 years old, Lucy, 26, and Jimmy, 9. See 1860 Montgomery County, Tennessee, Census.

38. Dover, Tennessee, is on the Cumberland River and is the county seat of Stewart County. Fort Donelson is in Dover. It is 30 miles west of Clarksville.

39. James was James William Frederick Macrae, uncle of B. W. Macrae.

40. James Johnson may have been James E. Johnson, who enlisted as a private in Company E of the 49th Tennessee Infantry on December 2, 1861, in Clarksville. He was taken as a prisoner of war at Fort Donelson, sent to Camp Douglas, Illinois, where he was hospitalized for pneumonia in March. He was exchanged at Vicksburg, Mississippi, with the rest of the 49th POWs. Since D. N. appears to have been near where the 49th was stationed, it would make sense that Johnson might ask D. N. to advance him twenty-five dollars. See Cross, *Cry Havoc*, 145.

41. One might hope that Ellen Galbraith finally found a second husband in Richmond after her failed flirtations with Dr. Charles Cooper, Bryce Stewart's brother Dan, and one of the Hillman brothers, possibly Daniel Jr. However, she does not seem to have succeeded there either. She is listed in a later census as living in the household of her daughter Ellen's mother-in-law, Marina Turner Dortch Cobb, widow of Dr. Joshua Cobb. The younger Ellen Galbraith married William T. Dortch (1833–1913), stepson of Dr. Joshua Cobb. The *Clarksville Weekly Chronicle* reported on December 14, 1860, that he was married to Ellen Galbreath [Galbraith] on December 11 in the home of John McKeage by the reverend T. Delacey Wardlaw.

42. Sarah was referring to the Hampton Roads Peace Conference. On February 3, 1865, President Abraham Lincoln and Secretary of State William H. Seward met with Confederate Peace Commissioners Alexander H. Stephens, John A. Campbell, and Robert M. T. Hunter on a steamer called *River Queen* at Hampton Roads, Virginia. They conducted negotiations but no peace treaty was produced.

43. Eli Lockert died in February 1865 of smallpox. Ursula S. Beach noted that Eli Lockert operated a tavern in Clarksville in 1819. See Beach, *Along the Warioto* (Nashville: McQuiddy Press, 1964), 164. He later opened a hotel. Eli and Amy J. Lacy Lockert were the parents of Dr. Charles H. Lockert, who died in November 1865 and of Mary Frances Lockert Bemiss.

44. Clarksville suffered a smallpox outbreak late in 1864. Dr. and Mrs. R. B. McMullen volunteered as nurses in Robb Hall at Stewart College and contracted smallpox. He and his wife Ann died in January 1865 and are buried at Greenwood Cemetery. Vaccinations for smallpox were first used in the eighteenth century;

doses were not standardized and the patient could contract a severe case of the disease from the vaccination. Therefore, many people opted not to be vaccinated.

45. Mrs. Bemiss was Mary Frances Lockert Bemiss, wife of Samuel Merrifield Bemiss, M. D. The couple had eleven children: Elizabeth Lacy, Sallie Lockert, Lillie L., Amy, Anne, Harry, Eli Lockert, Margaret, Maggie, Sammuel Hilton, and Bloomer. "Joss Family Tree," www.ancestry.com, accessed October 1, 2021. Dr. Bemiss was assistant medical director of the hospitals behind the lines for the Army of Tennessee.

46. John was probably an enslaved man that D. N. took with him.

47. By the end of the war, paper was scarce for Southerners and they often resorted to using inferior paper simply because that is all they could obtain. Out of desperation, Southerners would use wallpaper or fill the pages and margins as tightly as possible to maximize space.

48. Seatone is an edible extract from green-lipped mussels which is purported to improve joint health and to improve rheumatoid arthritis. This is an unproven treatment. Today it is widely available for purchase online. It is unclear what it was used for in the nineteenth century.

49. Hog jowl is cut from the pig's cheek.

50. This typhoid victim was possibly Colonel George W. Stacker's daughter, Mary, by his first wife, Martha West. Mary was born in 1850 and would have been fourteen or fifteen years old. George W. Stacker was the first commander of the 50th Tennessee Infantry Regiment, which was captured at Fort Donelson. Stacker had resigned on January 20, 1862, slightly less than one month before the battle.

51. Mollie Ward and her sister, Mrs. Fielding Williams, ran a girls' boarding school known as White Hall School in Ringgold, just north of Clarksville, beginning in the late 1840s; it resumed operation in March 1865.

## Epilogue

1. Beach, *Along the Warioto*, 226; Waters, *Historic Clarksville*, 208.

2. No first name was given for Colonel Smith.

3. Gildrie, "Dilemmas and Opportunities," 86.

4. Gildrie, "Dilemmas and Opportunities," 86–87.

5. Beach, *Along the Warioto*, 230–31.

6. Speer, *Sketches of Prominent Tennesseans*, 430.

7. Bergeron, Ash, and Keith, *Tennesseans and their History*, 178–79.

8. 1870 Montgomery County, Tennessee, Census.

9. *Leaf Chronicle*, June 7, 1873, 2.

10. 1880 Franklin County, Ohio, Census. The census listed each patient as "student" and marked each as "idiotic."

11. *Leaf Chronicle*, April 27, 1888, 1.

12. Speer, *Sketches of Prominent Tennesseans*, 431.

13. *Leaf Chronicle*, October 22, 1908, 1.

14. Speer, *Sketches of Prominent Tennesseans*, 431.

15. 1880 Montgomery County, Tennessee, Census.

16. The wedding announcement said she was closely related to US Supreme Court Justice Stanley Matthews. *Leaf Chronicle*, December 3, 1885, 5. Matthews served as a justice from 1881 to 1889.

17. *Leaf Chronicle*, December 3, 1885, 5.

18. Puerperal fever is caused by a uterine infection following childbirth.

19. *Leaf Chronicle*, December 7, 1886, 1.

20. The 1900 Shelby County, Tennessee, Census lists J. W. Clapp as a clerk for Light and Electric Company and notes he owned his house free of mortgage. In the household were Ellen K., 39; James A., 17; Kennedy Newton, 12; and Newton Kennedy, son of James T. Kennedy, 13. The census taker spelled the name Capp instead of Clapp.

21. *Clarksville Weekly Chronicle*, July 23, 1887, 7.

22. *Leaf-Chronicle Weekly*, June 13, 1890, 5.

23. *Leaf-Chronicle*, May 30, 1892, 1.

24. Beach, *Along the Warioto*, 246.

25. *Knoxville Sentinel*, March 19, 1908, 6; *Leaf Chronicle*, March 19, 1908, 1.

26. Now known as Mary Baldwin University, the school was founded in 1842 as the Augusta Female Seminary. It was named Mary Baldwin Seminary when Clara and her sister Ellen attended and later became Mary Baldwin College.

27. Speer, *Sketches of Prominent Tennesseans*, 431.

28. *Leaf Chronicle*, February 15, 1939, 1.

29. *Public Ledger*, October 26, 1881, 2.

30. *Tennessean*, June 18, 1897, 4.

31. *Leaf Chronicle*, October 25, 1893, 1.

32. For a discussion of this ironic phenomenon, see "History of the Tennessee Division of the United Daughter of the Confederacy," in *Tennessee Public Women in the Progressive Era*, vol. 2, *Constructing Citizenship: Education, Associations, Service, Suffrage* (Knoxville: Univ. of Tennessee Press, forthcoming) and Richard Kreitner, "The Confederates Loved America, and They're Still Defining What Patriotism Means," *The New Republic*, June 20, 2020, https://newrepublic.com/article/158305/confederates-loved-america-theyre-still-defining-patriotism-means, accessed August 20, 2021.

33. *Leaf Chronicle*, June 26, 1899, 3.

34. *Leaf Chronicle*, November 30, 1897, 1.

35. *Leaf Chronicle*, May 5, 1903, 8.

36. *Nashville Banner*, December 12, 1947, 18; *Bristol New Bulletin*, December 12, 1947, 3.

37. Annie E. Cody, *History of the Tennessee Division, United Daughters of the Confederacy* (Nashville: Cullum and Ghertner Co., 1947), 147.

38. Cody, *History of the Tennessee Division*, 266.

39. Cody, *History of the Tennessee Division*, 361.

40. Richard P. Gildrie and Thomas H. Winn, *A History of Austin Peay State University: 1927–2002 and Its Predecessors, 1806–1926* (Clarksville, TN: Austin Peay State University, 2002), 26.

41. Phyllis Smith, "Battling for Education, Tobacco, Women's Suffrage, Prohibition, and Democracy," in *Following the Faith: A Bicentennial History of First Presbyterian Church, Clarkville, 1822–2022* (Amazon Kindle Direct Publishing, 2022), 128–45.

42. *Leaf Chronicle*, April 22, 1904, 5.

43. *Leaf Chronicle*, April 24, 1904, 1.

44. *Leaf Chronicle*, April 27, 1904, 1.

45. *Leaf Chronicle*, May 30, 1904, 1.

46. First Presbyterian Church, *Meeting of Session*, May 2, 1904. Retrieved from www.clarksvillediyhistory.org.

47. A handwritten will is called a holographic will. The Kennedy will was signed and witnessed. Holographic wills are still legal.

48. The 1900 Montgomery County, Tennessee, Census, lists Laura Clardy, age 52, as a servant born in Kentucky, able to read, widowed with three children, two of them living.

49. Tennessee County, District and Probate Courts. Tennessee County Court (Montgomery County); Probate Place: Montgomery, Tennessee. Will Books, Vol R-S, 1869–1906, 700–703.

# BIBLIOGRAPHY

## Newspapers

*Bristol News Bulletin*
*Clarksville Chronicle*
*Clarksville Jeffersonian*
*Clarksville-Leaf Chronicle*
*Clarksville Tobacco Leaf*
*Clarksville Weekly Chronicle*
*Daily Tobacco Leaf-Chronicle*
*Knoxville Sentinel*
*Leaf-Chronicle Weekly*
*Nashville Banner*
*New York Times*
*Public Ledger*

## Government Records

*Census Records*
Brinkley Township, Monroe County, Arkansas (1880)
Carroll County, Mississippi, Census (1860)
Davidson County, Tennessee, Census (1860)
Franklin County, Ohio, Census (1880)
Jefferson County, Kentucky, Census (1870)
Montgomery County, Tennessee, Census (1850, 1860, 1870, 1880, 1900)
Montgomery County, Tennessee, Slave Schedule (1860)
New Orleans, Ward 1, Census (1860)
Prince William, Virginia, Slave Schedule (1860)
Shelby County, Tennessee, Census (1860) (1900)
Todd County, Kentucky, Census (1850, 1860, 1870)
Wilkinson County, Mississippi, Census (1840)

*Other Government Records*

Compiled Service Records of Confederate Soldiers Who Served in Organizations from the State of Tennessee. National Archives Building Washington DC.

Kentucky Compiled Marriages, 1851–1900.

Tennessee Bank Records, 1838–1945. Record Group 47, Box 7, Folders 37–44. Tennessee State Library and Archives.

Tennessee County, District and Probate Courts. Tennessee County Court (Montgomery County); Probate Place: Montgomery, Tennessee. Will Books, Vol. R-S, 1869–1906.

US Marriage Records 1780–2002 Microfilm. Tennessee State Library and Archives.

## Primary Sources

Barker, John Nicholas. Unpublished diaries (1843–1868). Microfilm 878. Brown Harvey Sr. Genealogy Room. Clarksville-Montgomery County Public Library, Clarksville, Tennessee.

*Born in Slavery: Slave Narratives from the Federal Writers' Project, 1936–1938.* Washington, DC: Library of Congress, 2001.

"Chap. CXCV—An act to suppress Insurrection, to punish Treason and Rebellion, to seize and confiscate the Property of Rebels, and for other Purposes." *U.S., Statutes at Large, Treaties, and Proclamations of the United States of America.* Vol. 12. Boston, 1863.

D. N. Kennedy Pardon Vertical File. Brown Harvey Sr. Genealogy Room. Clarksville-Montgomery County Public Library, Clarksville, Tennessee.

Drane Family Papers. Microfilm Accession Number 1143a. Tennessee State Library and Archives, Nashville, TN.

Federal Writers' Project. *Slave Narratives: A Folk History of Slavery in the United States from Interviews with Former Slaves.* Washington, DC: Library of Congress, 1941. https://lccn.loc.gov/41021619. Accessed October 1, 2021.

First Presbyterian Church. "Meeting of Session." May 2, 1904. http://www.clarksvillediyhistory.org. Accessed October 1, 2021.

"Home Again." Thomas G. Doyle. Bookseller, Stationer and Song Publisher, No. 297 N. Gay Street, Baltimore. Library of Congress website, https://www.loc.gov/resource/amss.as105400.0/?st=text. Accessed September 3, 2020.

Kennedy, Sarah. Unpublished letters. Civil War Collection Confederate and Federal 1861–1865. Confederate Collection, Box 9, Folders 6–8. Tennessee State Library and Archives.

Letters Received by the Confederate Secretary of the Treasury, 1861–1865. Pamphlet Accompanying Microcopy 499. National Archives Microfilm Publications. National Archives and Records Service General Services Administration, Washington, DC, 1967.

Lewis, Margaretta. Unpublished letters. Montgomery County, Tennessee, Archives, Clarksville, Tennessee.

Minutes of the General Assembly of the Presbyterian Church of the Confederate States of America. Augusta, GA: Steam Power Press Chronicle & Sentinel, December 4, 1861.

Minutes of the General Assembly of the Presbyterian Church. Montgomery, AL: Confederate States of America, May 1, 1862.

Minutes of the General Assembly, Presbyterian Church, Confederate States of America. Columbia, SC: Southern Guardian Steam-Power Press, May 7, 1863, 131–32.

Minutes of the General Assembly, Presbyterian Church in the United States. Columbia, SC: Office of the Southern Presbyterian Review, 1868.

Newspapers.com, https://go.newspapers.com/welcome.

"Proclamation Appointing a National Fast Day." Abraham Lincoln Online. http://www.abrahamlincolnonline.org/lincoln/speeches/fast.htm. Accessed August 20, 2021.

Titus, William P. *Picturesque Clarksville, Past and Present: A History of the City of the Hills.* Clarksville, TN: W. P. Titus Publishing Company, 1887. Reprinted by Ann Alley and Ursula Beach, 1973.

Uffelman, Minoa D., Ellen Kanervo, Phyllis Smith, and Eleanor Williams, eds. *The Diary of Nannie Haskins Williams: A Southern Woman's Story of Rebellion and Reconstruction, 1863–1890.* Knoxville: Univ. of Tennessee Press, 2013.

Uffelman, Minoa D., Ellen Kanervo, Phyllis Smith, and Eleanor Williams, eds. *The Diary of Serepta Jordan: A Southern Woman's Struggle with War and Family, 1857–1864.* Knoxville: Univ. of Tennessee Press, 2020.

"U.S., Civil War Soldier Records and Profiles, 1861–1865." Ancestry.com. Accessed September 26, 2020.

U.S. Find A Grave Index, 1600s–Current.

U.S. War Department. *The War of the Rebellion: A Compilation of the Official Records of the Union and Confederate Armies.* 128 vols. Washington, DC, 1880–1901.

Williams, Nannie Haskins. *The History of Clarksville Female Academy.* Clarksville, Tennessee, Library Committee, Women's Building, Tennessee Centennial. 1896. Reprinted by Montgomery County Historical Society, 1996.

*Williams' Clarksville Directory, City Guide and Business Mirror.* Vol. 1, 1859–60. Clarksville, TN: C. O. Faxon, 1859. Reprinted by Ursula Beach, 1976.

## Secondary Sources

"8th Regiment, Kentucky Cavalry (Union)." https://www.familysearch.org/wiki/en/8th_Regiment,_Kentucky_Cavalry_(Union). Accessed October 15, 2020.

Adoue Family Tree. Ancestry.com. Accessed February 22, 2013.

Allingham Family Tree. Ancestry.com. Accessed September 6, 2021.

Ash, Stephen V. "A Community at War: Montgomery County, 1861–65." *Tennessee Historical Quarterly* 36, no. 1 (Spring 1977): 30–43.

————. *Middle Tennessee Society Transformed, 1860–1870: War and Peace in the Upper South.* Knoxville: Univ. of Tennessee Press, 2006.

"The Battle of New Market, May 15, 1864." Virginia Military Institute website, http://www.vmi.edu/archives.aspex?id=3911. Accessed March 8, 2013.

Beach, Ursula Smith. *Along the Warioto: A History of Montgomery County, Tennessee.* Nashville: McQuiddy Press, 1964.

Beach, Ursula S., and Eleanor Williams. *Nineteenth Century Heritage: Clarksville, Tennessee.* Oxford, MS: Guild Bindery Press, 1989.

Bergeron, Paul H., Stephen V. Ash, and Jeanette Keith. *Tennesseans and their History.* Knoxville: Univ. of Tennessee Press, 1999.

Campbell Heyn Public Master Tree. Ancestry.com. Accessed October 27, 2020.

Candace Ricks Family Tree. Ancestry.com. Accessed October 14, 2020.

Charles, Harry K. "American Civil War Postage Due: North and South." Postal History Symposium, Nov. 2012. https://stamps.org/Portals/0/Symposium /CharlesPaper.pdf. Accessed September 28, 2021.

Civil War Philatelic Society. https://www.civilwarphilatelicsociety.org/. Accessed October 1, 2021.

Cody, Annie E. *History of the Tennessee Division, United Daughters of the Confederacy.* Nashville: Cullum and Ghertner Co., 1947.

"The Confederate Postal System." Smithsonian National Postal Museum. https:// postalmuseum.si.edu/exhibition/a-nation-divided/the-confederate-postal -system. Accessed October 22, 2020.

"The Confiscation Acts of 1861 and 1862." The United States Senate. https://www .senate.gov/artandhistory/history/common/generic/ConfiscationActs.htm. Accessed June 8, 2021.

Cooling, Benjamin F. *Fort Donelson's Legacy: War and Society in Kentucky and Tennessee, 1861–1863.* Knoxville: Univ. of Tennessee Press, 1997.

Cross, Wallace C. *Cry Havoc: A History of the 49th Tennessee Volunteer Infantry Regiment, 1861–1865.* Franklin, TN: Hillsboro Press, 2004.

————. *Ordeal by Fire: A History of the Fourteenth Tennessee Volunteer Infantry Regiment, CSA.* Clarksville, TN: Clarksville-Montgomery County Museum, 1990.

Daniel, W. Harrison. "Southern Presbyterians in the Confederacy." *The North Carolina Historical Review* 44, no. 3 (1967): 231–55.

Faust, Drew Gilpin. *Mothers of Invention: Women of the Slaveholding South in the American Civil War.* Chapel Hill: Univ. of North Carolina Press, 1996.

"Foraging and Looting." Encyclopedia.com. https://www.encyclopedia.com/history /applied-and-social-sciences-magazines/foraging-and-looting. Accessed June 8, 2021.

Gallagher, Winifred. *How the Post Office Created America*. New York: Penguin Books, 2016.

Gildrie, Richard P. "Dilemma and Opportunities, 1860–1900." In *Historic Clarksville: The Bicentennial Story, 1784–1984*, second edition, edited by Charles M. Waters and John L. Butler, 63–95. Clarksville, TN: Jostens Publications, 2004.

Gildrie, Richard P., and Thomas H. Winn. *A History of Austin Peay State University, 1927–2002*. Clarksville, TN: Austin Peay State University, 2002.

Glaser/Lang Family Tree. Ancestry.com. Accessed October 1, 2021.

Gorin, Betty J. *"Morgan is Coming!" Confederate Raiders in the Heartland of Kentucky*. Louisville: Harmony House Publishers, 2006.

Griffey, Irene. *Riverview Cemetery: Looking Back to Those Who've Gone Before*. Clarksville, TN: Montgomery County Historical Society, 2002.

Griffin Williams Family Tree. Ancestry.com. Accessed June 26, 2021.

Hern, Candice. "Regency Glossary." https://candicehern.com/regency-world /glossary/#:~:text=mushroom,starts%20up%20in%20the%20night. Accessed October 14, 2020.

"History of the Church." Archives of the PC (USA). Presbyterian Historical Society. https://www.history.pcusa.org/history-online/presbyterian-history /history-church. Accessed October 7, 2021.

Hooper, Candice Shy. *Lincoln's General's Wives: Four Women Who Influenced the Civil War—for Better or Worse*. Kent, OH: Kent State Univ. Press, 2016.

Hyatt, Paul, Marie Riggins, Ralph Winters and Thurston L. Lee. *One Hundred Years of County Fairs in Montgomery County, Tennessee*. Clarksville: TN: Clarksville-Montgomery County Historical Society, 1960.

John McQuaide Family Tree. Ancestry.com. Accessed October 13, 2020.

"Johnson's Island." Touring Ohio website. http://touringohio.com/history/johnson -island.html. Accessed June 8, 2021.

Jones, Howard. "Union and Confederate Diplomacy during the Civil War." Essential Civil War Curriculum website. https://www.essentialcivilwarcurriculum .com/union-and-confederate-diplomacy-during-the-civil-war.html. Accessed on September 28, 2020.

Joss Family Tree. Ancestry.com. Accessed October 1, 2021.

Kaufman, Trish. https://www.trishkaufmann.com/files/Knowles1.pdf. Accessed August 30, 2021.

Kanervo, Ellen, ed. *Following the Faith: A Bicentennial History of First Presbyterian Church, Clarksville, 1822–2022*. Amazon Kindle Direct Publishing, 2022.

Kemmerly, Phillip. "1862-1881: War, Reconstruction, and Cultural Upheaval: A World Turned Upside Down," in *Following the Faith: A Bicentennial History of First Presbyterian Church, Clarksville*, edited by Ellen Kanervo, 64–95. Clarksville TN: Amazon Kindle Direct Publishing, 2022.

Kreitner, Richard. "The Confederates Loved America, and They're Still Defining

What Patriotism Means." *The New Republic,* June 20, 2020. https://new
republic.com/article/158305/confederates-loved-america-theyre-still
-defining-patriotism-means. Accessed August 20, 2021.

Leonard, Devin. *Neither Snow nor Rain: A History of the United States Postal Service.*
New York: Grove Press, 2016.

"Masonic History of Montgomery County and Clarksville Lodge No. 89, Clarksville, Tennessee," http://clarksvillelodge89.org/index.php/history-of-cl89/.
Accessed on August 23, 2020.

McBride, Robert M., and Dan M. Robison. *Biographical Directory of the Tennessee
General Assembly, 1861–1901.* Vol. 2. Nashville: Tennessee State Library and
Archives and Tennessee Historical Commission, 1979.

McPherson, James M. *For Cause & Comrades: Why Men Fought in the Civil War,*
Oxford Univ. Press, 1997.

The Meriwether Society, Inc. http://www.meriwethersociety.org. Accessed February 22, 2013.

Morris, Wentworth S. "The Davie Home and the Register of the Federal Prison at
Clarksville." *Tennessee Historical Quarterly* 8, no. 3 (1949): 250–51.

"Nashville Female Academy." Nashville Sites. https://nashvillesites.org/re-
cords/01ae3439–3b8e-4ca7-b9ed-d568538a6321. Accessed July 29, 2021.

Ogle, Maureen. "All the Modern Conveniences." Cited in Sarah Zhang, "Showering Has a Dark, Violent History." *The Atlantic,* December 11, 2018, https://
www.theatlantic.com/health/archive/2018/12/dark-history-of-showering
/577636/. Accessed September 28, 2020.

O'Neal, Aaron. "Child Mortality in the United States 1800–2020." *Statista.* https://
www.statista.com/statistics/1041693/united-states-all-time-child-mortality
-rate/. Accessed October 27, 2020.

O'Neal, Jim. "Oaths of Loyalty to the U.S. Were Common at Time of Civil War."
*The IC Blog.* http://intelligentcollector.com/blog/oaths-of-loyalty-to-the
-u-s-were-common-at-time-of-civil-war/. Accessed September 12, 2020.

"Rudy's List of Archaic Medical Terms." https://glossarissimo.wordpress.com
/2016/05/26/en-rudys-list-of-archaic-medical-terms-antiquus-morbus
-home/. Accessed September 12, 2020.

"Sarsaparilla: Benefits, Risks, and Side Effects." https://www.healthline.com/health
/food-nutrition/sarsaparilla#benefits. Accessed February 9, 2021.

Sharpless, Rebecca. *Cooking in Other Women's Kitchens: Domestic Workers in the
South, 1865–1960.* Chapel Hill: Univ. of North Carolina Press, 2010.

Sidhu, Dawinder S. "Opinionator: The Birth of the Greenback." *New York Times,*
December 31, 2013. https://opinionator.blogs.nytimes.com/2013/12/31/the
-birth-of-the-greenback/. Accessed August 14, 2017.

Smith, Ernest A. "The History of the Confederate Treasury." *Southern History Association* 5, no. 1 (January 1901): 1–227.

Smith, Phyllis. "1902-1921: Battling for Education, Tobacco, Women's Suffrage, Pro-
hibition, and Democracy," in *Following the Faith: A Bicentennial History of First
Presbyterian Church, Clarksville*, edited by Ellen Kanervo, 64–95. Clarksville
TN: Amazon Kindle Direct Publishing, 2022.

Speer, William S. *Sketches of Prominent Tennesseans: Containing Biographies and
Records of Many of the Families who Have Attained Prominence in Tennessee.*
Nashville: A. B. Tavel, 1888. Reprinted by Southern Historical Press by Silas
Emmit Lucus Jr., 1978.

Tolbert, Lisa C. *Constructing Townscapes: Space and Society in Antebellum Tennessee.*
Chapel Hill: Univ. of North Carolina Press, 1999.

Tudor, Gerald R. "Fiction, Fact, and Embellishment: The Kennedys and Uncle
Tom's Cabin." http://freepages.rootsweb.com/~josephkennedy/genealogy
/Source%20Materials/Kennedy/fiction_fact_and_embellishment.htm.
Accessed October 14, 2020.

Uffelman, Minoa D. "History of the Tennessee Division of the United Daughters of
the Confederacy." Mary Evins and Minoa Uffelman, eds. *Constructing Citizenship: Education, Associations, Service, Suffrage—Tennessee Public Women in the
Progressive Era.* Knoxville: Univ. of Tennessee Press, forthcoming.

Waters, Charles, ed. *Historic Clarksville: The Bicentennial Story, 1784–1984.* Clarksville, TN: Jostens Publications, 1983.

Williams, Eleanor S. *Worship along the Warioto: Montgomery County, Tennessee.*
Clarksville, TN: First Federal Savings Bank, 1995.

Wink, Amy L. *She Left Nothing in Particular: The Autobiographical Legacy of Nineteenth-Century Women's Diaries.* Knoxville: Univ. of Tennessee Press, 2001.

Zieren, Gregory. Personal Interview. Austin Peay State University History Department, Clarksville, Tennessee. October 12, 2020.

# INDEX

Page numbers in **boldface** refer to illustrations.

Bailey, Mary Williamson. *See* Bryan,
Mary Williamson Bailey
Bailey, Maud(e) Lusk, 39, 59, 83, 128n94,
129n9
Bailey, Virginia Carney (Mrs. Charles
William), 5, 27, 107n49
Bailey, Wilmoth Boyd (Cousin Will)
(Mrs. Henry L.), 23, 28, 35, 54, 86,
120n20, 131n20
Balm of Gilead (tree), 16, 116n131
Balthrop (Williams), Fannie (Mrs.
Thomas W. Williams), 70, 136n4
bank assets, sent overseas, xxiii–xxiv,
96, 98n16, 133n40
bank notes, value of, 59, 76, 133n40
Bank of Tennessee, 59, 133n40
Banks, Nathaniel P., 118n9
banks, state, 59, 133n40
Barker, Aleck, 12–13, 114n113
Barker, Charlie, 37
Barker, Chiles Terrell, 5, 107n52
Barker, Edward Walton (Walton), 27,
30, 51, 123n52, 124n68, 129n7, 130n15
Barker, Ellen (daughter of John), health
of, 23
Barker, Ellen Watson Morris Carr
(second Mrs. John), 2, 5, 7, 51, 102n6,
103n16, 107n47, 112n98, 130n15;
health of, 4, 59
Barker, John Walton, 2, 5, 7, 9–10, 15,
22–23, 27, 33, 46, 51–52, 56, 61–62,
66, 73, 78–79, 102n1, 103n17, 107n47,
107nn51–52, 112n98, 114n113, 129n6,
130n15, 132n26, 135n56, 136n9; arrest
of, 13; family of, 5, 7, 15, 21, 33, 54,
62, 64, 78; health of, 59, 63, 75; and
supplies provided by, 5–6, 11–12, 39,
61, 73, 84; trial of, 21, 23
Barker, Louisa McTyler (Tex), 10, 30, 37,
112n98, 124n66

Barker, Mary Meriwether (Mollie), 5,
7, 30, 52, 54, 59, 63, 107n47, 124n68,
130n15; death of child Walton, 52,
54, 59
Barker, Mary Minor Meriwether (first
Mrs. John), 107n52
Barker, Walton (infant), 52, 54, 59
Beach, Ursula, 96
Beaumont, Frank S., 57, 60, 113n107,
132n28
Beaumont, Laura E. Conrad (Mrs.
Frank), 11, 113n107
Beaumont, Sterling, 60, 133n42
Beaumont house, 57, 60, 113n107, 132n38,
133n42
Bell, John, xxvii
Bell and Everett Club, xxvii
Bemiss, Mary Frances Lockert (Mrs.
Samuel M.), 15, 71, 86, 116n129,
140n42, 141n45
Bemiss, Samuel Merrifield, 71, 141n45
bilious (remitting) fever, xxxiii, 3–4, 54,
56, 105n33
births, xxii, xxviii, 5–6, 35, 39, 70, 83,
121n30, 135n2
Bivens, Mr., 22
Blain, Mr., 79, 138–39n29
Blair, Montgomery, xxix, 100n49
boil. *See* rising
bone felon, xxxiii, 5, 8, 106n45
Boone, William P., 33, 126n80
bowels, problems with, 32, 50, 74, 78, 84,
128n2
Bragg, Braxton, 49
Brandon (escapee), 22
Breckinridge Cannel Coal Company, 6,
107n57
Brentwood, Battle of (TN) (1863), 28,
124n58
Brer Rabbit, xxxvi, 101n71